CW00385971

IN THE MIDST OF THINGS

IN THE MIDST
OF THINGS

Neil Cameron

HODDER AND STOUGHTON
LONDON SYDNEY AUCKLAND TORONTO

British Library Cataloguing in Publication Data

Cameron, Neil. *1920–1985*
  In the midst of things.
  1. Cameron, Neil. *1920–1985*   2. Great
  Britain. *Royal Air Force*—Biography
  3. Marshalls—Great Britain—
  Biography
  I. Title
  358.4'1331'0924   UG626.2.G3

  ISBN 0-340-39081-6

Contents

Abbreviations

ACDS	Assistant Chief of Defence Staff
ACDS (Pol)	Assistant Chief of Defence Staff (Policy)
ADC	Aide-de-Camp
AFC	Air Force Cross
AHB	Air Historical Branch
AHQ BAFO	Air Headquarters, British Air Forces of Occupation
ALBM	Air-Launched Ballistic Missile
AMP	Air Member for Personnel
AMSO	Air Member for Supply and Organisation
AOC	Air Officer Commanding
AOC-in-C	Air Officer Commanding-in-Chief
ASC	Air Support Command
AUS (P)	Assistant Under-Secretary (Policy)
AVM	Air Vice-Marshal
BAOR	British Army of the Rhine
CA	Controller (Aircraft)
CAS	Chief of the Air Staff
C-in-C	Commander-in-Chief
CDS	Chief of the Defence Staff
CGS	Chief of the General Staff
CO	Commanding Officer
DCAS	Deputy Chief of the Air Staff
DGT	Director-General of Training
D/SACEUR	Deputy Supreme Allied Commander, Europe
DUS (Air)	Deputy Under-Secretary (Air)
GD	General Duties
IISS	International Institute of Strategic Studies
IRBM	Intermediate-Range Ballistic Missile
LAA	Light Anti-Aircraft
MRAF	Marshal of the Royal Air Force

NATO	North Atlantic Treaty Organisation
NPG	Nuclear Planning Group
OC	Officer Commanding
OTU	Operational Training Unit
PEG	Programme Evaluation Group
P/O	Pilot Officer
PPO	Principal Personnel Officer
PS	Private Secretary
PSO	Personal Staff Officer
PTS	Parachute Training School
PUS	Permanent Under-Secretary
RAFVR	Royal Air Force Volunteer Reserve
R/T	Radio Telephone
RUSI	Royal United Services Institution
SACEUR	Supreme Allied Commander, Europe
SASO	Senior Air Staff Officer
SEAC	South East Asia Command
SEATO	South East Asia Treaty Organisation
SHAPE	Supreme Headquarters Allied Powers, Europe
S/L	Squadron Leader
S of S	Secretary of State
SNCO	Senior Non-Commissioned Officer
VCAS	Vice-Chief of the Air Staff

Foreword by Marshal of the Royal Air Force, Sir Dermot Boyle

This book is remarkable for a number of reasons. Firstly it records the life of someone who from humble beginnings rose from the rank of Sergeant Pilot to the highest appointment the Services have to offer to a serving officer – Chief of the Defence Staff (CDS). Secondly it demonstrates, not for the first time in history, how someone who had an indifferent school record was uninterested in his future until he discovered what he wanted to do. In Neil's case it was to fly and from then on the great strength of his character emerged and his courage and outstanding ability were harnessed to a purpose. Thirdly Neil had remarkably varied operational experiences during World War II, in the Battle of Britain, in Russia, in North Africa and in the Far East where he ended the war operating Thunderbolt ground-attack aircraft against the enemy.

The reader will here find an interesting account of the working of the Ministry of Defence and some of the personalities involved while Neil was associated with it and the book includes a revealing account of his visit to China, the first ever made by a British CDS, and also to Iran in what turned out to be a critical time in that country's history.

On ceasing to be CDS Neil gave vent to his long-standing academic leanings by becoming the Principal of King's College London, an appointment which he filled with enthusiasm and considerable effectiveness. Also in the course of the book, we learn about Neil's Christian faith and how it affected his service career and his view of military strategy, particularly that relating to the nuclear issue.

This is a valuable account of the life of an outstandingly successful Air Force officer who combined humility and great ability with a strong, approachable and likeable personality. Furthermore, during Neil's life he had to face very serious illness and did so with typical courage and tenacity. This book will appeal not only to Neil Cameron's many friends and admirers but also to those who are interested in the lives of those military leaders who reach the top of their profession.

Introduction and Acknowledgments

Neil Cameron was born in Perth, Scotland, on 8 July 1920. His parents were poor and he had an undistinguished school record. But early in 1939, when the threat of another World War loomed ever nearer, like hundreds of other young men he joined the Royal Air Force Volunteer Reserve. This was a move which was to determine his lifetime's career.

He trained as a pilot, won his 'wings' but was not commissioned. In September 1940 he was posted to his first squadron, No 1, as a sergeant pilot; after a few weeks there, he was sent to No 17 Squadron, with which he flew during the closing stages of the Battle of Britain.

His subsequent rise to distinction as a fighter squadron commander was rapid: he served successively in Russia, the Middle East and the Far East, being awarded the DFC and then the DSO for his outstanding leadership.

After the war he decided to stay in the RAF and was given a permanent commission. He married a WAAF officer, and despite a serious illness which nearly cost him his life progressed steadily to high rank. By 1968 he had become an air vice-marshal; but subsequently his career seemed to stick at that point: he thought himself unlikely to get further promotion and seriously considered resigning from the RAF.

Then in 1974 his fortunes changed dramatically: he was appointed to the Air Force Board, with promotion to Air Marshal, and less than two years later was made Chief of the Air Staff as an Air Chief Marshal. Then, through the sudden death of the Chief of the Defence Staff, he succeeded to that post as a Marshal of the RAF.

When his Service career ended in 1979 he entered academic life: he was appointed Principal of King's College, University of London, in 1980 and three years later was made a Life Peer as Baron Cameron of Balhousie in the District of Perth and Kinross and in 1984 he was made a Knight of the Thistle. He was very much looking forward to playing an active part in the House of Lords.

In anticipation of his retirement in mid-1985 he decided to write an autobiography, to which he gave the title *In Medias Res – In the Midst of Things* – the Latin motto of No 258 Squadron which he commanded in the Far East. In August 1984 he visited the Air Historical Branch of the Ministry of Defence to seek help with the research and writing involved. The Head of the AHB, Air Commodore Henry Probert, suggested that the senior historian, Humphrey Wynn, who was about to retire, should undertake this task. Lord Cameron agreed and the work started in October of that year.

He had written several chapters himself; others were drafted and approved by him. Then, sadly, before reaching the date of his retirement he became seriously ill and had to be taken into hospital: he died there, of cancer, on 29 January 1985.

During the course of his discussions at the AHB he had expressed the hope that, should he not live to complete his autobiography, the assistance he had sought would be available – with the help of his family and the publishers – to see the work through to publication. Accordingly, during 1985 those who were involved in it – his son Neil and daughter Fiona, Air Commodore Probert, Humphrey Wynn, Mrs Sandra Gee (the Principal's Secretary at King's College) and David Wavre of the publishers Hodder & Stoughton – met to decide how to proceed to ensure the completion of *In the Midst of Things*. The result is a book which is in part autobiography, in part narrative and in part personal recollections of those who knew Lord Cameron at various stages of his career, and who agreed to talk about him to Henry Probert or Humphrey Wynn.

Wherever possible he has been left to speak for himself. Thus the first seven chapters, covering the wartime and early post-war years, are all his apart from the addition of some extracts from official records which it is thought will add interest to the story. These chapters therefore appear in the first person, as does Chapter eight, which after being drafted by Humphrey Wynn was seen and amended by Lord Cameron shortly before his death.

The remaining chapters covering his Service career have been mainly written by Humphrey Wynn and appear in the third person, though wherever possible they include extracts from Lord Cameron's speeches and writings. The chapter covering his time as Principal of King's College has been written by Professor Stewart Sutherland, who succeeded him in that appointment. Inevitably therefore there are differences of approach and style, owing to the circumstances under which the work was completed, and to the need to distinguish clearly between what Lord Cameron himself wrote and what others have since written or said about him.

Research for this book has in part relied on official records held either in the Air Historical Branch or the Public Record Office, together with Lord Cameron's personal papers and his taped interview with Air Commodore Tony Mason. It has also depended heavily on the assistance of many who knew and worked with him at various stages in his career; all requests for consultation have been most willingly and kindly met and our chief regret is that it has not been possible in the limited time available to talk to the many more whose names were recommended to us. Thanks go to Lord Mulley, Mr Denis Healey, Mr James Wellbeloved and Mr Brynmor John, the politicians under whom he served; to Sir Frank Cooper, Sir Patrick Nairne, Mr Cecil James and Mr John Blelloch, civil servant colleagues past and present; and to many RAF associates and friends: MRAF Sir Dermot Boyle, MRAF The Lord Elworthy, MRAF Sir John Grandy, Lady Humphrey, MRAF Sir Michael Beetham, Air Chief Marshals Sir John Barraclough, Sir Kenneth Cross, Sir Lewis Hodges and Sir Nigel Maynard, Air Marshals Sir Harry Burton, Sir Harold Martin, Sir John Rowlands and Sir Freddie Sowrey, Air Vice-Marshal I. J. Lawson, the Venerable Glyn Renowden, Air Commodores R. H. Palin and D. I. M. Strong, Group Captain J. A. G. Slessor, Wing Commander E. J. Strangeway, and Mr J. Sephton. Others who have assisted include Professor Sutherland and the Rev Richard Harries of King's College, University of London, Dr John Tanner, Mr Hugh

Hanning and Mr Alan Lee-Williams. Mrs Sandra Gee has provided invaluable administrative assistance. Of particular value has been the advice offered by Lady Cameron, and her son and daughter. Without their whole-hearted support this book could not have been completed.

1 BOYHOOD TO BATTLE

I was brought up poor. This is not a common qualification for a leader of Britain's armed services, but it is not a bad one. When, as Chief of Defence Staff, I visited Prime Minister Callaghan in his room in the House of Commons to put the case for an increase in service pay, I was able to speak with authority. I told him that my grandfather, in whose house I had been brought up, was Inspector of Poor for Perth and District. My father was his assistant. We were a poor family, just comfortable, I suppose, but my father died when I was three weeks old, and my mother, sister and I went to live with my grandfather.

These were the days before Social Security. From his office in York Place, Perth, my grandfather ran the poor of the area as best he could, and often he found himself putting his hand into his own pocket when some need was desperate. He had a soft heart when not dealing with his own family.

My father had been in the Seaforth Highlanders and later the Queen's Own Cameron Highlanders during the 1914–18 war. He had reached the rank of Company Sergeant Major and been awarded the Distinguished Conduct Medal. I still have it. The citation reads:

> Through the past six months this NCO has proved himself to be a most capable and energetic platoon sergeant. Cool in the presence of danger, skilful and resourceful in leading his men and directing work, he has at all times set the most magnificent example of courage and devotion to duty; notably during the fighting in the French zone at the end of July. On two occasions he displayed great courage and resource in the presence of danger, controlling his platoon under very heavy shell-fire and personally seeing to the evacuation of the wounded.

He only survived the war two years.

I was brought up by my mother, Isabella Stewart Cameron, who was a very strong-willed Christian Scottish woman. We lived in my grandfather's house which my mother ran, doing the cooking, cleaning and other chores. It must have been very hard for her. My grandfather was a small, tough Highlander, who spoke Gaelic before he learnt English, and I can remember him talking in his sleep in Gaelic; indeed I am sure that at times of stress he thought in that language. He had on occasions a very bad temper.

So all my early life, one way or another, I was influenced by work amongst the poor. The main office in York Place was two doors from the birthplace of John Buchan, where his son, the eminent strategist, Alastair Buchan, was brought up. I was to work with Alastair closely when he was the first Director of the Institute for Strategic Studies and later Commandant of the Royal College of Defence Studies.

The Poor House in Perth, which my grandfather ran, was a dark-stoned building where some of the poor of the district were housed in large, well-scrubbed dormitories with shining floors. The inmates had to clean for their keep. I hated it and was frightened by it, and went there as seldom as possible. But there was no avoiding it on many family occasions. The Governor of the Poor House was one of my referees when I put in my application to join the Royal Air Force Volunteer Reserve in early 1939.

The family – and there were many uncles and aunts and cousins – was a happy one on the whole. There was always someone coming or going. It was also a very strong Scottish Presbyterian Christian family and much involved in church work. The church was our social centre. On Sundays it was twice to church – for me, Sunday school after church in the morning, and no games or play with one's friends. It was best clothes, drawn blinds and the minimum of activity. Today it is difficult to comprehend the Scottish sabbath as it then was. The minister of the church was very much a power in the locality, though the children did their best to get around the restrictions of the 'day of rest'. I was a member of the Boys' Brigade attached to the church, and Friday was Brigade night. I enjoyed the games which usually finished the evening after the drill and discipline. I was also a member of the Crusaders' Union which met on Sunday afternoon. So Sunday, though a day of rest, left little time for idle hands except going to and from the various activities, and throughout it the Sunday kilt and suit had to be protected! This extremely strict early Christian upbringing helped to form my character and though I sped from the path of righteousness fairly quickly after leaving the family circle, the training and background remained and were summoned in aid later when things got tough.

Schooling started well; at the Northern District School, Perth, where I was from the age of five to ten, I was a well-above average pupil. From there I got a bursary to Perth Academy, partly on my own achievement, but partly also as a result of my mother's poor financial situation. Perth Academy is a school with a noted scholastic record, and many famous names started there. However, for me all seemed to go wrong from the start. I cannot explain it – adolescence perhaps, or lack of paternal guidance – but certainly I lost the will to learn, and struggled through the various forms at the bottom of the list, on one occasion totally failing. I have often tried to analyse this period, and what went wrong, but have failed to reach a clear answer. Although I was dedicated to games, I did not achieve first-team level in any of them, so that was not the cause of the failure. While after the war I was to play first-class club and some county rugby football, there was little sign of this talent at school. I had to struggle to gain my Lower Leaving Certificates (broadly equivalent to the present O-Levels) and was advised not to try to go on to higher academic things. I therefore left school at sixteen and a half with little regret, because I hated it and was ashamed of my lack of success. My sister, who was three years older, did extremely well.

The year was now 1937, and the question was what to do with this not very academic teenager. There were great family conferences, and eventually after an interview I was accepted by the then Commercial Bank of Scotland. I started work at their Newburgh, Fife, branch some twelve miles from Perth. I travelled by bus every day. I tried hard to enjoy banking and to apply myself to the Institute of

Bankers examinations. But it was a losing battle. I stayed
with them until the outbreak of war, and indeed they
continued to pay my humble salary throughout the war, for
which I was most grateful.

The yearning to fly first got a grip on me about the time
that I became a bank apprentice. The Trenchard short-
service scheme[1] to boost the strength of the Royal Air Force
was under way, and one of the Elementary Flying Schools
was at Scone airfield a few miles from Perth. Every day the
sky was full of Tiger Moths on some training mission or
another, and in the evening those who were learning to fly
could be seen in town displaying the panache one had come
to expect from those mixed up in aviation. It was another
world, and I longed to be part of it. Sir Alan Cobham's
Flying Circus, with Jim Mollison, Geoffrey Tyson and the
other famous aviators, visited Perth. What glamour, what
excitement!

I was determined to fly. The ultimate was, of course, a
cadetship at the Royal Air Force College, Cranwell, but I
had neither the academic qualifications nor the financial
backing to achieve this. My mother also took a good deal of
persuading that flying was a desirable activity for an only
son. But eventually I put in the application forms to join the
Royal Air Force Volunteer Reserve. This was the best of
both worlds. I could continue in banking, thus helping the
family budget, and fly at the same time. Eventually I was
called for interview at the Town Headquarters in Perth. By
some extraordinary piece of mismanagement, on the crucial day my alarm clock failed to go off and I woke up with
exactly twenty minutes to get dressed and travel nearly
one-and-a-half miles to the interview. I ran the whole way.
Immediately on arrival I was put in front of a medical officer
for examination. On checking my heart he looked somewhat puzzled, and suggested that I might return to see him
after the interview. The interview went well, and so did the
later medical examination. My heart was beating normally.
I was in.

The call-up for training came in May 1939. The war clouds
were gathering and the Royal Air Force was increasing its
strength as quickly as possible. We attended evening
ground school during the week: navigation, meteorology,

signals and the like. At weekends we flew, weather permitting. Scone was an airfield run by Airwork Ltd, who had a contract to train both short-service officers and members of the RAFVR. Now it was my turn to fly the renowned Tiger Moth. I was Sergeant Cameron, Pilot-under-training. My first instructor was a gruff, bad-tempered Flight Lieutenant who seemed to think that shouting at a student pilot would get results. With me it produced exactly the opposite effect: I reached twelve hours of dual instruction without flying solo, and showed little sign of having the confidence to do so. Then my flying instructor was changed. My new one was a kind, easy-going aviator, Flying Officer Bradley, a man of considerable experience who had flown in the 1914–18 war and had been instructing for many years. He gave me great confidence, and within two more hours' dual instruction I had gone solo and really never looked back. I owe him a great debt.

The Perth RAFVR contingent was called up on the 1 September 1939 and ordered to report at Perth railway station for transport to England, wearing our uniforms or as much of them as we had been issued with. It was a comical sight. I had a cap, a tunic, a pair of boots and a kit-bag. It was a very odd assortment of military figures that paraded at Perth station for the night train, seen off by tearful families, girlfriends and interested bystanders. Our destination was Hastings, where we were to undergo further ground training before getting into the regular Royal Air Force training circuit. I had never been out of Scotland in my life, and the whole journey was a great adventure. I was later to regard stations like Crewe and Peterborough with some horror, but on this occasion I was heading for adventure and excitement, away from the narrow Scottish family existence. I was just nineteen.

The English holiday resort of Hastings had been turned into a massive training camp for RAF aircrew. The two piers had been requisitioned, as well as many of the main hotels on the front. Some 2,500 RAFVR aircrew were to descend on this unfortunate place during the first few weeks of the war. Many of them, myself included, were to be there six months. This was the phoney war period, when few aircrew were being killed and the enlarged flying training programme had not yet got going. I was accommodated in the Marine Court Hotel – a splendid ten-storey building on the verge of completion when the war broke out. I was in a double room with three other aircrew from Scotland. We looked out over the English Channel – a waterway I was to get to know pretty well in the not too distant future. But it was a frustrating six months: drill, ground schools, lectures on air traditions and a whole variety of schemes to keep us interested, but no flying. Discipline was strict, which was just as well because several thousand young prospective airmen loose in a town like Hastings was a real challenge to law and order, both service and civil. The pubs must have done a roaring trade. The whole unit was commanded by Air Commodore Critchley, the famous golfer and business-man who had been put into uniform specially for this assignment. He had gathered around him quite a body of sportsmen – Wally Hammond and Len Crawley were amongst the officers; Len Harvey and Eddie Phillips, both former British heavyweight champions, were amongst the many sporting sergeants who joined the physical training group. But it was a time of great frustration for us all. We little thought of what might happen to us before the war was over. We just wanted to become operational pilots as soon as possible.

Eventually, as the war progressed and the flying training machine got organised, the log-jam was broken and we went off to fly. It was in March 1940 that I went to the Elementary Flying Training School at Redhill, where I passed with a good mark, and then at the beginning of June I returned to Scotland to No 8 Service Flying Training School at Montrose. This was an old World War I grass airfield, and the school had just been equipped with the new Miles Master trainer.[2] The teething troubles with this aircraft were numerous, and flying accidents were a regular occurrence. The sergeant who ran the sick quarters and the morgue put up a notice outside the latter, 'Standing Room Only'. His little joke had a horrible ring of truth about it.

The aircraft was later modified and did good service. There is always a temptation for a pilot who is gaining confidence – over-confidence perhaps – to indulge in some illicit low flying. I was in my own countryside and knew it well. The Tay Valley was a marvellous area since one could follow the river between the mountains and get the thrill of flying close to ground and water. One such sortie ended in near-disaster when, by an error of over-confident judgement, I flew through some telephone wires and trees and, though I managed to keep the aircraft in the air, finished up with some of the wires dangling from my tail. In addition, my radiator, which adjusted the engine temperature, was full of leaves; and the pitot head, which gave the pilot his airspeed, on the leading edge of the wing, was facing round the wrong way. The result was an engine temperature going off the clock and an airspeed indicator not registering at all. I managed to get the aircraft back to Montrose before the engine blew up, and made a landing without any idea what speed I was approaching the airfield. The morgue was cheated of a self-inflicted casualty that day. The aircraft was a terrible mess, and I was in very serious trouble. With me was another Sergeant Pilot, and he came in for equal chastisement. The outcome was that though both of us had been recommended for commissioning after FTS, we were both kept at the rank of Sergeant Pilot as a punishment for our indiscretion. It was touch and go whether we were court-martialled and possibly thrown out of the service. Certainly this would have happened in peacetime; but pilots were already being lost in large numbers and since we were almost fully trained we were reprieved.[3]

Then, at the end of August, I went to No 5 Operational Training Unit at Aston Down near Cheltenham to learn to fly the Hurricane. The fact that I had been selected for fighters was a great joy. The operational training unit was manned by many of the Officer and Sergeant Pilots who had been in No 1 Squadron during the Battle of France and thus had operational experience. The CO was Wing Commander 'Bull' Halahan, who had been its commanding officer. The Hurricane was a great advance on the aircraft we had used during training. It was, of course, a single-seater so that there was no opportunity for a dual flight before being sent off on my first solo. The experience of flying these aircraft was exciting because some of them were quite elderly; but one soon felt very much part of the machine and its weapons system. At the end of the course on 26 September, I was posted to No 1 Squadron. This was a particular honour for me because of the close association the OTU had with the squadron, and Halahan made a special point of telling me so.

No 1 Squadron at the time was at Wittering, near Stamford, on the Great North Road. After France it had been based in the South of England, but had been withdrawn further back to rest and take on a new complement of pilots. The Poles, Czechs, French and others were just beginning to come into the operational squadrons, and it developed into quite a cosmopolitan unit. At this time there was little operational work, and though the Battle of Britain was still in progress the squadron was not often called upon.

The station at Wittering was commanded by Group Captain Harry Broadhurst, who had already distinguished himself in the operational field and would continue to do so throughout the war. After I had been with the squadron for three weeks he sent for me. This was a sufficiently extraordinary occurrence for me to recognise that something was in the wind, and my first conclusion was that the authorities had relented on my commissioning. But I began to feel some foreboding when I was marched in front of the station commander by the station warrant officer as if I was on a charge. 'Hats off – right turn – left turn', etc. It turned out that my papers had arrived from my Flying Training School, and Harry Broadhurst felt that I had not been sufficiently punished. I tried to protest that I had lost my commission, but it didn't work, and he condemned me to one month's duty pilot. This was an activity which has long disappeared in the Royal Air Force, but it meant that I was air traffic controller both day and night, and generally looked after the activities of the airfield. This kept me pretty busy, and there was not much opportunity for sleep; the airfield was operational at night as there were German aircraft about, and Broadhurst used his black Hurricane (with some success) to hunt them. He and I have often laughed about this incident, but it certainly helped to knock the over-confidence out of me, and was intended to do just that.

During this short period, the CO of my squadron was killed in a flying accident and my own Flight Commander took over. He was a Canadian (later killed in Malta) and a good friend, who saw that the best way to get me out of my self-inflicted situation was to have me posted to another Hurricane squadron in the south of England. This was much to my liking because as well as getting rid of my local chores it was an opportunity for full operational activity. I was therefore posted in the middle of October to No 17 Squadron at Debden, near Saffron Walden. I packed my few belongings into the back of a Magister aircraft and was ferried down to Debden by one of the squadron pilots. I shall never forget his name – it was Pilot Officer Boot. When we got to the Debden area it was obvious that the airfield had just come in for some very severe treatment from the Luftwaffe. There were bomb craters all over the field, and it was clear that for the time being at least the squadrons had gone elsewhere. We hurried down to ground level in case some Messerschmitt 110 took a dislike to us, and set course for Martlesham Heath, near Woodbridge, an airfield we knew had sometimes been used by 17 Squadron. As it happened, the squadron had deployed there after the bombing of Debden and it was to remain there for several months. Before that eventful day was over I had met the CO, Squadron Leader Tony Miller, and been allotted to 'B' Flight.

Martlesham Heath was an airfield which the service had used for experimental work before the war. My flight, which was commanded by Flight Lieutenant Alf Bayne – now dead, but in these days a great hero and friend – was situated in commandeered civilian houses on the edge of the airfield. Our aircraft stood dispersed, but at readiness, on the heath outside. Since I had come from the famous No 1 Squadron, the first question Bayne asked was: 'Are you an Ace?' 'No', was the answer: I was a recently trained pilot of less than 250 flying hours with no operational experience. As he spoke the telephone rang, the hooter went, the room emptied like a flash and the squadron took off – quickly picking up formation and disappearing to the south-east in the climb. I was left to receive a few words of sound advice from the technical Flight Sergeant who ran the flight. He left me in no doubt of the lowly nature of my squadron status.

Even today the ring of the telephone and the sound of a hooter bring back much of the atmosphere of excitement and fear, and the wish not to let the squadron down. For me, at just twenty, it was an incredible experience. A few months before, I had never left Scotland. Now I was a member of a famous front-line fighter squadron with a long history and tradition. I knew I was insufficiently trained for the operational task; for instance, I knew little about deflection shooting[4] in the air-to-air battle. My main fear was not of the danger of being killed by the enemy or in a flying accident (and there were many at that time) but of not being able to make it, and being thrown out of the squadron – a failure.

I was given a few hours to get to know the operational area, and put in some dog-fighting practice, and was then declared operational.[5] It was a proud moment. This was the end of September, and the Battle of Britain – while past its climax – was still in progress. Some days we flew down to North Weald airfield, near Epping, and spent the day operating from there. Sometimes we operated from a field at Stapleford Abbots, not far from Debden. But the main operations were done from Martlesham Heath. Our day started before dawn, with early calls and the trip down to dispersal by truck. The aircraft would already be warming up, and the first task was to get parachutes and helmets into position and to make sure the aircraft were ready for immediate take-off. As dawn broke, the Flight Commander would report to Operations at Debden Sector that we were ready to go. Depending very much on the weather, it could be a long day, maintaining readiness right up till dusk, which was a favourite time for the Luftwaffe to start operating.

If the weather was reasonable we could perhaps be scrambled three or four times, either as a squadron or as a section of two or more. Often it was a case of stalking a Dornier, Heinkel or JU88 in and out of cloud. But in the early days of my operations with No 17 Squadron, if we were scrambled it usually meant that large numbers of German aircraft were attacking somewhere in the south of England. As an apprentice (and there were others) my task was to learn the art as rapidly as possible before an experienced operator on the other side claimed a victim. At that time most of our operations or scrambles were over the south coast, or into the Thames Estuary, to cover shipping convoys going up the east coast.

After I had been with the squadron some three weeks I was given the task of being one of the 'weavers'. The squadron normally flew as twelve aircraft in four 'Vs' of three in fairly close formation, with the 'Vs' in line astern. (The wisdom of doing this was much debated.) Two aircraft of the squadron were detached as the 'weavers', one above and one below the squadron. The purpose was to make sure that the squadron was not 'jumped' out of the sun, or indeed from anywhere, without warning. The job had its advantages and disadvantages. The main advantage was that though the 'weaver' had to stay in close proximity to the squadron he was not flying in formation, and thus was a more mobile platform and not such a good target. The disadvantage was that by criss-crossing above or under the squadron, and watching the sky behind, he could easily fall behind the squadron and become a prey to fighters above. Once behind, it was very difficult to catch up without using far too much fuel. Even 'weaving' close to the squadron one was inevitably covering much more sky than that squadron, and so used a good deal more fuel. My first two appearances in this role were unfortunate, and I narrowly missed being shot down by a Messerschmitt 109, a hail of tracer passing over me without warning. But having survived, I learnt quickly. The 'weaver' had to be as close to the squadron as possible, with great vigilance in case the squadron commander made a sudden turn.

During my early days with 17 Squadron there was much operational activity, but the squadron seemed to miss major action against any large German formation. The luck, if that is the right word, changed in early November. On mid-morning of the 8 November we were scrambled from Martlesham Heath to patrol a convoy just north of the Thames Estuary. We got there without delay in reasonable weather, but the damage had already been done, and several ships were sinking and others badly damaged. The naval escort and some of the ships gave us a nervous anti-aircraft barrage, but with little damage. We stayed with the convoy until our fuel was low. About mid-afternoon we were again scrambled to patrol the same convoy. This time we were put to the south of it, and ran straight into attackers – some twenty-five JU87 dive-bombers and fifty ME109s as escort.

It was a hazy autumn afternoon and I got the impression that our warships had lost touch with their charges. We did not; and the squadron gave the JU87 force a severe savaging without any effective interference from the ME109s. (I later flew a captured JU87 and understood why it might not be the ideal aircraft to have close combat with a fighter.) It was a great victory.[6] Later that evening we flew another sortie to the convoy, but it was not attacked. When we landed, there was a welcome signal of congratulations awaiting us from Winston Churchill. It was a good day, with many lessons learnt.

On 11 November the squadron had a similar experience, though not nearly so successful. It started just after dawn, with the terrible telephone from operations giving the scramble order to patrol a convoy coming out of the Thames Estuary. There was no enemy action, and we returned to base. But we were scrambled again in mid-morning and found a considerable air battle, with other squadrons involved, already taking place around the convoy. We ran straight into some thirty JU87s which were on their way to attack the ships, and this time the ME109 escort had kept in touch. The radar assessment was that a hundred and fifty ME109s were in the area. The Squadron Commander sighted the bombers and led our squadron into attack. As 'weaver' I then warned the squadron that a large formation of ME109s was diving to the attack and at the same time evaded a hail of lazily moving tracer bullets. The squadron acquitted itself well and destroyed three JU87s and two ME109s (plus four and one probables), but in doing so we lost two of our most experienced pilots. One dived straight into the sea and the other, with his aircraft badly damaged, was killed trying to make a landing in a field just across the Essex coast.

Later that day we were again scrambled to patrol the same convoy which had progressed further up the east coast. There was a good deal of cloud cover by then, and we were sent above the cloud whilst our sister squadron, No 257, was put over the convoy below. No 257 was commanded by Bob Stanford Tuck, already famous in the fighter world and later to become more so before being taken prisoner. Again I was the 'weaver', and as we emerged through the cloud I was shattered to see a formation of bi-planes heading in the opposite direction in a steep dive. I hesitated to report this to the Squadron Commander, thinking I was making an awful mistake. But this was the first appearance of the Italian Regia Aeronautica bombers in the battle against Britain. They took a bad beating. Later that evening we went out to see one of their bombers which had crashed on the heath not far from Martlesham. The air gunner had a bullet through his head, but the rest of the aircrew survived. In the aircraft there were empty bottles of Chianti and a large cheese, partly eaten. I did not see the Italians again for some time, and that was in another theatre of war.

I have not attempted to cover in any detail the Battle of Britain[7] and the last few weeks of it in which I participated. My aim has been to try to give an impression of a rapid transition from a very narrow life in Scotland to a humble part in one of the great battles of history. The squadrons took considerable punishment in pilot losses and injury, including bad burns and mutilations.

As the Battle progressed the experience of the fighter pilots dwindled. Earlier in the year, when a good many squadrons had gone over to the continent for the Battle of France, some of their commanders were aged between forty and fifty, but by the middle of the Battle of Britain the age-level had plummeted, and it was not unusual for a Squadron Commander to be under twenty-five. The 'oldies' left the scene fairly quickly, simply because the speed of events and the demands of air fighting were too much for them. But the career pattern in the Royal Air Force at that time meant that you were getting on a bit before reaching even the rank of Squadron Leader. The use of acting ranks met the problem, though this meant that at the end of the war it was not unusual for an Air Commodore to be reduced to his substantive rank of Squadron Leader.

For many of us, the Battle was not a self-conscious heroic

attempt to keep the Germans from invading our country, though this feeling was somewhere at the back of the mind. Much more it was a feeling of a great game, boosted by the squadron *esprit de corps* of that time and the wish not to let the squadron down. I have often thought back on those days, and still the feeling of defending this country against the Germans does not come through clearly. In my case this was probably due to unawareness of the main issues. The Czech and Polish pilots in the squadron had no doubt what the issues were, and felt a smouldering hatred against the Germans. At times this could lead to irresponsible acts of courage which put both their aircraft and their own considerable experience at risk.

By the time the Battle of Britain was over there were very few regular Air Force Officers left in the fighter squadrons. Most were Short-Service Officers, auxiliaries and Volunteer Reserve pilots like myself. Amongst these were many of the finest examples of British, Commonwealth and Allied manhood, and they took to command and leadership easily. There was no lack of fighting spirit. The squadron was the basic unit of loyalty. Often pilots in the squadron would not know the name of the Station Commander, and the command and staff organisation above him was a mystery. Occasionally we would receive a visit from a gold-braided Staff Officer – usually an unpopular occasion as the squadron would be encouraged to get its hair cut and generally try to assume a smarter appearance. Also, there were commanders and commanders. Some knew exactly how to talk to junior pilots and make them feel at ease, and could discuss the operations of the time. Others had no idea, and positively lowered morale because pilots were quick to detect someone who did not understand their problems. Certainly during the first year or two of the war, very few of the operational commanders had recent operational experience, and because of this many mistakes were made.

Notes

1. Under which an officer served for four or five years, followed by four years on the Reserve.

2. Pilots at Redhill were instructed on the Miles Magister, at Montrose on the Master.

3. Sgt Cameron had been awarded his Flying Badge on 18 July 1940.

4. I.e. making allowance for a moving target by firing ahead of it.

5. Sgt Cameron's name first appears in the Operations Record Book for No 17 Squadron on 16 October, when he carried out 'other flying' for thirty-five minutes. He was operational two days later.

6. According to the Squadron ORB, fifteen JU87s were claimed to have been destroyed, together with seven probables and one damaged. The squadron was congratulated by AOC No 11 Group, by C-in-C Fighter Command and by the Chief of the Air Staff for its achievement.

7. The Battle of Britain is officially considered to have finished on 31 October, but fighter activity continued afterwards.

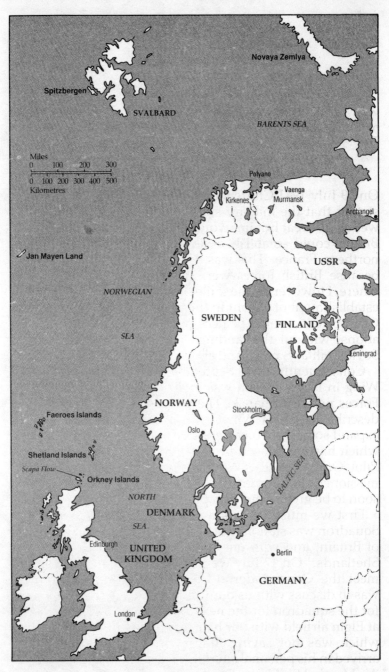

Map showing the route to Russia and the area of No 151 Wing operations

2   RUSSIAN INTERLUDE

On 19 July 1941 Churchill received a telegram from Stalin stating that the military situation of the Soviet Union, as well as of Great Britain, would be considerably improved if Britain could establish a second front against Hitler in northern France. This was of course a ridiculous request because British forces were in sore straits nearly everywhere. However, in the same message Stalin also urged the establishment of a front in the north, 'Here, on the part of Great Britain, would be necessary only naval and air operations, without the landing of troops or artillery', since Soviet military, naval and air forces would also take part.

Consequently, on 11 September 1941 a newly established Wing in North Russia was in action alongside Soviet Air Forces near Murmansk. The purpose of this chapter is to describe how this Wing – 151 Wing – got there and to expand somewhat on an episode of Royal Air Force history which has never been properly recorded. I was a humble Pilot Officer on the Wing, having only just been commissioned, but because of a serious flying accident, I was soon to be given a more responsible role.

First we must go back a month or two to when No 17 Squadron was stationed at Elgin in Scotland after the Battle of Britain, and with one flight at Sumburgh Head in the Shetlands.[1] On 17 July we were all summoned to Elgin to meet the Commander-in-Chief, Fighter Command who was to discuss with us our future and what the plans were for the squadron for the next few months. We all gathered at Elgin airfield with our hair cut and in our best uniforms, which was not saying much, and soon the great man arrived in his personal aircraft, covered in medals. This was Air Marshal Sir Sholto Douglas who had been a great hero in World War I and had now taken over Fighter Command from Air Chief Marshal Sir Hugh Dowding who had directed the Battle of Britain.

Naturally we all felt that something great was in the wind for us and we hung on every word that was being said. It was an occasion which I will always remember as an example of how a senior officer should not address his troops. We heard that we were to stay in Scotland at least for the next year, and that our role was to be to train fighter pilots who would soon be posted down to southern England where the action was going. It was a dreadful anti-climax for those of us who were anxious to get into the action ourselves, but clearly we were to be denied. The great man then got into his aircraft and disappeared to the south, leaving us to our fate.

However, before he was back at his own headquarters we had received a signal stating that the squadron was to be split up – one flight was to proceed to Royal Air Force Leconfield to form the basis of a new squadron, whilst the other flight was to proceed somewhere else for a similar purpose – in both cases the ultimate destination was unknown and the greatest secrecy was to surround our going. This was quite a turn-up for the books as we had only just dispatched our C-in-C who had quite a different story. Personally I was shattered by just how out of touch a senior officer could become and in the middle of a near-global conflict. It was a lesson that I was never to forget, though at the time I had no pretensions for high rank – the squadron was my life and I looked no distance beyond that.

The excitement grew when it became known later that evening that it was to be a volunteer-only operation and remembering the words that we had heard earlier from the C-in-C I had no hesitation in volunteering. Happily none of my special colleagues and friends had either, and we repaired to the Crown Hotel in Elgin to discuss the day's events and the possibilities for the future.

At that time I was still a Sergeant Pilot but the word had come through that I was to be commissioned along with another sergeant, though time was not on our side to complete the formalities before the new situation developed. We left our aircraft at Elgin where another squadron was to take over and departed by Harrow aircraft to

Leconfield on the 28 July. As soon as we landed there I
decided that if we did not get a move on we would go on
some operation still as sergeants, so applying for a few
days' leave we departed for London to persuade the Air
Ministry that they must hurry the commissioning pro-
cedure. But the civil service was not to be hurried even in
wartime. This put us in a bit of a quandary. It was clear that
we were destined for overseas somewhere but we did not
have in our hands the actual commissioning authorisation.
We decided that the only answer was to pay a call on Messrs
Moss Bros in Covent Garden, persuade them that our
commissioning was real, and get the necessary uniforms
and other kit. They were sympathetic to our persuasion and
we left the shop fully kitted as Pilot Officers. We celebrated
a little and then took the train to Yorkshire. Our only hope
was to put a bold face on the situation and hope that our
papers would come through before we left the UK. The CO
seemed pleased to see us in our new rank and went out of
his way to make us feel at home in the Officers' Mess.[2] I
think he was in a sense relieved that we had taken the
action that we had because we were both by then experienced leaders at least in the air. Happily before we left
England the commissioning papers came through and we
were made honest men, but it had been touch and go. The
peacetime air force would have been deeply shocked, but
times were not normal and occasionally action had to be
taken which was a little unorthodox. As I will explain in a
moment, it was just as well that we had gone ahead with
our own commissioning.

So at Royal Air Force Leconfield No 134 Squadron was
formed from what had been the famous No 17 Squadron. I
will not here recount what happened to the other part of the
squadron, beyond mentioning that they went to Burma
taking the squadron number with them and arrived in time
to take part in the dreadful events which had just struck
the Far East Air Force. Many of them became Japanese
prisoners of war. Such are the fortunes of choice and war.
134 Squadron was joined by 81 Squadron commanded by
Squadron Leader A. Rook and thus, with the HQ staff,
made up the Wing commanded by Wing Commander
H. N. G. Ramsbottom-Isherwood, AFC.

We had no aircraft but it was clear that wherever we were going we were to be flying Hurricanes. In the meantime we were receiving reinforcements in the shape of another flight's worth of pilots and new ground crew. It was clear that no sensible Squadron Commander was going to offer up his best pilots or indeed his ground crew when an order was received to help form another squadron, so quite a wide selection of half-trained pilots and ground crew turned up. It was a major task sorting out who was accept-able and who was not, and time was not on our side as we had been warned that we would have to move within a fortnight. The equipment section at Leconfield started handing out desert-style clothing so the rumour naturally was that we were off to the Far or Middle East. However the first intelligence breakthrough came when two Russian-speaking officers appeared and the options began to narrow, remembering of course that Russian territory had been invaded at dawn on 22 June 1941. It was not long before Russian dances were being performed in the Mess. There was however no official confirmation from higher authority and it was not until we were safely aboard ship that the final destination became known. It came as quite a shock.

On 12 August at 0300 hrs the main party, composed of HQ staff and 81 Squadron pilots and ground personnel, left by train for Liverpool docks where they boarded the *Llanstephan Castle*, 11,000 tons and built in 1913. They were joined aboard by officers of the Czech and Polish Missions to Moscow and journalists, including Vernon Bartlett, MP, and Charlotte Haldane, Moscow correspondent of the *Daily Sketch*; also a young Polish artist, Felix Topolski, later to become internationally famous. They arrived in Scapa Flow on 15 August leaving for Iceland on 16 August by which date we at Leconfield were more or less ready to move when the inevitable Harrow transport aircraft turned up to take the squadron to Abbotsinch airfield which stands close to the Clyde and the port of Glasgow. It was clear by now that some sea journey was on the cards but we had not reckoned on an aircraft carrier and HMS *Argus* at that. As we circled the airfield we could see in the harbour this tiny looking carrier which was to be our home for the next twenty-one days. *Argus* had originally been an Italian mer-chant ship which had gone to the Royal Navy at the end of World War I. The upper structure had been carved off and between the wars it had been converted to an aircraft carrier by putting a flimsy steel deck over the superstructure. It had also been used for launching the Queen Bee unpiloted aircraft which meant that there was a structure at the end of the deck which gave the Queen Bee a lift in life but did nothing for the Hurricane as we were soon to find out.

The Royal Navy were their usual friendly selves and did not seem to mind too much having sixteen eager fighter pilots to cope with. For them it meant doubling up in cabins during the journey north and the old ship was not very comfortable. The propeller screw vibrated the whole ship and at night sleeping was not easy to come by unless, as the RN medical officer advised, we drank a good deal of Plymouth gin. It certainly helped.

We sailed on 19 August and headed north accompanied by two destroyers. Our ultimate destination was still not known but it became clear fairly soon that we were heading in the short-term at least for Scapa Flow. We anchored there the following day. Scapa was full of the Home Fleet as would be expected, among which were the *Repulse* and the *Prince of Wales*, the latter having arrived there on 18 August from the USA via Iceland, with Churchill aboard after his meeting with Roosevelt. These two great ships were soon to go to the bottom off the coast of Malaya, not so far from where the rest of our squadron had gone. The wait in Scapa was wearisome, though helped by some sailing and numer-ous games of deck hockey – a game I became much addicted to as long as one was not catapulted over the side by an illegal tackle. I was to discover that the game could be played on almost any sized ship though some of the ob-stacles became quite a challenge. Eventually we sailed on 30 August and as we headed out into the North Sea we began to attract our escort. This included the aircraft carrier HMS *Victorious*, a variety of cruisers and numerous destroyers and minesweepers. It was a formidable armada.

When the coast of Scotland was behind us and the chance even of sending a message to Hitler in a bottle had dis-appeared, we were called to a briefing where we were told that our destination was to be the Soviet Union and that we were headed for an airfield called Vaenga which was close to Murmansk in northern Russia, and which had been used in Russia's war against Finland. As we already knew, there were sixteen Hurricanes on board and we were to fly these off and land at a Soviet base. None of us had done a take-off from a carrier before and on pacing out the flight deck we were not much encouraged. However, we were assured that it had been done before and that the Navy had thought of everything and provided an experienced Fleet Air Arm officer to help instruct us how to do it – in theory of course, as it was not a technique which could be practised in such circumstances. It had to work first time or not at all. As it was, the experienced deck operator was little use to us, giving quite the wrong advice on how to get a fairly heavy Hurricane off a deck which had a Queen Bee accelerator at the end of it. More of that later. In the meantime we heard that our other squadron pilots and the ground crews, together with the Wing Commander and his staff, were on the first trial Russian Convoy, code name 'Dervish', together with the rest of our boxed aircraft and equipment. The former were to be assembled in Kegostrov near Archangel prior to being flown northwest to Vaenga. As an aside I cannot see an expedition of this nature being entrusted to a Wing Commander in modern times. An Air Vice-Marshal might be the more likely nomination nowadays. A sad reflection perhaps.

We were soon in the Arctic Circle, then on again heading north still with a substantial escort. Our first stop was at Spitzbergen, or the Svalbard Islands as the Scandinavians call them. There a force was dropped off to deny what would have been a good strategic base for the Germans. Then we headed (or sailed) east to reach our fly-off position. We were due to leave the carrier on 7 September and the Captain was determined to get rid of us at all costs, as he was getting a little short of fuel.

The final briefings took place through 6 September and our take-off was timed for 0300 hrs on 7 September, it being light nearly throughout the twenty-four hours in that part of the world at that season. One of the difficulties was that the normal magnetic compass did not work accurately in such high latitudes and certainly not accurately enough to make for good navigation. And we were going to need good navigation because we were headed for an unknown coast with no navigational aids of any sort, and with some very inferior maps which the Russians had sent us. So the technique was developed that a destroyer should deploy on the horizon and after take-off we should set course over the carrier and towards the destroyer, at the same time engaging our Gyro compasses, and this would be the means of navigating to the Russian base. The plan was that the navigating officer of the carrier should rush out immediately before our take-off with the required information written on a blackboard. We hoped that the navigator got his sums right.

The first six aircraft to go were drawn up on the flight deck the night before, and after their departure the next six would be drawn up. We were awakened at 0200 hrs, with breakfast for those who felt up to it, and made our way to the flight deck where we found thick fog. As I mentioned earlier, the Captain of the *Argus* was determined to get rid of us as soon as possible (and indeed many of us were ready to go) so he decided to turn the carrier about and to sail back into a clear weather patch which we had passed through previously. He found the patch before too long and announced that he was ready to launch aircraft. The fact that our course was destined to take us directly through the fog did not seem to worry him. The first six aircrew got strapped in and ready to go, led by the Squadron Commander, Squadron Leader Tony Miller. The rest of us repaired to the safety nets to watch the fun, and we were not to be disappointed. The ship swung into wind and the first Hurricane set off down the deck and made a perfect take-off. We breathed a sigh of relief. However, the second aircraft set off and, remembering the briefing the so-called experienced deck aviator had given us, got his nose well up; having thus got into quite the wrong attitude he clipped the Queen Bee accelerator and promptly disappeared over the edge of the carrier. We all thought for sure that he had gone to a watery grave. But no, he managed to keep his Hurricane in the air though he had left a substantial piece of his propeller on the deck. Once the fly-off had started it could not really be stopped, and the next aircraft made exactly the same mistake; he too managed to stay in the air but with his undercarriage hanging down and useless. So it was a depressing start, and as the next six aircraft were brought up in the lift a very sad looking formation was seen struggling over the navigation destroyer.

I was in the second six and having learnt the lessons from the first-off we got away without trouble, formed up over the carrier and set course for the destroyer, at the same time engaging our Gyro compasses. Soon after passing over the destroyer we were in thick fog as we had expected and closed up into tight formation so that we would not lose each other. We were right down at sea level, just skimming the waves as we dared not go up through the fog in case there would be no chance of letting down again. After about thirty minutes of fog I was beginning to ask myself what would happen if the weather was like this all the way to Vaenga. Happily we flew out of the fog and into clear weather and the next problem was to make a good landfall and hope that our Gyros had not precessed too much as they were inclined to do after an hour's flying. But soon the Russian coast was in view and we set about finding the airfield, which in the end did not prove too difficult. However there were already two Hurricanes lying on their bellies as a result of the earlier carrier accidents. We landed without incident as did the other aircraft that followed us off the carrier. HMS *Argus* already seemed a long way away, as indeed she was and on course for home.

Soon we were surrounded by the Russian fighter pilots from the three Soviet squadrons already based there. They wanted to see the aircraft and to have a close look at the strange creatures that had flown them there. The difference between the two sets of pilots was quite staggering. The Russians always dressed in thick leather flying coats and carried revolvers at their sides, and they always wore their flying helmets whilst on duty. Their heads were shaved. On the British side, and speaking for myself, I had longish hair, suede flying boots and a new barathea uniform (recently persuaded out of Moss Bros against regulations).

The airfield was really a sandy strip which had been bulldozed out of pine forest and on it were to be two bomber squadrons and four fighter squadrons, of which two were British. We soon settled into the task of getting our aircraft operational as the airfield was raided almost daily by JU88s and ME110s escorted by ME109s and flying out of airfields in Norway. The Soviet operational area was commanded by a Major General of the Fleet Air Arm as it was in the maritime sector and we came under his direct control for operations. These were directed from a command post dug out of rock overlooking the Vaenga air base, and reminded me of my ideas of the Spanish Civil War.

Part of the ground staff had arrived by air and sea by 5 September and the remainder came by train and air, including the pilots of 81 Squadron who flew the reassembled Hurricanes from Kegostrov, refuelling on the way, by 16 September, on which date the Wing was complete. The BBC announced on 14 September our arrival in Russia. We learnt that two of our T Class submarines, *Trident* and *Tigris*, had been operating with the Russians at their large naval base at Polyano at the entrance to the Murmansk inlet since early in the previous month.

In the meantime we bedded down as best we could. Our home for the next few months was to be a newly and badly built house not far from the airfield which soon became known as the Kremlin. We had to walk some four hundred yards for our food. It was not quite to some people's liking, but to a restaurateur in the Belgravia area it would have been very acceptable. It was caviar in great amounts at breakfast, which usually meant at about 0600 hrs. This coupled with a great plateful of fried eggs was the staple breakfast diet. At midday we had some bread and soup and in the evening it was usually a fatty stew of some sort plus plenty of caviar. A fine mixture.

We were very closely guarded. There was no question of going off to the local village. The only time that we were allowed to leave the camp was to visit Murmansk fifteen miles southwest and that was under very heavy escort. The town of Murmansk was a bleak and desolate place, having to face German air raids nearly every day. There were no shops there of any merit and when we visited it was amazing to see the interest that was taken in our clothes. In the middle of Murmansk we became surrounded by the locals despite the police or NKVD guard and I found that I was being fingered to feel the quality of my uniform. Our visit was a local sensation, and much better than the Red Army Choir whom we had gone to see.[3]

Operations had started two days after our landing and as soon as our aircraft were fully operational. Unfortunately some bright equipment armourer had sent the wrong key part for our machine guns and we had to ask the Russians if they could help. They made replacement parts within forty-eight hours – a splendid piece of emergency engineering. Flight Lieutenant Jack Ross (who was killed later) and I did the first patrol with one of the Soviet squadron commanders – one Major Kharueonco. He was from Georgia and a great personality. The fact that we could not communicate between aircraft did not seem to worry him though it did us, and we set off to have a good reconnaissance of the sector that we should be operating over. As we crossed the front line we got the usual greeting of anti-aircraft fire, but the bigger problem was that my engine kept stopping and starting. This was due to the fact, as I discovered later, that the octane value of the Soviet fuel was different to the British fuel and the Merlin engine of the Hurricane was not used to it. I was sure that I was going to be the first casualty that the Wing in Russia was going to suffer. However, we made it and got a good idea of the rather inhospitable territory we would be operating over. The Germans had advanced to within about seventy miles of the port of Murmansk and the fall of this important port would have been a serious loss to the Russians and opened the door to an offensive on Archangel and down towards Leningrad as well as giving the Germans a base to attack reinforcement convoys with supplies from the west.

The absence of any radar in the sector was a great disadvantage to our operations. The most warning we got of a German air attack was when the Luftwaffe crossed the front line and they were spotted by the Soviet Army. But the usual warning was when bombs began to fall in and around the airfield – not ideal conditions for fighter operations. However, when we did get airborne in time we began to inflict losses on the enemy and elicited some admiration from the Soviets who were not having the same success. It was clear very soon that the Soviet squadrons were being given the first warning of an attack and when we saw the scramble it was time for us to get in the air. This was a very unsatisfactory state of affairs and drove us into an element of standing patrol – not a good way of operating because of the waste in engine hours. Also our aircraft were very vulnerable on the ground and we asked for shelters to be built for them. This was done in a remarkably short time by a vast labour squad being summoned. They were a sad looking gang of over a thousand of all nationalities from the length and breadth of Russia. One wondered what they had done to be given the privilege of working in these ghastly squads. At about midday, a donkey cart would appear with their rations which consisted of a small piece of black bread and a handful of rice. By mistake one day I wandered into one of their living quarters which was in a huge barn-like structure with hundreds of bunk beds going up to the ceiling. The smell was horrific (shades of the Gulags as we came to know them).

The shelters when constructed were a marvel of innovation. Soil was excavated so that the aircraft could be parked partly below ground level and the shelters were then built around them using some of the surrounding pine trees that had been chopped down. The roof was then covered by branches. They were very effective and we did not lose any aircraft on the ground; the cost must have been minimal (shades of the sophisticated shelters of today). The tricky part was to get the aircraft out of the shelter quickly if there was a scramble. This was done by getting two airmen to sit on the tail to keep the propeller from being damaged. This resulted in a tragedy during a German raid, when one of our aircraft took off hurriedly with two airmen still sitting on the tail. As it got airborne the aircraft went vertically upwards, stalled, and the airmen were thrown off and killed. This occurred on 27 September and was our first real casualty incident. The pilot, Flight Lieutenant Berg, crashed from fifty feet up, sustaining concussion, lacerations and a perforated fracture of the thigh. He was eventually evacuated to the UK by cruiser, via Archangel.

He had been one of our Flight Commanders and I was appointed in his place, still as a Pilot Officer.

Meanwhile operations continued, mainly scrambles, fighter patrols and bomber escorts.[4] We were often fired on by the Russian anti-aircraft guns and I watched one of their own bombers being shot down as it crossed the front line. No doubt the gunner joined the labour squad. The Germans were very active and the lack of radar cover proved to be a serious disadvantage.

Our quarters – the Kremlin – were virtually a prison. We were not allowed to move out except to go for a meal after we returned from the airfield which was about one mile away. We made our own entertainment. There were no lavatories and only cold running water in the Kremlin and the nearest latrine was a pagoda-type building about a hundred yards away. This was nearly acceptable when we arrived, but as it got colder, which it very soon did, it became a major expedition. The Pagoda was a down-to-earth construction in more ways than one and there was no plumbing at all.

Arrangements had been made for the Wing to have one bath a week in Vaenga – and most did, though it was not always possible. This meant an escorted expedition to the village bath house one and a half miles away – I suppose it could be called a sauna under modern parlance, but very primitive. The hot room was tiered and with the hottest temperature near the roof. You just sat there and perspired, and used the remaining soap sparingly. The old Russian hags who ran the house came along and attacked you back and front with birch twigs. This was not an unpleasant sensation if you could take it, but they were wont to make remarks about your physical attributes and roar with laughter! The next move was into icy showers and, if you survived this performance, there was a good chance that you were clean, but it did not happen very often.

There were two special social occasions. The first occurred on 8 September with an invitation from the admiral[5] to a banquet at the local large club at 9.00 p.m. in order that all our officers could meet their Russian counterparts. About 150 were present, all in their best uniforms.

The white-clothed tables were groaning with bottles and

the inevitable caviar (which I still love regardless), and the festivities soon got under way. The first toast was made by the Admiral in Russian champagne. I cannot remember the exact designation of the toast, but I think it was to the king of England. The reply which came from our Wing Commander was to Joseph Stalin. The eating started. The next toast soon followed which was made with a well-filled glass of vodka. The British team sipped in appreciation, but the Admiral was on his feet again with the challenge that the English must drain their glasses in one and made the accusation that he did not think that the English could drink. This was a severe challenge and I knew that we were in for trouble. And so it went on during the evening and into the early morning. The toasts were numerous and the drinks mixed in the most suicidal fashion. We were all in turn called to make a toast – those who could still speak – but it was very clear that the Russians were holding their drink rather better than those the Admiral called the English (being a Scot I absolved myself from this collective term). Soon after midnight the English began to slip under the table, but not before the Wing Commander and the Admiral together had given a superb display of Russian dancing between the two long tables! I suppose 'passing out' is the expression, and it was done with some dignity, but certainly cars and an ambulance had to be called to take away the most severely 'wounded' who were being helped to their transports by our Senior Medical Officer and his Russian colleague. When inebriated the Russians seemed to insist on kissing each other. We had to rescue the Wing Commander from the embraces of three officers before we could leave!

Next morning (or the same morning), we had just enough pilots operational in all senses of the word to fulfil our operational responsibilities, but it was a long day. Planning for a return match started fairly soon afterwards. We had brought out from the UK a fairly extensive supply of whisky, gin and white rum (why white rum I don't know). The invitation eventually was extended to the Admiral and his team to come to the 'Kremlin' to be received by us on 23 October, really as a farewell party. Six officers from our Naval units at Polyano came also as our guests. Long tables were set up on the first floor, containing many salads, tinned meat and salmon, together with a huge bar. Decorations essentially consisted of coloured balloons with HSA (Hospital Savings Association) printed on them supplied by the Wing adjutant.

The Admiral sent his apologies at the last moment, but the others arrived carefully escorted by a large posse of commissars, who refused our hospitality, but who were there clearly to fulfil another role. The bottoms-up technique which we had learnt from the Russians worked the other way round in this case. I had been given hosting responsibilities for one Lt Rodin (and I will always remember his name). We could only communicate in simple drinking language, though there were several interpreters about, but I offered him a glass of good Scotch whisky which he proceeded to down in good Russian fashion. He was then happy to accept a replacement which he dealt with in the same fashion. I stood back to watch results which were not long in coming as his legs began to buckle and he became the first victim for the commissars' recovery system. It was soon clear that the Soviets had little experience of British drinks and the same happened to them as had happened to the British contingent some weeks earlier. We felt that we had had our revenge. I saw Lt Rodin next morning and he was looking sorry for himself but bore no grudge.

Operations continued until the end of October when the task was to teach the Russians to fly and operate the Hurricane. We had shown them how to operate the aircraft but in a way the more difficult thing was to get them familiar with flying it. This was a bit of a problem because of language, but the arrival of some skilled interpreters from Moscow made the task easier. The pilots who had been selected to operate the Hurricane were specially chosen from many Russian squadrons and were skilled pilots. They were to be the nuclei of the 4,800 Hurricanes which were to be given to the Soviet Union during the war. Not much is heard of this effort by the British people nowadays. But the pilots were good and it was not long before they were familiar with the aircraft. The Admiral had in fact flown his Hurricane first on 24 September. The technique was for us to perch on the wing of the Hurricane with the interpreter on one side and the trainee pilot in the cockpit. So with a three-way conversation we were able to get them to know the controls of the aircraft. We watched their first solos with interest and I remember that the pilots that I had been training did their initial solos in the first snow storms of the Russian winter. They managed admirably and we were all impressed with their capability (as indeed they were with the Hurricanes), and why not, because they had an air force going before the British and some of the great achievements in aviation had been generated by the Russians? They had many fine designers and engineers.

Our airmen appeared to like their Russian counterparts and the food, and the mixing with their officers. One airman wrote home saying, 'Even Group Captains help to wash the aircraft.' (A Russian Senior NCO wore four rings on his sleeve!)

During our time in the Soviet Union one of their squadron commanders was shot up during an attack on German positions in Norway. He managed to make his way back to Soviet territory where he baled out and later died. His body was brought back to Vaenga and some of us were invited to his funeral. He had been a brave aviator and I attended. I confess there was an element of curiosity in how a Soviet funeral was conducted in this Marxist state. By the time we reached the cemetery the first snow of winter was beginning to fall. The coffin was draped with the red banner and at the graveside the senior commissar gave a eulogy about the Fascist hordes and how the Soviet forces were so bravely defending against them. He paid honour to the departed aviator by describing his career and, as the body was committed to the ground, the Soviet national anthem was played. There was, of course, no mention of any religious element at all. I confess to leaving the cemetery with an absolutely hopeless feeling that this good and brave man had been sent on his way to nothing. As we left to go back to our camp, a blizzard was developing.

About this time a most unusual incident occurred. The Admiral told our Wing Commander he had received twelve thousand roubles (about £180) to be handed over to our pilots who had shot down a certain number of enemy aircraft! The going rate at the time for Russian pilots was one thousand roubles per aircraft shot down. Our immediate reaction was to organise a large party. However, on more sober reflection, I understand the Wing Commander decided the money should be donated to the RAF Benevolent Fund.

With the main element of the Russians having gone solo in the Hurricane, our primary task was over and we looked forward to returning to the UK. But we had quite a wait. The plan was that part of a Russian convoy that was returning to the UK would call in at Murmansk and pick us up. However, on 12 October a signal had arrived from the Chief of the Air Staff to say the whole Wing, with a few exceptions, would move south across Russia to the Middle East. On reflection this would surely be impracticable, since it would entail crossing all the Russian lines of communication. Indeed it was not until 5 November that we learnt we were to be evacuated direct to the UK by courtesy of the Royal Navy from the ice-free Murmansk inlet.

The weeks went by and it was a challenge to keep the Wing occupied. The first Russian pilot in a Hurricane had shot down a German fighter on 29 October. We were lent some skis and as the snow was then ideal we had a good chance to learn the art. But as it was by then dark most of the twenty-four hours, such activities were a little limited. The Admiral, having bestowed numerous gifts on the Wing Commander, capped them all by presenting him with a young reindeer. A similar gift also had been given to Admiral Bevan RN commanding our Naval contingent at Polyano. The 'RAF' reindeer was named by our CO 'Droochok', meaning little friend. Most unfortunately and much to the Admiral's disgust Droochok died in three weeks despite the efforts of our two doctors, neither of whom had any veterinary experience! This tragedy was all the harder to bear, the BBC having announced a fortnight earlier that the 'Naval' reindeer, which had been placed aboard the submarine *Tigris* on her way home, had arrived safely and had been presented to Whipsnade Zoo!

A most unfortunate accident occurred on 8 November when Surgeon Lieutenant Chin, the only doctor at the RN Polyano base, fell when skiing and fractured a thigh, which meant our two doctors had to cope with the medical problems at the base, a launch trip across the estuary.

On 20 November news was released that Wing Commander Ramsbottom-Isherwood, the two Squadron COs, Miller and Rook, and Flight Surgeon Haw, had been awarded the Order of the Red Banner. Then, a week later, their awards were upgraded to the Order of Lenin. Later Squadron Leader Gittens, the Engineer Officer, was also given the Order of Lenin. All these awards were presented in London by Mr Maisky, the Soviet Ambassador, in 1942.

On 21 November, HMS *Kenya* and several destroyers had anchored in Vaenga bay and were awaiting our arrival. The pier was a mile and a half from the airfield at Vaenga and we asked the Russians for transportation to get us there. This was refused – we had done our stuff and they were not really interested in us any more. So we had to march in the snow down to the port. I fell my flight in and with the one or two drill commands that I remembered we set off for Vaenga. I gave a sympathetic thought for Napoleon's retreat from Moscow as we set course. But we made it and spirits rose wonderfully as the Royal Navy vessels came into view. We were soon on board, eleven officers and 220 airmen as the advance party, and though the accommodation was sparse to say the least, it was all a little piece of Britain, and with some luck we would be home for Christmas. We sailed eventually on 28 November, the remaining half of the Wing following in HMS *Berwick* on 1 December. In the meantime, however, Admiral Burroughs, who was flying his flag in HMS *Kenya*, had been ordered by the Admiralty to proceed to bombard the port of Kirkenes and particularly the iron ore mines there. I was aboard *Kenya* and five of us were sleeping on camp beds in the Admiral's day cabin.

We therefore set course for Norway on 24 November accompanied by three British and two Soviet destroyers (I had noticed when they were alongside that the Soviet destroyers had women crew members). The Admiral thought it would be a good idea if all his Royal Air Force passengers had a job of work to do, and I was made one of the aircraft spotters. That evening we reached the fjord of Kirkenes and proceeded up it to get within range of the target. All went well for a time until the shore batteries got the message and opened up. Then when the target was in range we opened up with *Kenya's* main armament and the destroyers added their fire support. The noise was fantastic. Fires had started on shore and they seemed to me to get horribly close, and I was much relieved when the Admiral ordered a return down the fjord. (In 1978, when I was Chief of Defence Staff, my Norwegian opposite number took me to visit the Soviet border and we spent the night in a new hotel in Kirkenes. The iron ore mines seemed to be going full blast, but I was shattered to see how narrow the fjord was, remembering that Admiral Burroughs had sailed a task force there, turned it around in the fjord, and returned unharmed into the Murmansk inlet.)

When we finally sailed from Vaenga a few days later, none of us was unhappy to see the back of it. Whilst there had been plenty to do, it had been exciting, but the waiting for the return home had been a bore, particularly because of the almost perpetual darkness (twilight was from 1000 to 1400, but we did not see the sun). The next day we picked up a convoy of merchant ships proceeding back to the UK and gave it escort in the most foul weather as far as Iceland where another force took over. I was on the bridge with the watch-keeping officer when we passed the Orkney Islands and moved down the coast of Scotland. It was a beautiful moonlight night and we were returning home for Christmas – a sentimental moment. Next day, 6 December, we docked at Rosyth and the Royal Air Force party took a train to Catterick in Yorkshire, which was to be at least our temporary home whilst we equipped with new aircraft. The rest of the Wing on HMS *Berwick* arrived in Scapa Flow a couple of days later having fought its way through a 110 m.p.h. hurricane. The Wing HQ staff finally entrained for RAF Ouston, Northumberland, and 81 Squadron for Turnhouse near Edinburgh. The squadrons disappeared on leave like a flash though a few of us were left behind to collect our new Spitfires. I note from my log book that I did my first flight in a Spitfire on Christmas Day 1941. It was a brand new Spitfire V and it was a great thrill even on Christmas Day. I thought then that we had seen the last of the much-loved Hurricane, but it was not to be so. More of that later.

Hardly was Christmas over than we were deployed to Northern Ireland to convoy the first American troops coming to this country for eventual operations in north-western Europe. I had never been to Ireland, though I recognised that the Celts had made their way to Scotland from there. Our base was Eglinton just outside London-derry, and the Irish did not seem to have suffered the same privations foodwise that we in Britain had. During the first week in flying from Eglinton on convoy patrols we had a mixture of new and old Spitfires. The old ones had been left behind by the Eagle Squadron, one of the first American units to operate from this country but in Royal Air Force colours.

Flight Lieutenant Jack Ross, who had been a Pilot Officer when I joined No 17 Squadron during the Battle of Britain, and who had been promoted to command a Flight in No 134 Squadron where I eventually became the other Flight Commander, had been a particular friend throughout this period. We had been in Russia together and he had well earned the DFC, of which he was very proud. Whilst based in Ireland he had to ditch in the Irish Sea because of engine failure. We searched for him for hours but the Irish Sea in early January is not exactly a friendly place and eventually we had to give up. His was a great personal loss to me and though I had got used to losing friends I felt his death very severely. He was a little man, indeed a very little man in stature, but very large in spirit and courage. I wrote to his parents along these lines. I found it difficult in wartime to know exactly how to frame some letters to parents who had lost loved ones, but this one was not difficult because I felt so strongly about it. But life goes on.

Notes

1. Sgt Cameron had served with No 17 Squadron from 15 October 1940 until 28 July 1941. Until 25 February 1941 the squadron had stayed at Martlesham Heath, largely engaged on defensive operations over the coastal area and in support of North Sea convoys, but once or twice carrying out offensive patrols across the Channel and on one occasion escorting a force of Blenheims attacking the docks at Dunkirk where Cameron described the ack-ack as 'hellish'. Then after redeploying to Croydon, the squadron re-equipped with Hurricane IIs and until the end of March operated patrols over the south coast – after one such, on 5 March, Cameron was compelled to land at Gatwick after his engine had packed up three times over the Channel. The beginning of April saw the squadron briefly back at Martlesham Heath before reverting to the Hurricane I and moving north. From then until July, No 17 Squadron operated from a number of airfields in the north of Scotland, principally Castletown near Thurso, Sumburgh in the Shetlands, and Elgin, from where Sgt Cameron and many of his comrades were despatched to Leconfield on their way to Russia.

2. In recommending Cameron for commissioning, Squadron Leader Miller had referred to him as a keen fighter pilot who showed promise of becoming a leader of great ability. His intense desire to engage the enemy and his undoubted courage had been an example to other pilots of the unit.

3. This visit to a 'House of Culture' took place on 5 October, according to the Squadron ORB.

4. On 6 October, the Squadron ORB records, six aircraft of 'A' flight had taken off for practice flying when a formation of JU88s bombed the airfield. Red 1 (P/O Cameron) attacked the leader, firing a five second burst from slightly below and on the stern quarter, opening at 300 yards and closing to 100. There was no return fire, and the starboard engine of the enemy aircraft emitted a stream of black smoke. Red 1 broke away and attacked the second aircraft, also from quarter astern, opening at 250 yards and closing to 50. No results were seen. He then attacked a third JU88 from head on: turning to port he saw the enemy aircraft going slowly at a steep angle, both engines appearing to have been hit. P/O Cameron was credited with one 'probable' and one 'damaged' for his part in this action.

5. Admiral Kuznetsov, Commander of the Soviet Forces in the Kola Peninsula.

3 WESTERN DESERT

It was clear that once the American troops were safely across the Atlantic, we would not stay long in Northern Ireland. Life was not unpleasant, with plenty to eat and drink, but we were all anxious to get back to the real war. The call was not long in coming. We had changed our CO. Squadron Leader Tony Miller left on 10 February on promotion to become CO of No 600 Squadron – the Auxiliary squadron he had been in before the war. We were sorry to lose him.[1] We also at that time lost all our Australian contingent who had played such a big part in the success of the squadron. They went back to fight the Japanese.

Then on 23 March 1942 a signal arrived ordering us to move the squadron to an airfield called Baginton, in the Coventry area, and we quickly realised that this was only a temporary posting. We left Northern Ireland on 25 March. The night before our departure was a merry one, and the locals saw us off in style. I did not manage to get to bed at all.

However, we put together a good formation of all sixteen of our brand new Spitfires and saluted the local area before setting course for the mainland. After refuelling at Woodvale, near Southport, where we had to stay for a day owing to bad weather, we flew on to Baginton on the 27 March and landed safely in smog. I was still a very junior acting Flight Lieutenant,[2] having been commissioned for only eight months, but I was told that I was to be in temporary command of the squadron until a new CO could be posted in. The news also came that we were to prepare ourselves to go to the Middle East. Our beautiful new Spitfires were to be crated and transported to the Western Desert by cargo ship. That was the plan; but we were never to see them again. The ship that was carrying them was torpedoed in mid-Atlantic.

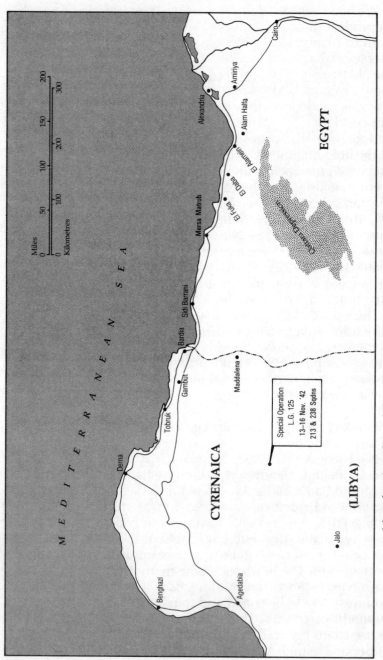

Map showing 'Special Operation' by Nos 213 and 238 Sqns in November 1942

We had been kitted up for the Middle East with the usual tropical clothing. After leave, we travelled on 10 April by train to Liverpool and the SS *Rangitata*. Sitting out in the Mersey estuary, she looked rather pathetic. She was one of the old freezer ships which carried mainly frozen lamb from New Zealand, and belonged to a New Zealand company. She was good for no more than fifteen knots, as we found to our cost later. The conditions on board were indescribably bad, particularly for our ground crew who were stacked up in the hold in tier-beds. There were four Spitfire squadrons on board plus units of the Army and some Royal Navy. We were a highly obstreperous bunch of aircrew, living in disgraceful conditions, and the four COs fell in before the OC troops of the ship to complain bitterly. He was a humourless man who had no idea how to deal with fighter squadrons or make the best of a bad job. I fear he was near distraction by the time we got to Durban, and was relieved to see the back of us. But we finally got there after an adventurous journey across the Atlantic, nearly to the coast of the United States, and then down to Freetown (29 April), which was the first land we saw after leaving Liverpool. On the journey our convoy had very little naval escort most of the time, and there were all sorts of scares of submarines and aircraft. We did all we could to keep morale up amongst the troops with concerts and the like, and they did wonderfully well, though it was all too much for one or two of them, who went over the side to a watery grave.[3]

One late afternoon as we were rounding the Cape of Good Hope, there were some heavy explosions and three of the ships in the convoy began to sink. The order from the leader of the convoy was full speed ahead on the assumption that we were being attacked by an enemy submarine. This put the poor old SS *Rangitata* in an unenviable position as we were the slowest ship in the convoy. As darkness fell we could see the rest of the convoy disappearing over the horizon, and were left very much to our fate. We survived a night spent mostly on stand-by. It later transpired that we had run through a minefield which had been laid by submarine. Three days later, on 18 May, we sailed into Durban harbour on our own, and with some pride. The rest of the convoy had already arrived.

The reception in Durban was wonderful. The ladies of the area had got themselves well-organised to entertain the troops. Buses were available to whisk them off – there were concerts, dances and swimming parties. A few years ago the main organiser received a presentation book which many of us had signed, including two Chiefs of Defence Staff and a Bishop of London. We were there for a week, billeted in a transit camp just outside Durban to await the arrival of the ship to take us up to the Middle East. The next part of our journey could not have been more different than the first. The ship was the SS *Mauretania*, and we were to make a fast, unescorted passage to Port Suez through the Red Sea. The ship was new and still in the trim for cross-Atlantic and other cruises, and we all lived in luxury, including access to a well-stocked bar. Even the ground crew were well looked after. In Durban a new CO, Squadron Leader Hartley, had turned up to take over from me as CO of the squadron, but he was not with us very long. The voyage was largely uneventful except for a very short stay at Aden on 1 June to drop off some airmen. When the great ship hove to, the heat of Aden really hit us, and we got some sort of idea what was in prospect. Travelling at some thirty knots we arrived safely at Port Tewfiq on 4 June where we disembarked and took the train for a transit camp at Fayid in the Canal area.

The transit camps where we stayed – Fayid, then Helwan and finally Kasfareet on the banks of the Suez Canal – were dreary places, and the squadron was soon suffering from the usual troubles, notably gippy tummy and sunburn. The kit which had been issued before we left the UK looked ridiculous; it might have been all right in the 1930s, but in 1942 it looked quite music-hall. I had been issued with a splendid topee mounted with an RAF flash, but I never wore it, and it soon found its way into the Canal. We were to be in those transit camps for nearly three weeks without any idea of what was going on in the rest of the world, even in the desert war, but I remember seeing with some horror the battleships HMS *Valiant* and *Queen Elizabeth* being towed through the Suez Canal after being damaged by Italian frogmen in the harbour at Alexandria. They were to be out of action for many months.

Eventually, on 2 July, the CO, the Flight Commander and the ten most experienced pilots were issued with transport and told to make our way up to Landing Ground 154 in the Western Desert, where we were to be affiliated to a somewhat war-weary Hurricane squadron, No 213. We would be operating Hurricanes – our own Spitfires being at the bottom of the Atlantic. All the other members of No 134 Squadron, including our splendid ground crew, were to go to Lydda, in Palestine.[4] This was bad news all round; but at least we were heading for action. We set course by road to join the Desert Air Force, passing through Cairo on our way. On the Cairo-Alexandria road it was soon clear that the flow of traffic was all one way, i.e. towards Cairo and the Canal Zone. On stopping at a 'char' shop ('Half-Way House' as it was known) we enquired of some Army officers what was happening and were told that General Rommel had won a great victory, and that if we had any sense we would go back the way we had come. But we had no sense, and continued our journey. In fact the traffic we were seeing was non-combat transport being withdrawn under the orders of General Auchinleck, to ensure that the Army would have to fight where they stood (i.e. El Alamein).

On reaching Amiriya, just south of Alexandria, we struck off into the desert to try to locate 213 Squadron. After learning some lessons about desert navigation by truck, we found them in their tented camp in the middle of a dust storm. They had no idea why we were there. Their rather sad-looking Hurricanes were dispersed around the sand strip looking very much the worse for wear. Soon after our arrival, on 4 July, the squadron took off for a sortie over the El Alamein position in a great cloud of dust, returning an hour later short of two of their number. I had known one or two of the squadron pilots before, so we got down to learning the ropes because it was clear that we were there to stay.[5] No 213 had seen almost continuous air fighting up and down the desert, and some of the aircrew clearly needed a rest. As we gradually took over, most of them were posted to non-operational tasks, though the more resilient ones continued on operations. To begin with it was not a particularly happy marriage and an odd way of doing things. The squadron clearly thought this new intake from the UK had a great deal to learn, as indeed we had. But things gradually settled down as we began to know the area and got some 'sand in our boots'.

The Western Desert was undoubtedly the right place to fight a war, that is if wars have to be fought. Wilfred Thesiger, one of the great desert travellers and writers, had said about the desert:

> No man can live this life and emerge unchanged. He will carry, however faint, the imprint of the desert, the brand which marks the nomad; and he will have within him the yearning to return, weak or insistent, according to his nature. For this cruel land can cast a spell which no temperate climate can match.

The desert can cast a spell. There was comradeship, the *esprit de corps* of a good squadron, the meeting up with many friends, the patrols and air fighting during the day, and sometimes at night. The celebrations after a victory in the air, the uplift with the arrival of the beer ration. The rising before dawn to get set up for a patrol. The smell of a dawn desert and of Merlin engines being run up as aircraft came to readiness. The nervous, queasy stomach, the mud-like tea, the breakfast eagerly eaten after a sortie. The return to readiness as the sun came up and the full heat of the desert came into the body. The hanging about waiting for a scramble or a set operation. The terrible heat of climbing into the cockpit of a metal aircraft at midday. The formation manoeuvring for take-off on the ground in dust clouds. The delicious sensation of cold air flowing into the cockpit as you gained height. The comfortable sight of your friends and colleagues forming up around you. The voice of the controller giving the first indication of enemy activity over the Alamein positions – the first tally-ho. The few hectic minutes of life and death. The order for home. Wheels down and back safely to the duty operations tent. The probing questions of the squadron intelligence officer and the Army Liaison Officer. This was a typical day. Perhaps you flew three or four times. Then came release as the desert dusk spread. A bath of some sort, a drink if there was one, some food and the camp bed.

There were few local people to get hurt. The Senussi nomads move freely about the desert, and they got the message that it was a good time to be elsewhere. The main sufferers were the combatants who introduced themselves into this strategic area. The surface of the desert is on the whole a mixture of rock and sand; but there are many areas of hard sand from which it is possible to operate an aircraft. Such places, some treated artificially, became the landing grounds for the Desert Air Force. The surface was very adequate, though aircraft systems could get badly eroded by the constant dust storms generated by vehicles, other aircraft, and certain meteorological conditions, like the khamsin – 'when the hot khamsin blows life becomes intolerable'.

As usual the Royal Air Force ground crews worked miracles to keep operations going. Most of the aircraft were old, and had been in the area for some time. Many of the reinforcements intended for the desert had been sunk in transit from the UK. The flow of Spitfires to the theatre had been abysmally slow, and the Hurricane IIC force was coping with ME109s and ME109Gs – both greatly superior to the Hurricane, except perhaps in manoeuvrability. Two of the four cannons had been removed from the Hurricane II C to give it a better performance. While it is useful to be able to turn inside your enemy in air combat, if the speed differential is too great it is difficult to take offensive action against him. Such was the case in the desert. This, coupled with the operational directive that the Hurricane force was to operate at about 10,000 ft, made our aircraft very vulnerable to the German and even Italian fighters. The reason for this directive was that the Commanders wanted the Army to see that they were being protected, particularly against JU87 dive bombers. It was quite common for a squadron or wing, from its patrol line in and around El Alamein, to see the German and Italian fighters taking off from their airfields at El Fuka and El Daba. Within minutes they had climbed above the Hurricane force, and could carry out their dive and climb attacks almost at will. The Hurricane tactic was to turn into the enemy while they were in their attack dive with the hope of securing a deflection shot on the turn, or catching one of the German fighters who got a little careless. This tactic, defensive though it was, got some surprisingly good results. But they could have been better. In its efforts to protect the Army from attacks by dive-bombers, the Royal Air Force got little advance warning because of the almost total lack of radar cover. We certainly succeeded in reducing the weight of attack against the Army; but in putting ourselves in such a vulnerable position in the sky, our force took heavy losses.

The morale of the Desert Air Force after the retreat to El Alamein was low, and no wonder. They had been on the move nearly every night, flying and operating hard during the day, and living very rough. So were the Army of course, but the Air Force had to keep some very sophisticated equipment working, while maintaining high operational flying skills amongst the aircrew.

Living conditions were tough, and aircraft standing out in desert storms had to take their chance of surviving. The tented camp was designed to be movable at very short notice. There was one HQ trailer, and another used by the squadron doctor as a consulting room; but otherwise it was tents for all of us. The officers and NCO pilots shared a mess, usually six to a tent. The first action on getting the tent erected was to dig some sort of slit trench fairly close by, so that refuge could be taken in the middle of the night when the desert airfields came under attack by JU88s or Dorniers – which was most nights. The equipment for hygiene was a canvas wash-basin and the occasional use of a canvas bath when the water supply permitted.

Before and during Alam Halfa and the Alamein battles the fighter squadrons were based back on the Cairo-Alexandria road in the Amiriya area. This meant that Alexandria was within a two-hour drive. After the desert tent, the fine suites of the Hotel Cecil in Alexandria were another world, and driving into the clear air of the sea coast as one approached Alexandria was an unforgettable experience. These excursions did not last long, but every moment was made to count, and if the squadron did not manage three night clubs during the evening they felt they had failed. In particular, two Lebanese sisters performed at all three night clubs, and they were assured of a following if the squadron was in town. I never hear the Serenade from *Harlequin's Millions* by the Italian composer Drigo without recalling this music which they used in their act.[6] Alexandria, the summer home of Egyptian kings and queens, was a great refuge.

As the El Alamein position consolidated, Cairo and Alexandria became the main goal posts standing behind the 8th Army and its associated Air Force. If the Afrika Korps had driven through to these goal posts and touched down on the Nile Delta, the war would have taken a very serious turn. Few realise how close the Axis came to achieving this aim. At the time of the Battle of Alam Halfa, in September 1942, they were within a day's drive of Cairo. Yet life went on in these two cities as if nothing much was happening. Though some of the braver Staff Officers were beginning to burn their papers and think longingly of the Levant, the hoteliers and club-owners in Cairo and Alex were made of sterner stuff.

It was always a levelling experience to fly back from Cairo to your landing ground in the desert, straight from a bedroom and bath to a dusty tent shared with several others, bully-beef and biscuits for supper, and a patrol over Alamein at dawn.

The Desert Air Force has never had its due recognition from historians and students of the Desert campaign. The Army had its historian in Monty himself. The RAF account should have been written by Air Marshal 'Mary' Coningham, a New Zealander, who was Commander of the Desert Air Force, but he was killed in the Tudor IV 'Star Tiger' which crashed near the Azores in January 1948. His memoirs were never published, nor his analysis of the operations of the Desert War. They would have made interesting reading.[7] The Desert campaign saw the start of the close cooperation between the Army and Royal Air Force which was carried over to the great operations in North-West Europe.

Much credit is due to Montgomery, a dedicated advocate of Army-Air cooperation, and the techniques that emerged in Africa were largely developed between him and Coningham. Relations between them were sometimes turbulent, but no more than you would expect from two powerful personalities.

There is no doubt that the Desert Air Force won air superiority when the 8th Army was on the retreat, and it made the later offensive a great deal easier. But certainly in the Hurricane squadrons, who were really outclassed and were having to operate at a difficult height for them, the losses sustained in the Desert War were greater than during the Battle of Britain. The lack of real radar cover was a great disadvantage. On one occasion a small formation of ME109s penetrated our defences and shot down three of the aircraft of 213 Squadron just as they had taken off and were trying to gain speed and height, and on another we lost six aircraft in one day. Things became a little easier when the Spitfires began to appear in some numbers because they gave the top cover to the Hurricanes flying at a lower level.

During the retreat to the Alamein position and during the battle of Alam Halfa and thereafter, the Desert Air Force kept up a continuous assault against the Afrika Korps positions. Without this assault there would have been no Alamein and the course of the war could have been very different. The air cover produced by the Hurricanes and the few early Spitfires, and the constant attacks by Bostons, Baltimores, Tomahawks and later Kittyhawks (and Wellingtons by night), not only established air superiority, but helped the Army to fight the land battles.

The Battle of El Alamein started on the night of 23 October with the first penetration of the enemy minefields, an intensive artillery barrage, and a wide variety of air attacks. The early morning Alamein fighter patrols witnessed an incredible landscape of burning tanks and vehicles and clouds of smoke rising to air operating height. The battle was to continue for nine days.[8] By 12 November the German and Italian Afrika Korps were in retreat, and Montgomery and Coningham decided the moment had come to step up the air harassment. They agreed to base two Royal Air Force squadrons well behind the German lines to carry out attacks on Rommel's communications. It was a bold and imaginative plan.

As I have explained, it was possible for a wide-undercarriage aircraft like the Hurricane to operate from a hard sand surface. The task force was to consist of

Hurricane squadrons, Nos 213 and 238, armed with two 20mm cannons. Its members were exceptional for their experience in ground attack operations as opposed to aerial combat. Clearly, the main problem would be navigational. Landing Ground 125 (as it was numbered) was deep in the desert, and the area had few conspicuous guide-marks. Radio silence was to be maintained, as far as possible, for the whole operation. There were no navigational aids. The map was useless. The compass and the watch were virtually all we had to go by.

The two squadrons were to be led to LG125 by a Lockheed Hudson, an American aircraft much used by the wartime Royal Air Force in the Western Desert in an air transport role. The Hudsons would also ferry in essential supplies to keep the squadrons going as long as they remained behind enemy lines. This was expected to be three or four days, depending on how long it took for the enemy to find out where the attacks were coming from.

The two squadrons were allowed to take only the bare necessities. These included a large supply of 20mm ammunition, as it was expected that considerable quantities would be expended in our attacks. Pilots were allowed the basic minimum of personal equipment. Most of us slept in our aircraft. Shaving was not required; there was precious little water for even the most basic hygiene. Two cooks came with the minimum of emergency rations. Some aircrew managed to find room in the Hurricane for a few cans of beer and these characters became extraordinarily popular. But supplies did not last long.

The three Hudson aircraft alighted on our departure airstrip on 12 November. Loading operations started immediately and went on all night. There was no denying the adventurous nature of the operation, and only the more experienced pilots were selected to take part. The whole thing could end in a total debacle if our landing ground was discovered. There was much apprehensive excitement in the aircrew mess that night.

The intelligence was clear. Rommel and his forces were retreating, and our task was to make life as difficult for them as possible. The whole concept of subversive operations was new to us all. Some of us had been involved in the

Battle of Britain and the first offensive sweeps over France, but an airfield behind enemy lines was quite different, and something (virtually) new in the history of the RAF.

At dawn on the morning of 13 November we set course for Landing Ground 125. We settled into loose formation with the Hudsons and hoped their navigators were on the ball. The flight was due to last about two hours. The Hurricanes were fitted with long-range tanks, but even so the operations envisaged were going to stretch fuel capacity to the limit.

Before the operation started the Long Range Desert Group had carried out a reconnaissance of the area, and the RAF No 2 Armoured Car Company had been selected to provide ground support. The origins of this famous RAF desert unit dated back to the Trenchard concept of the 'Air-Pin' – the use of air forces to control local tribes in Iraq without requiring large numbers of soldiers. The technique had worked well, and the RAF Armoured Car Companies were kept in existence, later becoming part of the RAF Regiment. No 2 was commanded by a fabulous character called Squadron Leader Casano, who had been in one desert or another for many years. He knew his Senussi desert well, and the Company boasted several other experienced desert warriors.

Squadron Leader M. P. Casano had joined the Royal Air Force, like most of us, to fly. I don't know what happened to his flying career, but on the ground he was one of the great characters of the Western Desert. He was a man of medium height with jet black hair and a black moustache. He could have been taken for an Arab. His uniform was profoundly unconventional, at least in the Desert, but some declared that they had seen him in Cairo looking quite smart, and he seemed to know where the ladies were to be found. As the Commander of No 2 Armoured Car Company, which he led for two years, he became a legend, and even the Army were prepared to acknowledge his operational effectiveness. He had operated with the 11th Hussars – the Cherry Pickers – and been decorated with the Military Cross for an action when his Company had been attacked by a force of German and Italian bombers in the open desert.

I cannot do better than quote from his operational log when he accompanied us behind the German lines. It ran like this:

11 November	At 12 15 hrs S/Ldr M. P. Casano MC received order to proceed to a secret forward landing ground well into enemy territory. Company moved off at 12 30 hrs (no waste of time).
12 November	Company reached 'the wire' (the Egypt/Libyan border) at Fort Maddalena. At 14 15 hrs a German Warrant Officer who was proceeding back to his unit was taken prisoner, having walked five days due west.
14 November	Company arrived at LG 125 at 12 00 hrs and immediately formed a defensive screen 50 miles from airfield to observe hostile air or surface enemy forces.
16 November	Half section under F/LT Palmer proceeded to area 60 miles SE of LG 125 to search for crashed aircraft.
17 November	Withdraw from area at the end of the operation.

Squadron Leader M. P. Casano was later badly wounded in Tunisia and had to hand over command of the Company. The Royal Air Force has some exciting characters who do not necessarily fly aeroplanes.

So the armoured cars had worked their way behind the German lines and thrown a defensive screen around Landing Ground 125, ready for the arrival of the aircraft. The screen had a radio warning link with the main control car, situated close to the airfield.

Our course took us well south of the area of operations, and after two hours flying over featureless desert the Hudson leader led the formation down over the strip that we were to use. The strip was marked out by a line of petrol drums, and it was on this patch of relatively hard sand that the Hurricanes landed. Once on the ground, the first task was to disperse and refuel the aircraft from petrol drums already flown in by Hudson. There was very little cover.

The refuelling was achieved by using stirrup pumps originally intended for putting out fires during the Blitz. This
method was to prove extremely handy in the days ahead.
The second task was to dig slit trenches so that there would
be some sort of protection if things started to go wrong.

That afternoon 213 Squadron, operating as two flights,
one of which I led, took off for an attack on road communications in the Agedabia area. It was an eventful sortie.
We set out in a loose grouping since this was less tiring on a
long trip. After about forty-five minutes I called my flight
into closer formation. When we were about ten miles from
the target I took them down to about 200 feet so that the
radar at nearby Agedabia airfield would not pick us up. As
our formation lost altitude, one of my pilots, a Canadian,
flew straight into the ground. Whether he was hit by
German fire or it was an error of judgement, we shall never
know; but I had lost a fine, aggressive operator and the
crash resulted in a huge fire and an oil-smoke plume visible
for many miles. We had little time to worry about this, as
the road we were to attack was already in view.

As we approached it, with the coast in the distance, we
switched on our gunsights and placed the firing button on
the control column to fire. The formation started to fly an
erratic course to put off enemy gunners. This was the
moment when you forgot fear, and an exhilarating sense of
total commitment took over. The harder you attacked, the
less chance there was of being shot down. We approached
the road at right angles, only pulling up at the last moment
to get a sight on a target. There were targets in profusion
because the Afrika Korps tanks and vehicles were nose to
tail, some in 'lager' brewing up. We picked on batches of
vehicles, and soon we had explosions going and a large
number of fires. It is never wise to go back on a target a
second time unless absolutely necessary, so I indicated a
turn to the north, where further soft-skinned vehicles could
be seen in large numbers. Again our attack brought fires
and explosions. Unfortunately the Afrika Korps were beginning to wake up. Anti-aircraft fire, particularly heavy
machine-gun fire, was criss-crossing our course with the
occasional burst of lazy-looking red tracer. It was about this
time that I lost another aircraft, but in the heat of the action I

did not see exactly what happened. I had exhausted my cannon ammunition and imagined that others in the formation were in much the same situation, and as all surprise had now been lost, I made a right turn back into the desert, calling the flight on R/T. That was my last call. The important thing was that the enemy should not monitor our radio transmissions and thus discover where we had come from.

As we left the target, and the excitement of the action subsided, I wondered how, as leader of the formation, I was going to find LG 125. To get there we had to cross 200 miles of featureless desert with no sort of navigational aid. We were at fairly low level, lest the enemy radar got some idea of the location of our base. So it had to be the watch and compass. Fortunately it was a clear day, and we were able to spot the patch of almost white sand which was the only real feature close to our landing ground. The whole sortie had taken two hours. The other flights had also lost an aircraft to ground fire, so we were already three aircraft down.

That evening was spent digging in and briefing for the following day's operations. I slept in the cockpit of my aircraft, not the most relaxing couch, and woke several times during the night. By dawn I was stiff and uncomfortable. But the operation was never designed for comfort. Next day the plan was to attack Agedabia airfield, which was known to be active. Again the operation was to be undertaken in separate flights. After breakfast of soya sausages and beans (which several of those with nervous stomachs could not face) we were off again, heading west.

The flight to the target was uneventful. As we approached, I ordered my flight down to low level and into a loose formation to give maximum manoeuvrability for strafing attacks. Locating the airfield was made simpler by sighting an Italian SM82 transport circling over it. I detached two aircraft to deal with it, hoping it was full of Generals. There were several Italian CR42s parked on the strip. We swept across them with cannon fire and then turned our attention to the airfield installations. It was a successful attack and we claimed the poor SM82 and the CR42s. But light anti-aircraft fire from emplacements surrounding the airfield was quite intense, and one of my aircraft was shot down. It was with some relief that I headed the flight back to the desert.

This was to be an eventful journey. As one of my wing-men came abreast of me, I could see that his port long-range tank was on fire. What should I advise him to do? He was leaving a long trail of smoke across the sky. The danger was that the fire would reach the main fuel system and the aircraft would explode. I was about to tell him to make a speedy forced landing, and hope to be picked up, when the problem was solved for me. An explosion in the burning tank blew it off the wing. I did not know what damage this might have done, but as we were by now over some pretty inhospitable desert, I felt that the pilot, a level-headed Australian, should try to carry on. Our troubles had only just started. The sky was by now overcast and the desert had taken on a grey colour. Again I tried my best dead-reckoning navigation; but this time, when my watch told me that we should be in sight of the landing ground, there was no sign of it. There was no white sand dune showing up against the grey of the desert. There was nothing for it but a 'square search' in the hope that one of us would pick up the strip. Still we could not find it. With considerable self-condemnation concerning my navigational technique, and anxious glances at the fuel gauges, I decided that our only chance was to bear north in the hope of running into the British 8th Army, which I knew to be advancing fairly rapidly in the direction of Benghazi.

The aircraft that had been on fire now seemed to be under control, so off we went. I hoped to strike the coast some-where near Tobruk; but had we enough fuel? We climbed to obtain better visibility and conserve fuel. We pulled back our engine revolutions and put our fuel control into 'weak', only clearing the engines occasionally to stop rough running. Our course took us over a large element of the retreating Afrika Korps, though because of the dust haze we were unaware of this until it was too late. Luckily there were no enemy fighters in the air; had there been, we would have been sitting targets, as no one in my flight had any ammunition left.

The whole sortie to Agedabia airfield should have taken

about two hours. We had now been in the air over four hours. Things were getting pretty desperate. A landing in the desert and possible capture were very much on the cards. Then, through the haze in the distance, I saw the coast appear. We now had to see whether we could make it on the fuel we had left, and, if we did, whether we could find a landing ground in allied hands. Luckily the answer to both questions was Yes. We struggled to Gambut airfield, which had just fallen to the allies. All pilots landed safely, although the aircraft which had been on fire was a write-off.

At dawn next morning, after some sleep and refuelling, I set off with my remaining aircraft to try to find LG 125. I was a little apprehensive about what sort of reception I would get, and felt that my navigation might come in for some criticism, especially since my squadron CO, leading the other six aircraft, had been due to attack the same target a few minutes after us. Once more we headed behind the German lines, and this time I took care to steer well clear of the Afrika Korps. It was a clear morning and my navigation put me right on to the strip. We landed without further incident. To our surprise we learnt that the CO and his flight had also failed to return. As far as the ground crew were concerned the whole of the squadron had been lost, and near-total catastrophe had struck the operation. Our return brightened the situation somewhat. I had a pretty good idea that the CO had got into the same sort of trouble that had affected my navigation, and that he and his flight were down in the desert somewhere, so we refuelled our aircraft and set off to search for them. With a stroke of inspiration we took along two stirrup pumps.

We spent about an hour searching likely areas for a forced landing when we spotted Very lights. We found five Hurricanes (one having been shot down over the target) which had apparently landed in the desert with wheels down and were in reasonable order. They wasted no time in marking out a safe landing strip for us. By skilful and energetic use of the stirrup pump we transferred fuel from our long-range tanks into their empty main tanks. The aircraft batteries were all in good shape, and twenty minutes later the whole circus was back at LG 125. What had at first looked like a total catastrophe for the squadron had been to a large extent retrieved.

During our adventures in the desert the other squadron, which had not been with us on the airfield raid, was briefed to make further attacks on the Benghazi-Agedabia road. On their way to their target they spotted an Italian armoured column of over fifty vehicles some sixty miles from our strip. The column had obviously been sent to winkle us out of our secret landing ground. Our security was blown. The squadron abandoned their sortie and got stuck into the column; we joined them as soon as we refuelled and remained at the task until all the Italian vehicles had been destroyed. That particular column was no longer a threat, but chancing on it had been a great stroke of luck. Given a few hours, the Italians might have made a terrible mess of our whole operation. We had to accept that they had sent out a wireless warning. We spent a restless and vigilant night, on guard against another possible attack, as other columns might be in the vicinity. Time was clearly running out for us.

On the next day, the fourth behind German lines, the morning's task was to attack the airfield at Jalo which was being used by both the Germans and Italians. It was situated just outside an oasis of the same name. Jalo was on the edge of the Great Sand Sea and dominated by an old Italian post. It was about 250 miles south of Benghazi. It had changed hands several times during the Desert War and the Sudan Defence Force was the usual allied occupier. Jalo was about an hour's flight almost due south into the desert, without even a coast line to help us judge our target position. On this occasion, however, the navigation was good and we found and attacked a very surprised airstrip. There were few aircraft on the ground, but a lot of transport and many swiftly scattering troops. It was possibly the HQ of an enemy long-range desert group. Ground fire on this occasion was not intense and we had no losses.

After the previous navigational experience the journey back was made at greater height, with the aircraft spread well out to give maximum desert coverage. The day was clear, and on the hour the welcome white sand dune was in sight. We were soon on the ground.

During our absence two Hudsons had appeared with orders for us to pull out before our strip came under air attack itself, or we were attacked from the ground. As soon as refuelling was complete we were off, and a two-hour flight brought us back to our slightly more established desert base, and the comforts of a shave and a camp bed in a tent. Even now we had to forego a bath.

During the operation, our squadron had lost five aircraft with their pilots. Three of these in fact survived to become prisoners of war. No 2 Armoured Car Company were left to make their way back to more friendly territory. This they did by disappearing into the desert and flanking the southern elements of the German Army. They had done a great job, and their redoubtable commander's reputation as a real desert hawk was further enhanced.

Military historians have often accused Montgomery of failing to harass the Afrika Korps sufficiently during their retreat. But the Desert Air Force played their full part, and though we were only a small cog in the overall air assault, we helped to damage and demoralise the enemy. Our squadron took fourteen aircraft on the operation and lost five, with one write-off. I don't know what Rommel thought about it all, but I would guess he must have been worried about his flank and the knowledge that relatively short-range fighters were already operating against his rear. It was a good plan and it succeeded. In addition, some fighter formation leaders learnt a thing or two about desert navigation!

The squadrons that operated from LG 125 would agree wholeheartedly with Thesiger's sentiments, quoted earlier: 'No man can live this life and emerge unchanged'.

After the operation the desert battle moved on, and the Hurricane squadrons were left behind to cover the local areas and to escort convoys supplying the 8th Army on its way to Tripoli. But first we were to see the debris of a defeated army. After the Alamein line broke we moved as a squadron to El Fuka, one of the German airfields which had been a thorn in our side during the Alamein operation. The field was littered with wrecked enemy aircraft, Italian and German. There were dead bodies everywhere, and in the full heat of the summer the corpses had swollen to twice their size. It was a gruesome sight; the smell was indescribable. The Italian units seemed to have left their positions in some panic, with letters from wives and girlfriends strewn all over the place. For the rest of the desert campaign I wore an Italian jacket which helped to supplement my meagre supply of Royal Air Force clothing. The squadron also captured several Italian vehicles, not unlike some you can see in Rome today, and these too were to stay with us for the rest of the campaign. They were robust and serviceable, even without an immediate supply of spares.

Also at one of the German airstrips we found not only many aircraft destroyed by Allied bombing and strafing, but also a JU87 which was caught short in the process of having an engine change. The old engine had already been taken out and the brand new one was standing alongside waiting to be installed. My Flight Sergeant Sam Hoare was always good at innovation and suggested we should do all we could to make the Stuka serviceable. The Germans, a race who make things as simple as possible, had invented a technique whereby every pipe or system was marked by a colour – matching the part to which it should be joined. This made the engine installation easy. After getting the cowlings back on the aircraft we ran it up to our satisfaction and then looked for a volunteer pilot to make the first take-off. Flying Officer George MacKay, who had been at flying school with me and was a very able pilot, as well as a little mad, offered his services. After taxiing it on the ground, he took it into the air first time, with great cheers from the ground. He made a successful flight and landed safely, and later several of us went solo on it. We carefully painted out the Iron Crosses on the sides and replaced them with the squadron letters – followed by a large question-mark. The aircraft then proceeded to register some 250 hours between desert airfields and Alexandria, fetching beer and other goodies for the squadron. We took all the armour plate out and the performance became very reasonable. The Egyptian anti-aircraft guns always fired at us as we approached Alexandria, but they were so far off target that we did not take them into account. The aircraft was good for squadron morale in that it proved a link with civilisation as we progressed up the desert. 'Baron' MacKay, as he became known, survived the war, but has since died.

We were one of the first squadrons into Tripoli, landing at Castel Benito airfield. This had been one of Mussolini's showpieces when he was master of Libya. It had good facilities. On the outskirts of the airfield was a Chianti vineyard with adjacent vats. When we arrived, the main vat was nearly full and hardly having had a drink of anything for several days we paid it a visit with our captured jerricans. It was not the best wine, nor was it ready for drinking, but we were thirsty and keen. We came back every day and the vat level went steadily down until on one of our visits we were a little surprised to see a pair of army boots beginning to show at the bottom. It emerged that a New Zealand soldier, anxious to slake his thirst, had got to lapping. He had slipped in – boots, equipment, rifle and all – and drowned. Chianti drinking from that source dropped sharply.

The task of the squadron, which was based for most of the time at Misurata, now became the day-and-night defence of Tripoli harbour, where much of the supply for the 8th Army was being landed. The enemy air raids were mostly at night and we did not have much success. Soon the time came for me to leave the squadron, having completed this operational tour, and at the end of March 1943 I was summoned back to Middle East HQ in Cairo to hear my fate. Apart from sea journeys, I had been on operations since the later days of the Battle of Britain, nearly two-and-a-half years. I was very sorry to leave the squadron, but perhaps it was time for a rest.

This took the form of training No 335 Hellenic Squadron at Mersa Matruh, where I arrived on 3 April 1943, posted for 'advisory duties'. It was no rest from the desert, but it was promotion,[9] and the next six months were to be an exciting period and nearly as challenging as operations.[10] The squadron had been assembled in October 1941 at the request of the King of the Hellenes,[11] and the titular CO was a Squadron Leader Pangalos, whose father had been Prime Minister of Greece. His name was well-known in Hellenic circles. Operationally, I ran the squadron, but Pangalos did the administration. I am a great admirer of Greek pilots, but at times their panache made life more dangerous than facing the Luftwaffe. Serviceability was not one of their strong points, and on the first operation, against Crete, one of the Sergeants lost his long-range tanks on take-off. Though he had no possible chance of getting to Crete and back without them, he pressed on, and not surprisingly failed to return with the squadron, though I believe he carried out some brave attacks. We gave him up for lost. Two weeks later, he turned up in a Greek caïque having persuaded its owner to sail him to Libya.

Within six months my training task was complete, and I made my way to Cairo, hoping to persuade the authorities to send me back on operations. They agreed. But it was not to be quite what I was expecting.

Notes

1. On 19 January the officers and sergeant pilots of the squadron were present when Flt Lt Cameron presented Sqn Ldr Miller with a silver spoon and fork for his new-born daughter.

2. His promotion was dated 4 December 1941.

3. On 6 May they 'crossed the line', and the ceremonies were carried out in Flt Lt Cameron's cabin. The repercussions took most of the following morning, resulting in a threat to close the bar if such goings on were repeated (134 Squadron ORB).

4. At Lydda they found themselves helping to service recently arrived Liberators and Fortresses of the United States Army Air Corps. They retained their identity as No 134 Squadron and were eventually re-equipped with Hurricanes.

5. Flt Lt Cameron took part in his first patrol over El Alamein on 7 July.

6. The Serenade comes from *Les Millions d'Arlequin*, a ballet by Ricardo Drigo (1846–1930).

7. The Squadron ORB records AVM Coningham visiting the squadron on 15 October, when he addressed all its personnel, expressing his

confidence in the outcome of the impending battle and wishing everyone 'Good Luck'. The following day Lord Trenchard came to see them – 'those who had not before had the pleasure of hearing him realised something of the driving force behind this great man' as they sat listening to him in the middle of a sandstorm.

8. The squadron was visited informally by Sir Arthur Tedder on 5 November, and subsequently received a special message from him congratulating them on the excellent work they had done.

9. Promotion to Acting Squadron Leader was dated 18 April 1943.

10. During his six months with No 335 Squadron, Squadron Leader Cameron not only flew the Hurricane and Spitfire, but also the Hawker Hart, the Harvard, and the Tiger Moth.

11. Most of the personnel had left Greece when the Germans invaded in April 1941 and many had fought against the Italians. Based in Egypt, the squadron's main role was convoy protection.

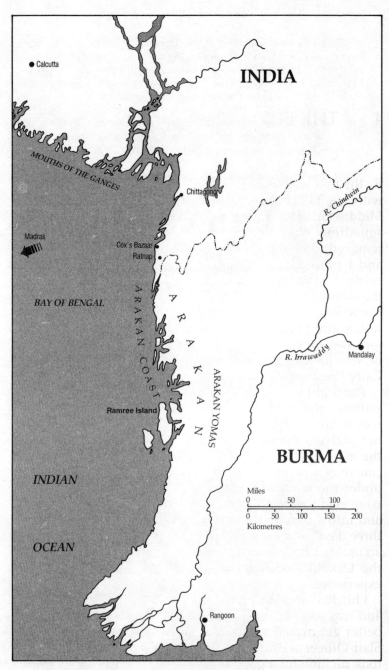

Map showing the No 258 Sqn area of operations

4   THE BURMA FRONT

By the first week in September 1943 I had finished my stint
with No 335 Hellenic Squadron and I was summoned to
Middle East HQ, Cairo, for an interview. Six new Spitfire
squadrons were forming in the Burma theatre and I was
required to command one of them. This was good news,
and I proceeded swiftly to the usual haunts in Cairo to
celebrate. I wanted to get to India as soon as possible; and in
the famous Shepherds Hotel that evening I ran into an old
friend who told me that he was tasked to ferry a Dakota to
India, and needed a second pilot or navigator. I quickly
took the opportunity to assure him that I was just the man
he was looking for, and we arranged to meet next day at
Cairo West airfield, where the aircraft was being prepared.

The flight was via Habbaniya in Iraq – a famous old RAF
station – and thence to Shaibah, Sharjah and Karachi. This
was an area well known to many old sweats in the RAF. It is
not perhaps the most pleasant part of the world to serve;
the main enemy were still the local tribesmen, and in the
course of a night stop at Sharjah the aircraft was pulled in
under the walls of the fort against a possible attack. We
were glad to leave. The next afternoon we were in Karachi
and into a different world. The whole flight had taken us
three days, and my navigation had been safe, if not highly
accurate. I had also gained a good idea of how to drive
the Dakota – an aircraft of which I had absolutely no
experience.

I hitched another lift to Delhi via the old city of Jaghpur,
and was soon advised by some old friends there that I had
better get myself smartened up quickly as the Senior Air
Staff Officer wished to see me to talk about my future. It
took no time for a good bearer to have me looking reasonably smart, and I departed to call on the SASO (Air Vice-

Marshal John Baker) and have lunch with him. The awful news soon emerged that the Spitfires destined for the Burma theatre were to appear fully manned from the UK, and the best I could hope for was a Hurricane squadron. Not even a good lunch, the glorious lawns or the wonderful architecture of New Delhi could soften this disappointment. I was instructed to proceed to No 224 Group at Chittagong not far from the Burma frontier. Again it was an airlift hitchhike, and though I was to come to love the area, the first sight of Chittagong was a little depressing. But from an operational point of view things began to look up, as the Japanese were on the offensive towards India and had begun to bomb Chittagong and the airfields of the Arakan. For a spell I was to be part of the fighter operations cell in the HQ. My immediate boss was Wing Commander H. M. Stephen, DSO, DFC, who had distinguished himself during the Battle of Britain and was later to become Managing Director of the *Daily Telegraph*. I marvelled at his facility in directing fighter operations, writing reports, and preparing papers. Staffwork was new to me, as my whole war had been on operational squadrons. I was a very bad staff officer then; but before my career was over I would spend rather a long time on staffwork, particularly Plans and Policy.

My staff stint this time was not to last long, as on 4 January 1944 I was sent to take over No 258 Fighter Squadron after an incident which required a change at the top. This was good news and a great relief, and I was to spend the rest of the war in command of 258. We had a wonderful team of aircrew drawn from all over the Commonwealth and I managed on the whole to keep this fine group of men together.[1]

258 Squadron was based at Elephant Point.[2] It must have been one of the more original of wartime airfields. It was not far from the Japanese front on the Arakan Coast, and we landed and took off from the beach which, when the tide was out, was a wonderful spread of sand. After landing, the aircraft were pulled back into the jungle where camouflage was complete. It was important not to get caught by the tide, and its movements became an important part of our lives. The squadron camp was in the jungle in bamboo huts. At times Elephant Point lived up to its name;

on several occasions the camp was trodden down by herds of elephants. One of my Canadian pilots was stupid enough to take a pot shot at the herd, and only just lived to remember it.

It was a busy and fascinating life. The Japanese were on the offensive and had reached the entrances to India at Kohima and Imphal. In the Arakan they had nearly reached the line of the Maungdaw-Buthidaung road. The line of the Arakan Yomas had been tunnelled in the 1930s between Maungdaw and Buthidaung for ease of access across the mountains. These were small villages, but when it came to the fighting, the tunnels in the area became vitally important. The Japanese had dug in on the mountains as only the Japanese knew how. It was very difficult to winkle them out.[3]

There was also a war going on in the Kaladan valley. Here the West African Divisions were facing a considerable Japanese force. The West Africans were wonderful. They were at their best during daylight when they could see the enemy, or at least knew where he was. But during the hours of darkness the Japanese took advantage of the spooky sensibility of many Africans, and at times frightened them out of their wits. The Japanese were past masters at this kind of psychological warfare. But the West Africans won in the end.

The squadrons in the area were operating from airstrips which the engineers had made out of the Burmese paddy, or rice fields. Around the strips they had built bamboo huts, with living accommodation on some of the numerous hillocks in the area. Life was quite civilised. I learnt to make curry from one of our Indian cooks. In the non-monsoon period the weather was most pleasant, and the huge teak forests added to the delights of the country. But as the monsoon approached the weather got desperately hot and sultry; and when the rains started we had to move the squadrons off the paddy-field strips to more solid runways, or back to the rear for rest and training. Operations against the Japanese did not come to a halt during the monsoon, but the very heavy rainfalls made coherent military activity difficult.[4]

As the monsoon broke I was instructed to move my

squadron to an airfield called Yelahanka, just outside Bang-
alore in South India, so as to re-equip with American P-47
aircraft (the Thunderbolt, as the RAF was to call it). Six of
the Hurricane squadrons were to be so re-equipped. This
was great news, because though the Hurricane was a
marvellous fighting aircraft it was getting a little long in the
tooth for the latest Japanese fighter aircraft and air defences. By now Mountbatten had been in the theatre for
some nine months, and the forgotten Army and Air Force
were beginning to receive every facility that could be made
available.

We flew to South India via Calcutta on 23 May 1944.[5] The
first task was to get the squadron off on leave after a hard
period of operations on the Arakan front. I had the opportunity to go off to Kashmir and the Vale of Shalimar with
another squadron commander. Transport at that time, and
I suppose at any time in that part of India, was not easy. But
in wartime regulations were a little easier than they are
now, and we took a Vultee Vengeance – the two-seater type
which my colleague was operating in his squadron. Loaded
with our humble but necessary possessions we set course
for the hills to fish and shoot and breathe some cool air. The
first night was spent in Delhi as a staging and refuelling
stop; and it proved to be more eventful than we had
planned.

We booked in at the famous Maidens Hotel and got set to
savour the joys of civilisation which Delhi, with real baths,
bearers and reasonable food and drink, could provide. The
evening started well, and after a drink we set off for the
hotel dining room for our first civilised meal. As we were
half way through it a waiter came hastening to our table and
reported that our room, which was in a bungalow in the
grounds, was on fire. We arrived in haste, and the building
was well alight, with no sign of the local fire brigade. We
lost all our kit and spent an unpleasant night with the
Indian police, who wanted to know how the blaze had
started. The prospect of spending our leave in a Delhi cell
was very much on the cards. However, we were released
without prejudice and allowed to continue our journey next
day, minus all our kit except for the clothes we had dined
in. But this was a minor snag in India in those times, when

clothes could be run up overnight by a good 'dhersi'. We landed at Rawalpindi airfield and left the aircraft in the hands of our good friend Group Captain Chater, who had been our Wing Commander in Burma.

We made the trip to Kashmir next day in a rickety Kashmiri taxi, through some of the finest and most rugged country in the world. The first stop was Murree at 5,000 ft, the home of the famous Murree beer. Suitably refreshed we were better prepared to face the more exciting part of the taxi ride into Kashmir. The Vale of Kashmir seemed to me the most beautiful part of the world and this, coming from a Scot, is high praise. We selected our houseboat in Srinagar, the capital of Kashmir State, and then were poled up the canal to the Nigin Bagh lake. Once we reached our selected site on the lake, a variety of merchants in their Shakaris (small boats propelled by paddle) drew alongside and tempted us to sample their wares. A cook and bearer had been provided by the company who owned the houseboat. This had three bedrooms, a dining room, lounge, and bathroom, even if the plumbing was a bit suspect. Anything more different from the hustle and dust of the Burmese front would be difficult to imagine.

After three days getting straightened out and acquiring new clothes, we set off for the Madmutti valley with a miniature expedition: tents, a cook, a bearer, fishing rods, and the guns which we had brought with us. It is not easy to describe the peace of a valley in the Kashmir State. Today in some areas this peace has been disturbed, but then it was complete. We pitched camp by the side of a trout stream at a height of about 3,000 ft. The day started with fishing, which was not difficult since the trout seemed to be prepared to give themselves up. So it was fresh grilled trout for breakfast, and with good Indian tea and toast at 3,000 ft, this was difficult to beat. One remembered at times the nervous sort of breakfast one had in Burma before a sortie against the Japanese.

The rest of the day was spent in the mountains looking for bear. This meant climbing anything up to 10,000 ft through the most marvellous country. Except in bad weather the bear rarely came down below 5,000 ft. We had a good Shikar with us who knew where the bear might be found.

Sometimes, when gasping for breath, we doubted his skill; but on our first day we got a wonderful sighting of a bear crossing a stream on a fallen log just as it got dusk. We came down the mountain in the dark, an eerie experience, assaulted by many strange sounds which made the hair stand on end. Back at our tented camp a late supper was ready, and after a good 'dram' it was curry and rice as only the Kashmiris can make it. Then it was the camp bed and sound sleep, lulled by the rushing of the trout stream outside.

But soon we were back to war and the task of re-equipping the squadron with Thunderbolts. Our first aircraft arrived on 8 September and with them two American instructors who had a lot of experience on the aircraft. What a delight it was to have brand new aircraft and a type which we knew that the Japanese would respect. As it was a single-seat aircraft, my pilots could only have a comprehensive ground briefing before being shown the cockpit and sent off on their first solo. It was all managed with the minimum of incident. One problem was that the aircraft was heavy and fast and had a powerful engine. One of my more adventurous Australian pilots thought he would try to dive it with full throttle and see how fast it would actually go. He should have known better, and he spread the aircraft and himself over most of the southern states of India. It was difficult writing to his mother in Brisbane to explain exactly how he had met his death. I did not attempt to give the details.

This was the first experience many of us had with the sound barrier, or Mach 1 as it came to be known. The word then was 'compressibility'. It meant the same thing, but aviators were just beginning to learn about the problem ahead of them.

The Thunderbolt offered our first experience of fighter-bomber operations, and the squadron had to be trained in this technique. We had by then moved back to Arkonam (8 October) and word was sent to me that I had to have the squadron ready to go back to operations in Burma within three weeks – fully trained in fighter-bomber operations. There was much to be done. Since there were no bombing ranges on which to drop practice bombs, I decided the only answer – bearing in mind that practice bombs did not actually explode – was to make a range and target in the middle of the airfield. Luckily higher authority never found out that this was the way we met their requirements: to think of this sort of thing happening in peacetime makes the hair stand on end! There were over thirty Thunderbolts on the airfield but none of them was hit by wayward bombs. The drill was to bomb-up with practice bombs, climb to the dive-bombing height, drop the bombs and get back to the ground as quickly as possible for another load. The whole sortie took about fifteen minutes. Thus we got the squadron operational in time to return to Burma for operations. The method proved effective, and the fact that my pilots distinguished themselves later in the field was a cause of some satisfaction.

By the end of November we were back in Burma and operating against the Japanese.[6] The new aircraft proved a real success. Its great range brought many new targets in Burma into our radius of action. At the same time the ground offensive was beginning in a big way, and the Mountbatten changes were being felt.[7] These included the introduction of the Liberator strategic bomber, which was to be used for taking the war deep into Burma. One of the roles of the Thunderbolt was to escort these bombers and defend them against Japanese fighters. The Liberator force included both RAF and USAAF squadrons.

My squadron was again based on the Arakan coast, operating from a hardened rice paddy-field. We had the range to get east into the Irrawaddy valley and carry out fighter-bomber attacks there, returning to the Arakan to refuel. Alternatively we would fly over into the Irrawaddy valley at dawn and attack a target before landing in that area, and then refuel, spending the day there supporting the Slim offensive.[8] To climb into the cockpit of an all-metal aircraft at midday with the temperature at some 110° was a test of endurance and fitness. We had to wear a flying overall full of gadgets for making an escape in the event of being shot down. Prickly heat affected everyone. The relief of reaching cooler air around the 10,000 ft mark was quite indescribable. In the evening we would return to our base on the coast, which in the Thunderbolt was about one hour's flying. A bath, or a bathe in the Indian Ocean, worked wonders. Then the same performance would be repeated next day. It was a long day – dawn till dusk in difficult conditions. We could not be based in the Irrawaddy valley where the action was, because water and rations there were short and there was already a wide variety of other squadrons already stationed there. We were happy to return to the coast every night even though this meant an extra hour's flying.[9]

The Thunderbolt was proving an excellent ground-attack aircraft, as well as a pure fighter and long-range escorter of bombers. It was heavy, and once it was put into a dive, few aircraft of that period could stay with it. The Japanese fighters of the day were light and very manoeuvrable and could easily turn inside even the Spitfire or the Hurricane. But the Thunderbolt could dive away or use the extra speed to climb out of range.[10]

Soon the operational focus was turned to the twin-pronged drive to Rangoon, by way of the Arakan coast and the Irrawaddy valley. This first of all meant the capture of Ramree Island, off the west coast of Burma – strategically an essential forward base for operations against Rangoon and beyond. The Japanese held Ramree in some strength. But a massive assault on 21 January 1945 using strategic and fighter bombers, and amphibious forces supported by the battleship *Queen Elizabeth* and other naval forces, won a foothold and eventually on 17 February the capture of the Island was complete. The Engineers then moved in to construct a main airfield. This was achieved in remarkably quick time considering the heat and terrain, and I flew in my squadron as soon as it was ready towards the end of April.[11] Living conditions were very rough, but as usual the initiative of the British soon asserted itself and by making skilful use of the boxes our long-range tanks came to us in, life became a little more pleasant.

Ramree Island was a strange mixture of jungle, scrub, rocks, cliffs and sea. It could have been made into a tolerable resort under modern conditions. In 1945 it was a mosquito-ridden patch with a long steel-planking airfield used by three Thunderbolt squadrons. There was a minimum of army support, as the forces that had taken the island disappeared to India to prepare for the invasion of Rangoon.

Our operations now included the dropping of napalm, a weapon which has since been associated with all the worst in warfare. But using it against the Japanese at that time seemed to us acceptable, having regard to the vicious manner the British, US and other Allied prisoners of war were being treated.

Our capability to operate with napalm went back to some time before the invasion of Ramree. Communications were not all that efficient within South East Asia Command and one day several American officers turned up at our airfield with jeeps and what appeared to be long-range fuel tanks. Had we heard that the squadron had been selected to be given a napalm capability? No, we said, and anyway what was napalm? We soon discovered that it was a highly inflammable jelly-like petroleum product which, if pressure-driven into a long-range tank, with a detonator attached to it, and hung from our bomb positions, would produce, when dropped or jettisoned, a mini-inferno on the ground. The purpose was to drive the Japanese out of their foxholes or suffocate them if they stayed inside. It seemed to be a pretty effective weapon, and rumour was that we were the first squadrons on the Allied side to be equipped with it.

At that time the Japanese were well dug into the Arakan Yomas – a range of hills guarding the route to India along the Arakan coast. The Army artillery had a great deal of difficulty in targeting these deep foxholes in jungle country. It was decided that with our napalm we should burn down areas of the jungle so that the Army could get its artillery and tanks into action. Our first sortie was against a feature which we had all come to know well, and I took twelve aircraft, all of them carrying two napalm tanks – one under each wing. I had no difficulty in identifying the feature and soon fire was raining down upon it. There was no real way of aiming the napalm tanks. We were briefed to fly as low over the feature as possible and jettison the tanks upon it; they had no ballistic qualities. Soon the jungle was in flames, and some limited success was claimed. We repeated the performance later in the day and certainly a good deal of bare rock was exposed. The 14th Army were grateful for our efforts and friendly signals were exchanged. So forthwith we had a napalm capability. But it was difficult and treacherous stuff to handle in those days, and if a sortie was aborted, the tanks had to be unloaded from the aircraft. Even then I had an Australian pilot whose tanks on one occasion began to leak badly and ignited on take-off, leaving a burning trail right along the airfield and spraying napalm across friendly jungle. It seemed only a matter of moments before the whole aircraft blew up, but luckily the sea was at hand and the Indian Ocean received its first shot of napalm. A slightly singed Royal Australian Air Force Sergeant Pilot landed safely with a damaged aircraft.

This was an eventful period. On several dive-bombing attacks aircraft blew up and pilots were lost. We thought these losses might have been due to enemy action, but this was soon discounted because a similar incident occurred during a practice sortie. Were bombs exploding prematurely? It was a mystery to know what was happening and good pilots were being lost. Soon afterwards, as I set course with the squadron for a support target in the Irrawaddy valley, one of my pilots (now a solicitor in Cardiff) reported on the radio a strong smell of petrol in the cockpit. I told him to return to base as smoothly as possible, go round corners quietly, and do a long level run-in for landing. He stuck to the instructions and later, when taking the aircraft to pieces, the engineers found that the 'header' tank in the aircraft (i.e. the tank in front of the pilot and above the engine) had a split running from the filler cap deep into the tank. If he had put his aircraft into a steep dive, as we did for dive-bombing sorties, the fuel from the damaged tank would have poured on to a very hot engine and exploded. We had no more mystery explosions after that, but, after extensive inspection, several 'header' tanks with splits had to be replaced. I mention this episode to indicate how sloppy craftsmanship, thoughtless storage or bad fitting killed several valuable pilots before we discovered the root of the problem. These losses we could ill afford.

Preparations for the invasion of Rangoon were now well in hand, and the convoys sailed from India. General Slim's operations down the Chindwin and Irrawaddy valley had gone well, and the 14th Army was poised for the final thrust. Slim's leadership at that time has been well recorded elsewhere and needs no further praise from me. Suffice it to say that the conditions under which his forces had operated were exceptionally difficult. During this period the Thunderbolts from Ramree were carrying out attacks closer and closer to Rangoon and we were escorting Liberators to hit targets in the area. Four and a half hours flying in a Thunderbolt sitting on a dinghy with plastic bellows inside it did my backside permanent damage. On the way home, when out of enemy range, I would open the squadron out into wide formation and finish the journey sitting on my right and left hip bone alternately. The fat ones fared best! Other hazards included Far East cumulonimbus clouds which could be deadly. One Spitfire squadron was forced by deteriorating weather conditions into such a cloud, and only three out of twelve survived. The rest were hurled in all directions by the atmospheric pressure. A Hurricane squadron commander thought he would try his luck and flew voluntarily into one of these cloud formations. He woke up three hours later hanging from a jungle tree by his open parachute without ever having pulled the rip cord. He did not try again.

Our attacks in and around Rangoon continued as the invasion fleet approached, and I began to get suspicious of the strategic situation because of the lack of Japanese reaction. It was some time since we had seen a Japanese fighter, and the anti-aircraft fire was decreasing.

D-Day (2 May) was a nasty one for weather. A parachute force had dropped at first light at Indaw at the mouth of the Irrawaddy river, well beyond Rangoon to try to give the landing craft a fair passage. We took off just after dawn to give them support. There was much activity on the ground – I could see fires burning in Rangoon, but the invasion force was going well and seemed set for success (the Japanese had in fact withdrawn from Rangoon before the invasion went in).[12] We had a difficult journey back across the mountains to Ramree Island. I had eleven aircraft with me but the weather had closed in behind us with cloud going up to 25,000 ft and down on to the mountains. I did not have the engine power to go over the top, and the cumulonimbus clouds looked menacing. So I chose to try to find a way back through the low cloud and the valleys. It was the right decision as it happened, but twelve aircraft dodging around peaks in and out of cloud without any sort of radar control left an empty feeling in the stomach. The weather cleared as we got to Ramree and the news of the Japanese withdrawal from Rangoon greeted us.

With the almost premature fall of Rangoon, on 3 May 1945, there was a period of anticlimax, because operations were moving faster than the Joint Planners in SEAC HQ had anticipated.[13] But I was soon instructed to withdraw my squadron from Ramree Island and take it back to South India to prepare for Operation Zipper. This was to be the Allied invasion of the Malay Peninsula. I had completed several tours of operations, and as I had been overseas for four years I was due for repatriation. However, when we arrived back in India in the early part of June, I reported to my Air Officer Commanding (Air Vice-Marshal the Earl of Bandon[14]), who gave me a broad outline of the plans for the assault. The Thunderbolt force (with its considerable range, using three long-range tanks) was to spearhead the attack, which was to go in around Port Swettenham. This meant a flight of some five hours from Burma down the coast, and then hopefully somewhere to land at the far end. (One of the airfields being used by the Japanese was to be made operational quickly by the assaulting engineers.) Bandon also pointed out that he was a little short of experienced Thunderbolt leaders. I volunteered to stay on until the operation was over. I confess to having felt at the time that this was a high-risk operation – a long flight out in the Indian Ocean with few landing grounds which could be used as diversions, and something of an uncertain reception at the end. But I had a good and experienced team, and training began.

[Editor's Note:

Operation Zipper, as the invasion of Malaya was known, was scheduled for 9 September 1945, but the dropping of atomic bombs

on Hiroshima and Nagasaki precipitated Japan's surrender on 15
August, and Zipper was converted into a reoccupation. By then,
however, Squadron Leader Cameron was already on his way back
to the UK, having handed over his squadron on 8 August.
Reflecting on his period in command, he wrote:]

To divert for a moment, one of the problems for squadron commanders in wartime was to judge whether their pilots had become fearful of operations against the enemy (goodness knows, anyone with any intelligence was scared stiff most of the time). The symptoms were sometimes quite clear, such as the return from a sortie because of engine trouble or some other excuse of unserviceability. Sometimes it was more difficult and a pilot would manage to keep clear of actual engagement when his squadron was fully committed. The situation was complicated by the fact that several experienced pilots did not recognise themselves when they had had enough. Rightly, the service rules about being willing to attack the enemy where and when he could be found existed. This was supported by what was known as the 'lack of moral fibre' rule which virtually meant cowardice in the face of the enemy. I would argue that aircrew faced a hazard additional to those of the other two services. This meant not only the operational hazard, but also a reasonable chance of being killed in a flying accident or in some other unexpected incident. But the 'moral fibre' rules existed and any aircrew asking to come off operations unless for good medical reasons had to face the board which had been set up to judge 'moral fibre' cases, and generally this meant the finish of a career if one was a regular officer: The dilemma which faced the squadron commander at this level was to assess when the time had come to put an individual, who no doubt was himself wrestling with his conscience, through the process. On the other hand, the pilot or member of aircrew who was not pulling his weight on operations was sooner or later going to let his colleagues down and someone other than himself was going to get killed because of his problems.

As a squadron commander, I had several cases of this type to deal with. One was an Australian pilot who came to me and said he could not face it any more. He had not completed even half a tour of operations and I must admit that I had not detected this apprehension in his operating performance. I arranged for him to disappear from the scene in a matter of hours without his having to go through the questioning of the other pilots. I often wonder how the whole incident affected his life and if there was any permanent damage. I fear that there must have been.

The other case was a Canadian pilot who had very nearly completed a tour of operations. He was a great character in the squadron and he would have hated to have been taken off operations in the dubious circumstances surrounding 'moral fibre'. His symptoms were starting to drink too much and lacking concentration in some of his flying. It was a difficult case to judge and I believe in retrospect that I let him go on too long. Before his tour was over he killed himself in the Thunderbolt on a practice flight by losing concentration and speed on the final approach to landing. I watched this incident happen from a distance and willed him to put on some more speed, but the aircraft stalled, turned over and dived to the ground. When I reached the spot the aircraft was already a blazing inferno and the ammunition was going off. We buried him or what was left of him on Ramree Island. The grave had been dug on the far side of the airfield and the body was wrapped in an old blanket. There were three of us at this odd funeral. I hope that the body now lies in more pleasant surroundings. I have often pondered over this incident – should I have taken him off operations, with all this meant for his self-esteem, pride and his future state of mind, indeed for the rest of his life? It was a difficult decision and one which I am not sure about even now, but there was not too much time then to ponder on such matters as the next operation was coming up and squadron morale was the important thing.

[Editor's Note:

It seems appropriate to add here what those who knew Neil Cameron best thought about him as their Commanding Officer. The words are those of Flying Officer Johnston, who wrote up the squadron ORB in July 1945: 'A great blow to the Squadron is the news that our Commanding Officer, Squadron Leader Neil Cameron, DFC, has to leave us. After trying all he knew to stay with the Squadron for this next season he has been ordered to return home as he has done more than his share of operational flying. The Squadron loses a Commanding Officer whose whole thought was for 258 Squadron. Joining the Squadron in February 1944, he has led it through two operational seasons, firstly in Hurricanes, and then in Thunderbolts, to the rank of a really first-class squadron. He commands the greatest respect and loyalty from the AC2 upwards which has been reflected in the work of all personnel. As a leader on Ops the pilots wish for none better. It is with regret that we lose a great skipper and a good friend. We wish him every success on his return to the Old Country.'

A few months later, on 2 October, his achievements were to be more formally recognised in the award of the Distinguished Service Order and the brief phrases of the accompanying citation: 'This officer has a long record of operational flying and has served in England, Russia, The Western Desert and Burma. Since the award of the Distinguished Flying Cross he has led his squadron on many sorties over Burma. An outstanding leader, Squadron Leader Cameron has always displayed keenness, determination and courage, setting an inspiring example to the other pilots in his squadron.']

Notes

1. Within three days of taking over command, Squadron Leader Cameron gave what the ORB describes as 'an inspiring talk to all ranks'.

2. Elephant Point is a few miles south of Cox's Bazaar.

3. The squadron's main role was to support the land forces in these operations. As recorded in detail in the squadron ORB, it did so by strafing Japanese positions, by escorting bombers during their

attacks, and by protecting transport aircraft that were dropping supplies. It also provided air defence. On 23 February, for example, eight aircraft led by Squadron Leader Cameron and escorted by Spitfires made a low-level attack on the main landing ground at Akyab. LAA was experienced and Cameron's aircraft sustained superficial damage. On 5 March he and Flying Officer Brown were carrying out a reconnaissance when they discovered a group of bashas suggestive of a Japanese rest camp; three hours later 'he led a flight in a vigorous and well-concentrated attack during which the main block of bashas was completely destroyed'. On 14 and 15 March – determined to see at first hand what it was like on the ground – he and three of his officers spent an exciting forty-eight hours with the forward troops during which time they were shelled, mortared and sniped. The good relations he was clearly determined to establish with the Army were reinforced on 27 March when, after leading twelve aircraft to attack Imbauk, he received congratulations on well and truly strafing the area and thus enabling the advancing Army to reach its objective. Throughout these months the squadron flew at high intensity – the ORB for April for instance, records its sixteen aircraft completing over 500 operational sorties, of which Squadron Leader Cameron himself carried out thirty – his full share.

4. In 1983 Lord Cameron wrote a piece about Group Captain George Chater, who commanded his Hurricane Wing at this time, for inclusion in *Wings of War*, edited by 'Laddie' Lucas (Hutchinson, 1983). This offers an interesting sidelight on the conditions in which they operated.

5. The squadron deployed first to Arkonam, near Madras, before proceeding to Yelahanka on 13 August.

6. The squadron aircraft left Arkonam on 17 November and reached their new base at Ratnap on 26 November. That same day a signal arrived announcing the award of the Distinguished Flying Cross to Squadron Leader Cameron. His citation read: 'S/L Cameron has a fine operational record. He has served in England, Russia, the Desert Air Force and more recently in the Far East theatre of war. He has built up his squadron to a high standard of operational efficiency and has led them on numerous sorties, invariably displaying a fine fighting spirit, reliability and great devotion to duty.'

7. Lord Mountbatten visited the squadron on 19 December 1944.

8. Almost every kind of target was attacked: troop positions and observation posts, gun batteries, barracks, ammunition and supply dumps, airfields and airstrips, railways, bridges and ferries. Hardly a day passed than the squadron was out in force against one or more such objectives, usually with Squadron Leader Cameron leading it. On 21 February, however, he was unable to do so, since he was

suffering from a poisoned arm caused by one of the variety of ferocious insects found in the country. According to the Squadron ORB, he underwent much painful treatment with remarkable courage and fortitude, and was back leading his squadron on 2 March.

9. The Squadron ORB, which contains a great deal of detail on all these operations – itself a tribute to the thoroughness of its CO – recounts an incident on 31 December 1944. Eleven aircraft were attacking a village where the Japanese were gathering and the CO put two bombs in the centre – starting a good fire. Pilot Officer Stead then dropped his bombs next to the fire, putting it out with the blast. On his return he apologised to the CO, but assured him that he had restarted the fire when he strafed.

10. The Squadron ORB describes one of Squadron Leader Cameron's combats as follows: 'On 11th February the squadron took off from Cox's Bazaar to rendezvous with three RAF squadrons of Liberators at the south tip of Ramree Island and act as close escort to Rangoon with 134 Squadron (P-47s) in the role of medium cover and 459 Squadron (USAAF) (P-38s) as top cover. When Rangoon was reached six 'Tonys' (Kawasaki single-seat fighters) approached from head-on at the same height as our aircraft – 15,500ft. The Tony's method of attack was a half-roll and dive straight through the bombers. As the second enemy aircraft went into his dive, Squadron Leader Cameron went into attack giving a burst of three seconds with 70° deflection from 400yd. The enemy aircraft was lost to sight for a second but, on looking round the pilot was observed to bale out.' Squadron Leader Cameron did not claim this aircraft as he did not observe the strikes and considered it only as a 'possible'. His logbook, however, credits him with half a Tony confirmed as destroyed, and the ORB later supports this.

11. Reflecting in the Squadron ORB on this move, he felt bound to criticise 'the usual embarkation inefficiency which is so prevalent in this theatre' – none of the moves of the squadron's ground personnel was accomplished without considerable difficulty, often including the loss of technical equipment and personal belongings, and it speaks much for Squadron Leader Cameron's qualities of leadership that morale remained so high.

12. One of the first indications that the enemy had gone was a message on the roof of the notorious Japanese jail in Rangoon sketched out by allied prisoners. One wondered what British intelligence had been up to.

13. The squadron's last operational sorties took place on 14 May.

14. An extrovert Irishman, Bandon was famous for his direct and unconventional ways of getting things done.

5   PEACETIME

So the war was over; in a way it was an anticlimax and in a way, a disappointment. Anticlimax in that there was to be a period of not knowing exactly what was going to happen, disappointment in that the happy comradeship days of squadron life, when there had been a common threat which seemed to bring individuals together, were over, and that soon the splendid teams which we had built up in the squadrons were to be dispersed back to their civilian tasks if they had any, and soon the *esprit de corps* would have gone. On the other hand, the chances of being killed were reduced, though one seldom thought of that.

It was with great sadness that I took farewell of my squadron. Many of the pilots and airmen had been with me from my first days and I had developed a great affection for them. We understood each other. The fear was that when we all got back to civilian life the comradeship and the spirit to face a common danger would disappear. It did. Since then there have been squadron reunions and it has been great to meet the people who faced the dangers together and to remember the 'old days'. Yet I have never cared very much for reunions and inevitably there is disappointment and a blurring of the marvellous times of the past. Much better I suggest that remembrance is a personal matter and the best memories grow better with age as long as they are not disturbed by the present and the changes that occur in personalities and circumstances.

After great farewell celebrations which seemed to go on for several days built on the alcoholic qualities of Hayward's (Calcutta) gin and Carew's (Bombay) rum, both ghastly vintages which the liver did well to survive, I left to join a transport aircraft at Bombay which would return me to the UK. I was in no desperate hurry, and it was just as

well. I had come to love India and I had never been to
Bombay. However, the days dragged on and I was beginning to run out of money, so I decided to make my own way
back. I managed to hitch an airlift to Delhi and put up in one
of the transit hotels which I knew was used by the aircrew
passing back to the UK. I had not long to wait because in the
bar that evening I ran into a Lancaster crew who were on
their way home having been demonstrating the Lancaster
bomber in India. By midnight they had offered to add me to
the crew for the return passage. I was duly grateful and
joined them next morning on the journey to Palam airfield
where their Lancaster was positioned. I was a little anxious
at seeing the pilot sitting in the truck which took us to the
airfield with his head in his hands. A Delhi bug was the
story, but I wondered what sort of a flight we were in for. I
had never been in the famed Lancaster until that day and
was suitably impressed. The pilot, who had a fine war
record, seemed to recover and we reached Sharjah without trouble but there a fault developed in an engine, and
I left them to get it sorted out and managed to get a seat
on a York that was staging through. This went well until
we got to Malta and, in meeting some old friends from
fighter squadrons there, I missed the York which disappeared to the UK without me, but bearing all my humble
possessions.

I was stuck in Malta for two days and the next lift that was
available was a converted Stirling bomber which was proceeding via Algiers. We spent the night there and next day
made the UK. We landed at RAF Lyneham, a station that in
later days was to come under my command, but in 1945 I
was one of the boys and treated accordingly. As we crossed
the English coast and let down over the fields and valleys of
West Country rural England, I found this return deeply
moving after some four years abroad. The green fields and
the thoughts of what had been going on in this fair country
in wartime – the liberation of Europe and many other issues
– went through my mind as well as the fact that I had come
through the war after nearly five years of flying and operational activity. I soon located my miserable kit and was on
my way to London by Service bus. The journey thence was
one of rediscovering the beauties of the English countryside

after four years of desert and jungle – it was a great and wonderful joy.

I booked in at the Park Lane Hotel which had been a haunt of our squadron before we went overseas. Not many of those who had started the journey of operations were left and their presence and personalities were much in my mind. I felt lonely and disorientated and wondered what the future would hold for me personally. I was not a regular officer and the chances were that I would be returned rather smartly to civilian life. The thought appalled me and I decided to take myself off to Shepherds Bar in Shepherd Market which had been another haunt of the squadron when in London. It was not until I was enjoying the delights of my first English beer that I realised that I was rather oddly dressed, and that people were staring at me. It was no wonder. Civilian clothes were to me quite a novelty and having been wearing tropical kit for some four years, I had not worried too much about my wardrobe. I was wearing a suit which had been made for me by a tailor in Kashmir and its construction looked like it. Whilst I had got away with it in India, in fashionable Shepherd Market in the West End of London it looked a little odd to say the least. I hurriedly finished my beer, felt more lonely than ever, and set course for Simpsons where I hoped that, in fitting me out with an English-type suit, they would not laugh too much at what I was wearing. I reflected on the situation of at one moment being a Squadron Commander with fairly substantial powers of life and death and the next a lonely creature in London looking for a new suit and feeling slightly ashamed. I soon pulled myself together and blamed a lingering hangover since the farewell parties.

During wartime I always found leave in Scotland difficult. I came from a strictly temperance household and to slow the living pace down (if that is what you might call it) was a strain and not what leave was meant to do. It was always a relief to get on the train back to England and to duty. Though I was a Scot through and through and always will be, it was the comradeship of the squadron life with people facing the same dangers that I missed. It was rather a disturbing time immediately after the war with many RAF folk not knowing exactly what the future held and with training flying being a poor substitute for the real thing. I was lucky in that I was soon posted to the School of Air Support at Old Sarum – a famous old World War I airfield. This was my first staff job and the task was to instruct people in the art of close support for the Army. It had been laid down by Lord Tedder (then CAS) that both the RAF and the Army must never forget the technique of air support operations which had taken so long to learn during the war just ended. I had had considerable experience in the technique and it was to be put to use.

Soon after my arrival at Old Sarum I was offered a permanent commission in the RAF which I accepted.[1] This was done without any assessment of career prospects or of the future of the RAF. I was an acting Squadron Leader. It was difficult to settle down after wartime to the routine of peacetime and the conventions of the service. I seemed to be in a series of troubles and 'adventures' and it was suggested to me by those in charge that I settle down and live a respectable Service life. The Commandant of Old Sarum at that time, and indeed for a considerable period after, was AVM Sir L. O. 'Bingo' Brown – a South African who had been in command of one of the Groups in 2nd Tactical Air Force at the end of the war. He knew his air support and he also understood the problems of a youngish squadron commander trying to adjust to peacetime conditions. He was very patient with me, even when I shot the top off the hat of a distinguished Admiral who was on one of our senior courses. The outcome was a visit to Messrs Gieves to pay for a new one, plus some friendly advice. But it was touch and go whether my RAF career was to be ended there and then.

I had never given a lecture in my life; plenty of squadron briefings – yes, but no formal lecture lasting forty-five minutes. But this was to be the pattern at Old Sarum. Staff Colleges and other establishments now give tuition in lecturing but then it was a matter of learning as you went along. I did my best. During my period at Old Sarum I arranged to do a course on jet aircraft – in this case the Meteor. It was at a time when the Meteor had only about half an hour's endurance. On my second trip my airspeed indicator started reading the wrong way round: when climbing the speed went up and when diving it went down. I was led into land by another Meteor formating on me and I landed safely. The engineers could find nothing wrong and began to look at me somewhat suspiciously. But the same thing happened to someone else on the next flight and it was discovered that a wasp had got into the pitot tube which served the airspeed indicator and was causing the problem. As it happened my activity on jet aircraft was limited because of a medical problem which I will be discussing later.

My conversion to being a reasonably civilised RAF officer was taken in hand by the then Group Captain E. G. Gordon-Jones (later to be Commander-in-Chief Middle East). He also suggested that I might start playing games again and spend less time in various bars. I had not played rugby football since I was at school and then not very seriously. However, on his advice I took up the game seriously, playing second-row forward. We built up a good station team and I played for the Salisbury Club on Saturdays. This eventually led to my being selected to play county rugby and learning some very quick lessons on the game from such sides as Cornwall, Somerset, Gloucestershire and Devon. I only played once for the RAF though not in an inter-Service match. Later I was to become Secretary, Selector, Chairman and finally President of the RAF Rugby Union and to have a lasting joy in the game which gave me so much, including a dedication to getting really fit which in a way was to become my downfall, but more of that later.

I was three years at Old Sarum. It was a good period to adjust to service life but the transition was not easy. Salisbury is one of my favourite places in England and the Cathedral Close is hard to beat in any assessment of environment. Whilst at Old Sarum I was to marry the WAAF officer at the station who had been an operational plotter during the Battle of Britain. During the great air raids on RAF Debden she had been persuaded to take shelter, and as I mentioned earlier, overflying Debden to go and join 17 Squadron we had very nearly met in 1940. However, it was not until 1947 that we met and married and the then Station Commander at Old Sarum did not really approve of an officer and his wife living and working on the same station. How times have changed. However, I had a good friend in Group Captain Teddy Donaldson who understood the affairs of the heart.[2] Teddy had been the holder of the world speed record for a number of years and when he retired from the RAF became Air Correspondent of the *Daily Telegraph*, and a very good one too. Teddy arranged that my wife should be posted to RAF Andover which was a station quite close to Old Sarum, indeed the next stop by train on the way to London. So we conveniently had a small but adequate flat in Salisbury and my wife got the train to Andover whilst I made my way to Old Sarum. It all worked very well. However, the time came for me to move and things got a little more complicated.

Much to my astonishment I had been selected for the 1949 RAF Staff College course at RAF Andover but there was to be a six-month waiting period. I was asked by the Army if I would go to HQ Rhine Army which was then at Bad Oeynhausen, to be the RAF liaison officer because, even though the war had only been over for three years, the understanding of air support for the Army was beginning to be forgotten. I gladly accepted this offer and spent what I think was a useful six months in Germany reminding people of the merits of close air support. It was a good life in Germany at that time. Good for some, certainly, as far as the occupying forces were concerned, but Germany lay in ruins and the Control Commission were working hard to get it on the move again and to lay down new rules of democracy and a plan for the future, including the future of the trade unions, which we managed to get right for the Germans before getting ourselves sorted out. But the main cities were still devastated. In my travels through the Ruhr at that time I felt that if anyone wanted to get an impression of what air power could do to a nation it was there for all to see. Hamburg, the city where the great fire storm had been caused by RAF Bomber Command in 1943, was particularly depressing. It was a scene of complete destruction. Though the conquering nations lived in some comfort in the few hotels that had escaped the holocaust, the Germans were existing in cellars and in holes in the ground, and the speculation was, would they ever recover? Their recovery is now a matter of history and the near miracle of the Marshall plan and all that went with it. But in those days the future Germany that we see today was difficult to envisage.

At that time I had the opportunity (if that is the correct expression) to visit Belsen and see at first hand the atrocities that the German nation, or at least part of it, had inflicted on the Jews and others who did not find Nazi favour, and of course on many who had as Germans been totally against the Nazi regime. Belsen is still there if anyone has any doubts about what a totalitarian regime can do to people.

It was my privilege to meet Sir Arthur Harris on many occasions after the war and to talk with him about the days of his offensive against the Axis. Sadly Bomber Command was never to get the credit for the defeat of Germany and Italy it deserved – a campaign medal for the Battle of the Atlantic, North Africa and Burma, but nothing for the aircrew who carried out the assault on the heartland of Germany with grievous aircrew casualties: a bad error of bureaucratic judgement.

Notes

1. Squadron Leader Cameron was posted to Old Sarum on 13 October 1945 and his permanent commission was dated back to 1 September. Substantive promotion to Squadron Leader did not come until 1 January 1950.

2. Lady Cameron recalls that, a mere six weeks after she had been posted to West Raynham, Group Captain Donaldson – who was Senior Air Staff Officer at HQ No 12 Group – organised her posting back to Andover. She left the WAAF early in 1948 and was thus able to accompany her husband to Germany, where they lived in a requisitioned house at Bad Oeynhausen.

6   HOSPITAL

In 1949[1] I was playing first-class rugby football in London and at county level in the West Country. I thought I was very fit, and certainly I trained assiduously. One day in December I was playing in an RAF Cup match for the Air Ministry. We won, and I remember that I scored a try. In the dressing room after the game I suddenly felt dreadful. My brain could not transfer my thoughts to speech. I left quickly without arousing suspicions that I was unwell.

The train journey home to Welwyn Garden City, where we were living at the time, was a nightmare. I lay full length on the seat, the carriage being empty, and felt sorry for myself. I tried to think of a piece of poetry to recite, in case my speech was coming back, hoping that I had simply had a knock which was wearing off, but it got no better. By the time I reached home I could only speak gibberish. It was the most horrible feeling. My wife was shocked, and I could not even try to explain the theory that it was only a knock. It was all most frightening. We spent a disturbed night. This was to be the start of two years in hospital.

By the next morning my speech had returned, and I went off to London to see the RAF doctor. After a full examination, including a brain X-ray, he could diagnose no illness. I went back to work. But I was far from well, and was eventually persuaded by the local doctor to go into hospital for tests. He had listened to my heart and detected a serious murmur. Eventually my trouble was diagnosed as sub-acute bacterial endocarditis – a disease of the heart valve. I had chosen to go into the local hospital, rather than a Royal Air Force hospital because it was nearer to home and my wife was expecting our second child. This was a mistake which cost me many extra months of hospitalisation.

The discovery of penicillin and who should get the actual

credit for it has been covered in many books and learned articles. There is no doubt that Sir Alexander Fleming did the original work way back in 1929 but afterwards it was not until the great drive of an Australian – Howard Florey – that this antibiotic was developed into something that could be used clinically. This takes us up to 1941–42 – which means that a passage of some thirteen years had gone by without real development into what was to become perhaps the greatest life-saving drug of all time. Florey and his team worked first at Oxford and later Cambridge and in the most difficult wartime circumstances and in very poor laboratory conditions. By 1941 there was just enough penicillin available to begin clinical tests on a few patients.

One of the diseases that it was hoped might be mastered by the use of penicillin was bacterial endocarditis. In this disease the valves of the heart become invaded by bacteria – usually a particular strain of streptococcus – which, at that time, could not be dislodged by any known treatment. In consequence the blood is constantly affected, the valves themselves are destroyed, and the patient dies within a few weeks or months. Clinical trials began in late 1940 on three patients who were suffering from this disease, giving them what were very small doses of penicillin. The patients did not respond to this treatment and all eventually died. It was not until many years later that it was discovered that only massive doses of the antibiotic could effect a cure. The trouble was that penicillin remains effective in the body for only a very few hours before being excreted. Also, given small doses of the antibiotic, what usually happened was that the germs became resistant to penicillin and then the patient was in real trouble, sulphonamides being useless for this particular illness.

This is exactly what happened to me in a county hospital just outside London. Though the diagnosis which was eventually made was correct, i.e. bacterial endocarditis, the treatment given was small doses of penicillin. There was some improvement in my condition in the first week or so but soon the bacteria became insensitive to the treatment.

The local consultant had put me on a small dose of penicillin, and told me that in his opinion I would never fly again. The weeks began to pass. Life in a county hospital in the early 1950s was pretty rugged. One felt that the expertise level was low and that certain drugs were just not available. There were deaths in the ward which I felt might have been prevented.

The fact of the matter was that the local consultant, who was only a GP doing part-time work in the hospital, did not really understand the nature of my trouble, and a small dose of penicillin was as good as anything to assure the patient that he was being treated. It might even effect a cure! After some eight weeks of this treatment my temperature had gone down and I was determined to get out of the hospital and get home. I still felt far from well and looked rather like a Belsen victim. I was discharged, but was soon seriously unwell again, and on 6 September a Royal Air Force ambulance came to whisk me off to the RAF Hospital at Halton in Buckinghamshire. There was a comfortable feeling about being back in the RAF family, and I felt confident that I would be well looked after.

I was not to remain long at Halton. The local RAF consultant recognised that I was in a desperate condition and put me on the 'dangerously ill' list, which of course frightened my wife and prompted chaplains of various persuasions to visit me and give me words of comfort. By the time the third – who happened to be the Anglican chaplain – arrived, my morale was sagging and I realised that something pretty serious was up. He, poor fellow, was sent packing with the sharp edge of my tongue, and this suggested to him that I was far from being a write-off.

Next day, 9 September, I was told that I was to be transferred to St George's Hospital, Hyde Park Corner, to be under the care of Dr (later Sir) Kenneth Robson, one of the civilian consultants to the Royal Air Force. So began a close friendship which was to last until his death in 1979.

At that time, sub-acute bacterial endocarditis was not really curable except, in some cases, by massive doses of penicillin. The prognostication for survival was not good. My earlier treatment with small doses of penicillin had caused the organism perching on my heart valve to become insensitive to the drug. This was bad news. There were, however, one or two new antibiotics on the market and I was put on an eight-week course of aureomycin – a new drug, discovered in the USA, which worked to keep the level of penicillin high in the blood stream. This brought my temperature down, and for a time all hoped that the bug had been slain. But after two weeks off the drug the blood culture began to show that it was active again. Several of the newer drugs of the early 1950s were tried but always after a few weeks off the drug I would have a relapse. The days of waiting after a course of treatment to see if it had been successful were testing periods for the nerves. Sir John Conybeare, the great physician of Guy's Hospital, at that time Chief Consultant to the RAF, came to examine me and made some suggestions for further treatment. But the fact of the matter was that all known drugs had been tried and the heart condition was beginning to deteriorate.

Williams Ward in St George's Hospital held some twenty people, most chronically sick, and there were many deaths. I was used to death as I had seen something of it during the war but at no time did I really feel that the next victim might be me. The ward itself saw a great cross section of London life pass through it: tramps who had been brought in from the Embankment and had to be scrubbed by the nurses from top to toe, a general practitioner who was a drug addict, professional men, children, a sailor with bad dysentery, several with cancer of the lung, and a wide variety of other people and sicknesses. It was an education for me in more than one sense. The place could have been a centre of gloom but for the cheerful and intelligent ministrations of Sister Nora Aldred – the ward sister who became a personal friend. After a year and a half I had become easily the most senior inhabitant of the ward, and quite expert in diagnosing every case that was admitted, but my own condition was getting more serious. The Royal Air Force had given me two years to get better on full pay before retiring me as unfit. This was a great relief because it meant that my wife, with two babies to look after, could at least pay the bills. It was not easy for her to visit, and it was to be a testing time for her.

From Williams Ward I could just see the traffic on part of Hyde Park Corner; people going off to work and returning home in the evening; the Royal Garden Party invitees making their way to the Palace in their finery. I looked down with deep envy for their health and freedom. Garden Party days usually meant that the sandwiches and cakes which were not consumed were sent round to St George's. Little events became vitally important. The visit of the local church choir on Sunday evenings after their own service was an emotional experience when they sang some of the old hymns from my childhood in Scotland. I was often sad in spirit when they left, wondering what the future would bring.

I had been in St George's for over a year when Dr Tom Pilkington, who was Sir Kenneth Robson's registrar, decided it would be interesting to perform blood tests on me every three hours, day and night, to try to assess the bacterial level at different times. Not long after this process started, I was being wheeled down to the bacteriological laboratory at 3.00 a.m. by Dr Dai Davies of the bacteriological staff. He was well known for his strong Welsh Chapel Christian beliefs and as we left the ward he said to me: 'Have you ever considered that you might not leave this hospital alive?' This remark rocked me somewhat, but I did not reply because I was full of sleep, having just been awakened.

Next day I remembered, and began to ponder his remark quite carefully. I recognised that I was slipping downhill, and that all forms of treatment had failed. This led me on to the thought of dying, and what it might entail for my young family, and for the first time I began to feel the real need of Christian comfort and the hope that after this life on earth there might be something to look forward to. Soon I was recalling my strict Christian upbringing, and decided that it would be a good idea to talk things over with the hospital chaplain, a mature curate from St Paul's, Knightsbridge. About the same time I had an unannounced visitation from Captain Hartley-Holmes, who I discovered was the Secretary of the Officers' Christian Union. I have to this day no idea why he turned up, but we talked about the issues of life and death and he left me with a New Testament which I still have now, much battered. He was a saintly man whom I got to know well later.

I decided that I should be confirmed into the Church of England. I had been baptised into the Church of Scotland as a baby, but the outbreak of war soon put my religious upbringing well into the background. I was quickly prepared for confirmation by the hospital chaplain. There was no great conversion in my case, but certainly fear of the unknown and recognition that I had been a real sinner and the sooner I made my peace with my Maker the better. The motives for confirmation were questionable, but in mitigation I can say that my faith has grown daily. Now my Christian conviction is the central part of my life.

A Confirmation Service was arranged in the hospital chapel. I was the only candidate, and I was confirmed by the Bishop of Kensington in my pyjamas and dressing gown, with Sister Aldred as my supporter. The Matron gave us a cup of tea afterwards and I returned to daily life in Williams Ward.

But now it was different. The message of my confirmation was beginning to seep through, and there was a new perspective to my life which had to be carefully assessed. Important events were about to take place, and they all happened at the same time, shortly after my confirmation. First the blood tests began to show that the organism affecting my heart valve had suddenly become sensitive again to penicillin. This was a miracle in itself. Secondly, it was decided to try aureomycin again. This drug was flown from America and my treatment began, using huge doses of both penicillin and this penicillin-retaining drug. The course of treatment was to last eight weeks. Soon my temperature fell and the fever seemed to go, but I had seen all this happen before. At the end of the period the treatment stopped, and the awful waiting began to see if I was going to relapse yet again. It was then that I drew on my new Christian alignment by calling on God, through prayer, that I should be cured. First one week passed, then two, and still the blood cultures were clear; then it was three weeks and optimism began to rise as I had never gone that long before. Soon I was allowed out for a short walk in Hyde Park escorted by a nurse from the ward. I cannot describe the joy of being in the fresh air, of smelling the grass and gazing at the gardeners and others going about their business. It was an experience I shall never forget.

When later almost daily passing the spot, I murmured a prayer of thanksgiving.

Soon it was time to be sent home. I had been in hospital altogether for two years, and a slight sense of panic struck me about how I was ever going to cope without the support of the hospital staff. I am told this is a common feeling, and I soon got over it. My doctors, though not totally optimistic of my recovery, felt that there was a good chance that I had been cured. I returned home to the weeks of waiting, the regular blood tests, the two or three days before the results were known. It was quite a harrowing time and I drew heavily on my strengthening Christian faith to sustain me through this period.

After some weeks of convalescence the doctors were prepared to say that I was clear of the disease, though some heart damage remained. The dreaded blood tests were stopped.

I will always maintain that this was a miracle. I knew a lot of people had been praying for me. After my confirmation I had prayed for myself and my recovery, and indeed for all sick people and I had seen plenty of them. The fact that the organism became, after two years, sensitive to penicillin, and that the new drug had been discovered in America, all came together in my view – and one which I still maintain – as a miracle cure.

My case was written up in the medical journals and the treatment I had received became the recognised one for the once dreaded disease of sub-acute bacterial endocarditis. It is still a very serious illness but the recovery rate is now good, depending on the patient's general state of health.

The next important issue was to persuade the Royal Air Force that I was fit for further service. I had no ambitions for high rank but a keen desire to get back to the service I loved. I was content to stay at the rank of Squadron Leader for the rest of my career, but the service were a little unhappy about re-employing me. I was a pilot without (at that time) any sort of medical flying category. Whatever happened, they argued, I would be on the ground for the rest of my life.

However, thanks to the help and intervention of Sir Kenneth Robson, who was much revered by the uniformed doctors, I was slowly rehabilitated and allowed to stay in the service ('at least for the time being'). The Royal Air Force works on various grades of medical flying category. I had none at all for the six months after I left hospital but with Ken Robson's help, I was gradually allowed to start flying again, first as a passenger, then as second pilot, then as first pilot if accompanied by an experienced second pilot. After several years' rehabilitation I was allowed to fly certain aircraft solo. The feeling of total recovery swept over me. I was reinstated in the ranks of the flying branch and thus took my chances of promotion with the others, though the fact that I had been on the sick list for over two years when others were learning to fly high speed jets was thought to be something of a handicap. The stress of high G-levels, the doctors said, was not for me but the service had other aircraft which were not so physically demanding.

As it happened I was appointed, at the end of 1953, to the Directing Staff at the RAF Staff College, Bracknell, as an acting Wing Commander.[2] This was an important appointment, and I was grateful for the chance to be fully back in the swim. I had very much enjoyed my time as a student at the Staff College some years before, and it had made me think about some of the great issues of air power. So the chance to be at Bracknell as an instructor was most welcome. The College had a fine library and it was a wonderful opportunity to read deeply into the subject. I could also fly on occasions, because in the 1950s all aircrew were encouraged to keep in flying practice when on a ground tour, and communication flights existed to support this policy.[3]

It was a fascinating period in the development of air power. The Royal Air Force were just coming into the deterrent business, with the introduction of V-bombers and British nuclear weapons. It was the time of John Foster Dulles and his doctrine of 'massive retaliation'. Those were heady and exciting days. Theories of the use or non-use of nuclear weapons were being hotly debated in the highest government circles; and with something like a hundred students and twenty instructors, the RAF Staff College was very properly an expert forum for such discussion. It was a period when the RAF – being the service entrusted with Britain's nuclear capability – were of the opinion that they held the master card, and that the tasks of the other two services were secondary and in some cases unnecessary. Across the Atlantic new institutes were beginning to grapple with the great issues that the Hiroshima and Nagasaki weapons had raised.

The Staff College course lasted for one year, and each member of the directing staff was tutor to six students.[4] I was to be at Bracknell for three years, first in the tutorial role and then as one of the exercise writers. The latter task was an exciting challenge because I was involved in preparing the first major nuclear exercise relating to the defence of Europe and the support likely to be given by Strategic Air Command of the United States Air Force. It was to be a joint exercise with the Army Staff College at Camberley, and I worked with Lt-Colonel Colin Paddock, RTR, who was the exercise writer at Minley Manor. The discerning eye of Colonel (later General Sir Mervin) 'Tubby' Butler was kept on our more outrageous ideas.

Getting the material for the exercise meant visits to Supreme Headquarters Allied Powers Europe (SHAPE) – in those days just outside Paris – and to various units in the field, both army and air. It was the period of Field Marshal Montgomery's time at SHAPE as Deputy Supreme Commander (or Inspector General of NATO, as he liked to call himself) and of the start of his annual exercise SHAPEX. That year Monty and his exercise team were covering much the same ground as we had chosen for our exercise at Bracknell/Camberley, so we managed to cut some corners. The power of Strategic Air Command, then under General Curtis Le May, and the whole plan for its application were a real eye-opener for us. Much of the information was top secret, but eventually I felt it necessary to ask if I could brief the whole staff at Bracknell about these momentous developments in the defence of Europe. The exercise was a great success and ran for many years at Bracknell/Camberley. Its main purpose was to jerk the war-weary thinking of the British into line with US nuclear concepts and capabilities.

For practically my whole stay at Bracknell I ran the small chapel there and it was a great joy to see it full most Sundays. The Commandant for most of my time was Sir

Douglas Macfadyen, supported by his charming wife, and it was a happy family.

When I came to the end of my stint at the Staff College in August 1956, I determined to get a flying appointment of some sort, notwithstanding my restricted flying category. I was sent to the University of London Air Squadron, then based at the old Battle of Britain airfield at Kenley in Surrey.[5] One of Lord Trenchard's many inspired ideas when setting up the Royal Air Force had been to form air squadrons attached to the main universities. The aim was not solely one of recruiting, although the regular service got some marvellous officers from this source (and still does); it was also to inculcate a feeling for the 'air' amongst undergraduates who were likely to play an important part in our national life. Oxford and Cambridge were the first, later followed by London and Glasgow. The squadrons were equipped with light training aircraft.[6] Flying was done at weekends and occasionally during the week when undergraduates could spare the time. One evening a week was devoted to ground training. The squadrons all had summer camps, usually on a well-established RAF station such as St Mawgan where the members got a real whiff of service life.[7]

One of my first duties was to call on the Vice-Chancellor and Principal of the University, at that time Sir Douglas Logan, who took a keen interest in our activities and usually joined us for a few days at summer camp. He was always popular, not least because he was no mean performer on the piano. He and I were to become firm friends; long after his retirement he continued to be active on the fringes of university life. I also called on the heads of the main colleges, and was well received. (I had little idea when calling on the Principal of King's College in the Strand, that one day I was to occupy his position.) The appointment gave me a great chance to get to know university life, coupled with a regret that, having lacked motivation as a schoolboy, I had not qualified for a University education myself. But there had been a war, and if I had, events might have moved rather differently.[8]

In the middle of 1958 I was warned that I would shortly be required to go to the United States to join the NATO Standing Group there. At that time, the Standing Group consisted of planning teams from the United States, the United Kingdom, France and West Germany, and played an important role in the longer-term planning for NATO. (Two years later it moved to Paris, where perhaps it should have been in the first place.) The family were delighted with the prospect of seeing something of the United States and extending their experience. All preparations including the packing of furniture got under way and tickets for the boat passage were organised. Places for the children in English schools had to be cancelled, and they were looking forward to tackling United States education. Then, two weeks before departure from Liverpool, I was told that the move had been cancelled, and that I was to become the Personal Staff Officer to the Chief of the Air Staff, Air Chief Marshal Sir Dermot Boyle.

Before taking the story further, I would like to reflect on the difference my conversion made to my subsequent career.

Notes

1. After returning from Germany, Squadron Leader Cameron had attended No. 6 course at the RAF Staff College Andover, where he met again a number of his wartime colleagues and also had the opportunity to work with students from other countries. Afterwards, on 22 May 1949, he was posted to the Directorate of Organisation in the Air Ministry as 04, and he and his wife went to live at Welwyn where their first child was born.

2. Previous to this, Squadron Leader Cameron had spent the best part of two years on aircrew selection duties in London, he and his family living in Bromley.

3. At that time Staff College continuation flying training took place at White Waltham.

4. One of his students at Bracknell, Squadron Leader (now Air Marshal) Freddie Sowrey, recalls the great respect and admiration he had for Neil Cameron, who was his first-term Directing Staff. He had an open mind which embraced all elements of a problem and possessed an instinctive gift in summing up and sensing how to draw the best out of people. He was particularly keen to encourage thinking and writing about broader defence matters; he himself was already

writing and he believed the RAF had too few officers who were really articulate. He also took his full part in the social and sporting life of the College; while he could not play rugby he was now Secretary of RAF Rugby, a task which took up much of his spare time and entailed a lot of travel both at home and abroad.

5. The Camerons lived in quarters, first at Kenley and then at Biggin Hill when the squadron moved there in April 1957.

6. The Chipmunk for most of Wing Commander Cameron's time.

7. The permanent staff of the squadron numbered about thirty officers and airmen; its members included some ninety pilots and forty fighter controllers at any one time. In December 1957 the Slack Trophy, presented annually to the best University Air Squadron, was won by London; it was Air Marshal Sir Douglas Macfadyen, formerly Wing Commander Cameron's Commandant at Bracknell, who presented it to him. The squadron won it again in 1958, the first time any squadron had done so two years running.

8. At one point during this tour of duty, during late October and early November 1956, Wing Commander Cameron was attached to the staff of the Assistant Chief of Air Staff (Operations) in the Air Ministry, for duties in the Operations Centre at the time of the Suez Crisis.

7   ON BEING A CHRISTIAN

Being a Christian in the armed forces and to be known as such can be quite a challenging stance. There are of course the large percentage of members of the armed forces who have to declare a religion on their documents on joining and only a very small percentage will declare other than a Christian belief. However, in most cases that is the end of it, and it is useful to the authorities to know what sort of burial is required should they get killed whilst still serving. There are also of course many hidden Christians who though they believe quite deeply do not let the subject become known – their religion is to them a very private matter. I have some sympathy with this view.

The teaching of Jesus suggests that the good Christian news should not be kept to ourselves, but the message should be passed on. The passing on is perhaps one of the most difficult tasks in a fighting service. All too often the Christian can get carried away with himself and his faith and get quite the wrong reaction from his service. Thrusting Christian beliefs at brother officers and subordinates is poison and we have many examples of those good intentioned folk who thought they were putting across the message but were getting entirely the opposite reaction. There is a fine and precarious balance in a fighting service. As officers we have an inescapable responsibility for the morale and welfare of our subordinates, both officers and men. Without a moral standard in our services it would be impossible for long to maintain a high disciplinary standard. Of course by far and away the most important way of discharging this responsibility is by personal example. By humanity, by going out of our way to help because we want to do it. And I suggest this applies to Christian leadership over the whole range of life and not just in the armed forces.

The Christian has got to show something a little bit extra, or try to show it and show it in the right way.

I have rather a good example of what I mean by Christian leadership in a member of my staff some years ago. He was a youngish squadron leader and a test pilot who was and is a very devout Christian. His office had various texts from the Bible pinned up here and there and many thought that this was overdoing it. He read his Bible in his office during the lunch-break, but he did not thrust his views at his colleagues. Of course people were inclined to snigger as they passed his office, and joke about his beliefs. Poor old so and so has become a religious maniac. But I noticed that when some of his colleagues had family problems that troubled them, a son on drugs, a daughter keeping the wrong company, it was to this chap that they turned for advice. He had some quality about him that they knew they could trust in their uncertainty – they knew that he was in touch with God, they felt that he had some rather special spiritual knowledge, he had an understanding which they lacked. They were troubled, they needed help and he did not fail them.

Sir Arthur Bryant writing some time ago said that he never found himself in the company of modern British servicemen of any of our three services without being surprised and moved by the contrast between the working philosophy with which they govern their lives and society and that of the permissive, competitive and confused world outside. They steer as he said by compass, and for all their individuality it is the same compass. They know where they are going and despite all the uncertainties and upsets, discomforts and dangers of their dedicated lives, they go there together. It is the togetherness which counts – a togetherness based on selflessness and consideration for one another.

We all in fact have access to that compass Sir Arthur refers to. God gave us a conscience which can be a very sensitive instrument and pointer to the way. Sometimes the indications may seem a little blurred and the right heading difficult to discern. But I believe that with every reading that we take the way becomes clearer and we begin to acquire a little of that Christian worth we describe as character. Emerson said 'beware what you set your heart upon for it shall surely be yours.' One treasure we can set our hearts upon is character. It cannot be bought or manufactured – it comes as a product of thousands of daily strivings to live up to what is best in us. This for me is what trying to be a Christian is all about. I fail time and time again, but take encouragement even from a slightly confused and imperfect faith to try and try again.

I have found it interesting, instructive and encouraging to look back to the Christian faith of some of the great leaders of the last war. No one is more qualified to speak on the effect of Christianity on courage and morale than Field Marshal Sir William Slim (later Lord Slim) who commanded soldiers of many beliefs during his great campaign in Burma. He has written, 'The Christian religion is above all others a source of enduring courage which is the most valuable of all components of morale.'

Another valuable illustration is revealed in Field Marshal Lord Alanbrooke's Diary. After Churchill had offered him the appointment of CIGS at a moment of crisis in the war Alanbrooke was temporarily left alone with his thoughts. Of this moment he wrote, 'I am not ashamed to confess that as soon as Churchill was out of the room my first impulse was to kneel down and pray to God for guidance and support in the task I had undertaken. As I look back on the years that followed, I can see clearly how well this prayer was answered.'

Field Marshal Lord Montgomery has written in his memoirs, 'I am not in the least ashamed to say that every night I go on my knees and pray to our Father in heaven for help in the days which lie ahead.'

Marshal of the Royal Air Force Sir John Slessor (who held many important appointments during the war), when told at the end of 1949 that he had been selected to be Chief of the Air Staff during a particularly difficult period in the history of our nation, prayed 'that God will give me the nerves to carry out the great task which has been given to me.'

Though I hold myself in no way comparable to these great operational wartime commanders with their heavy responsibility for life and death, I confess that when asked to become Chief of Defence Staff my immediate reaction was to pray to God that I would be given the courage and ability to carry out this frighteningly responsible task.

Clearly for a Christian in the armed forces the ethical situation surrounding the use or non-use of nuclear weapons is important. If I was preaching a sermon on the issue I think I would start by taking as my text one from Deuteronomy:

> Only take heed, and keep your soul diligently lest you forget the things which your eyes have seen.

My eyes saw the Battle of Britain fought to keep Nazi tyranny from dominating and occupying this country. I have seen my friends killed or badly burnt in their fighter aircraft. They were young men full of life, but conscious of the threat Nazi Germany posed to this country. I have seen the war graves in the Western Desert where so many brave and courageous soldiers, sailors and airmen are buried in a foreign land so that their homes might be kept safe. I have seen the Belsen gas chambers and seen in detail Hitler's grisly attempt to exterminate the Jews. I have witnessed the Japanese atrocities in fighting against them in Burma. I have seen the labour gangs of the Soviet Union at first hand. I have seen recent satellite photographs of the greatest rearmament programme in history now being carried out by the Soviet Union. I will not forget what my eyes have seen. But as a committed Christian, though I have forgiven, I am determined that attempts to destroy our freedom to worship God as we like must be resisted and if pressed to the limit even by the use or the threat of use of nuclear weapons. I am a man of peace, a dove not a hawk, a multi-lateral disarmer; but I believe to the depths of my soul that we must defend our Christian way of life.

What can we say of the ethical teaching of Jesus on some of these great issues, and can our Christian leaders help us in our thinking on the subject? It is clear that Jesus recognised that an individual had a responsibility to the State and this comes out clearly in the New Testament. Jesus was not a pacifist and this is also quite clear.

I feel the words of the Dutch jurist and theologian Hugo Grotius are worth considering:

> If the right of . . . defending the citizens by arms against robbers and plunderers was taken away, then would follow a vast licence of crime and a deluge of evils. Wherefore if the mind of Christ had been to induce such a state of things as never was heard of, undoubtedly he would have set it forth in the clearest and most special words, and would have commanded that none should pronounce capital sentence, none should wear arms; which we nowhere read that he did: for what is adduced to this effect is either very general or obscure.

I would argue that a state of stability has been built upon nuclear deterrence and we must be vigilant to see that this balance is not disturbed by getting behind technologically or philosophically. There are some very responsible people in the peace-keeping business who every hour of the year are watching the situation carefully. Robert Osgood of Johns Hopkins University in the USA has written:

> What is novel in contemporary crisis management is the intensity of aspiration to exercise a far greater control over these critical junctures in state relations than men have exercised in the past, and the confidence that this may be done through exhaustive analysis, imaginative speculation and careful planning for future actions.

Richard Harries, Dean of King's College London and an enlightened thinker on these issues, has written:

> Granted that Jesus did not advocate armed revolution – is his ethical teaching really to be interpreted as a set of rules which can and ought to be put into effect in a straightforward way? Jesus taught that God himself would bring in the Kingdom and that this transformation of the whole fabric of human life was already beginning.
> Had Jesus's conviction about the imminent rule of God any effect on his ethical teaching? I believe it had in the sense that if he had known that life would continue for another 2,000 years, he would have spoken more fully on subjects that he almost left untouched.
> What I am trying to say is that it is wrong in my view to

accept totally and blindly that the words and sayings of Jesus 2,000 years ago necessarily apply to the defence and deterrence situation of the year 2,000.

I do not intend to discuss the Just War theory, much has already been written and spoken about it and whether it has a real application to the present situation. There are however one or two issues around this area that I would like to cover. A man deeply involved in both World Wars was Archbishop Temple. In September 1939 when Archbishop of Canterbury he wrote:

'The prevailing conviction is that Nazi Germany and oppression are destroying the traditional excellence of European civilization and must be eliminated for the good of mankind.'

At that time he came under great pressure from pacifists and others to give a lead to the Christian conscience. To one pacifist he wrote:

'Though you cannot advance the Kingdom of God by fighting, you can prevent Christian civilization or a civilization on the way to becoming Christian from being destroyed and that is what we are engaged in. If you look at the New Testament carefully, there can be no doubt that there is a theology of the State as well as a theology of the Church and that it is our duty as citizens in support of the State to do things that would be inappropriate to do as Churchmen in support of the Church, and its cause. It is quite wrong to say that Christians ought not to fight.'

On the bombing of the Ruhr dams in 1943 Temple was to give his opinion:

'The decision to go to war or to support a country in war is a desperately serious one. But which ever way it is answered, the answer must be regarded as carrying with it the full consequences. If we answer *no* – we ought to have been naturally ready for the establishment of the Nazi regime, Gestapo and all the rest of it in Britain, rather than fight. If we answer *yes* – we must be ready for what is required to defeat the enemy other than the infliction of useless suffering. I think there is no doubt that the bombing of the Ruhr dams was a perfectly legitimate act of war. There is a great deal to be said for refusing to fight, but I think myself that in this case, it would be shirking a duty. There is still more to be said, I think, for fighting in support of freedom and justice, but there is nothing to be said for fighting ineffectively.'

And what do the present hierarchy of the Church say about the issues of nuclear weapons and the Christian conscience? In a report published in 1983 the Bishop of Salisbury supported in his committee by a Quaker and two unilateralists, and with little dialogue with others, recommended that this country should unilaterally get out of the nuclear weapons business. When the paper was put before the General Synod of the Church of England it was given a thumbs down on some particularly sensible arguments. The present Archbishop of Canterbury said in his contribution to the debate:

'I do not believe that unilateral measures . . . will in fact have the effect of getting multi-lateral discussions going. My fear is that the kind of action being advocated will actually undermine the negotiations now in progress in Geneva. It would be a tragedy if the Soviets' will to make progress, for example in eliminating the most threatening weapons in Europe, was to be weakened by the spectacle of the NATO alliance in disarray and the tempting prospect of gaining great diplomatic advantage by consolidating a nuclear as well as a conventional superiority in Europe.
Since I believe that the unilateralist approach would undermine disarmament negotiations in progress without exerting much exemplary influence, I cannot accept unilateralism as the best expression of a Christian's prime moral duty to be a peace-maker.'

And what is the message from Rome? The Pope's statement to the UN Special Session on disarmament in June 1983 highlighted the key point. He said:

'In current conditions deterrence based on balance, certainly not as an end in itself but as a step on the way towards a progressive disarmament, may still be judged morally acceptable.'

Personally I find that as a Christian I can live with the deterrent philosophy but this has to include the possibility of the use of nuclear weapons if we are faced with Soviet aggression. I do not agree with the theory that the first use of two or three nuclear weapons if we were clearly losing the conventional battle would mean an immediate global nuclear holocaust. The issues are much too grave for that to happen and I am sure the Soviets have no doubt in their minds that nothing is to be gained by the destruction of their 'empire.' As things stand at the moment the nuclear deterrent picture is a stable one and that is how it must be kept. Perhaps not too comfortable for the Christian conscience but, as the Bishop of London has said, we live in an imperfect world and at times an imperfect solution may have to be acceptable to the Christian. Some years ago the *Economist*, in an interesting and absorbing article, asked the question 'Is Satan Dead?' The writer went on to argue that he did not think Satan was dead, but concluded that God was not either.

8   INTO THE CORRIDORS OF POWER

I greeted the news of my appointment as Personal Staff Officer to the Chief of the Air Staff with mixed emotions; on the one hand, I had only once (in 1949–50) served in the Air Ministry, and here I was going to a job at the centre of power and policy making. On the other hand I knew that any wing commander selected to be PSO to the CAS had the opportunity of a lifetime: if he did well, his further Service career would benefit, for the job was a stepping stone to advancement; if he failed, his future would be 'bound in shallows and in miseries', as Shakespeare has put it. But I was proud to have been selected.

The CAS, Air Chief Marshal Sir Dermot Boyle, a tall, handsome Irishman with a sense of humour, of whom it was once said that 'no air force could have had a more persuasive propagandist', was the first ex-Cranwell cadet to become CAS and one of those legendary pilots who had flown in the pre-war Hendon Displays as a member of the Central Flying School formation aerobatic team. Now, some thirty years later, the problems with which he had to deal were much more complex than those of the comparatively simple 1920s and 30s. He was having to 'fight to preserve the fabric of the Royal Air Force' (as he himself put it) after the Duncan Sandys Defence White Paper of 1957 and the pressure to cut defence spending whilst still maintaining commitments worldwide. He was responsible for a force that wielded greater destructive power than ever before in its history, that had entered the missile age, and that had closer links with the United States Air Force than at any time since World War II. The Air Staff had probably never been so busy, and anyone joining it – as I was being asked to do – would find himself very much at the sharp end of things.

The officer whom I was to succeed – Wing Commander

Desmond Hughes – would be a hard man to follow. He had had a brilliant wartime career, winning three DFCs for night-fighter operations and then being awarded the DSO for 'great skill . . . unsurpassed determination' and 'brilliant leadership', but it was not only his operational record which had brought him this post: a native of Belfast and pre-war member of Cambridge University Air Squadron, he had been commissioned in 1939 and his experience and character fitted him well for the job. We had been on the Directing Staff of the Staff College together. He was thorough in my briefing, which I valued because I had had little previous experience of how the Air Staff worked and because the Department headed by CAS was a large one, its members – both Service and civilian, with the latter forming a kind of permanent secretariat – all being involved in shaping RAF policy. When I joined it towards the end of 1958 (my appointment dated from 10 November) its staff totalled some 341 officers and civil servants, all of them experts in their particular fields and with great practical knowledge of how the RAF should respond to the tasks it was called upon to perform. CAS himself was answerable to the Secretary of State for Air – George Ward, a distinguished figure, wholly committed to the RAF and ever ready to champion its views in the political arena. As George Ward's principal adviser on the direction of the Air Force, and responsible also for its fighting efficiency, Sir Dermot Boyle was supported by his Vice-Chief and Deputy Chief. When I joined the Department the VCAS was Air Marshal Sir Edmund Hudleston and DCAS was Air Marshal Sir Geoffrey Tuttle, both extremely able and hard-working officers.

In Edmund Hudleston, CAS had an ideal Vice-Chief, a 'thinking airman' in the tradition of Lord Tedder: he occupied this post with great distinction and longer than any of his predecessors or successors, for four and a half years. In general terms it can be said that he was mainly concerned with questions of the current effectiveness of the RAF and plans and policy for its employment on operations, while the Deputy Chief's main interests were with training and the long-term equipment of the RAF to meet foreseen strategic and tactical requirements. In his work as

DCAS, Geoffrey Tuttle combined thoroughgoing keenness and determination, characteristics which had distinguished his Service career. His tour of duty, however, came to an end about halfway through my time as PSO and he was succeeded by Air Marshal Sam Elworthy who had only seven months in office before going off to Aden as Commander-in-Chief Middle East Command in July 1960; he himself later became CAS and then Chief of Defence Staff.

Throughout the CAS's Department there were many men who had distinguished themselves in the war years, now Air Vice-Marshals (John Grandy, 'Zulu' Morris, Sydney Bufton and 'Digger' Kyle, for example) or Air Commodores (Fred Rosier, Peter Wykeham and John Searby, for example), and some of them likely to rise still higher. Of course, in such a large Department one got really acquainted with only a few fellow officers in a normal tour of duty, but being at the centre point I was in a good position to meet many of my colleagues. My immediate ones, in CAS's office, were his private secretary and his ADC. R. F. Butler, the PS, I found to be an admirable colleague both professionally and personally: he was extremely efficient (as he needed to be, because of the streams of papers which came in requiring CAS's attention) and always courteous, the epitome of a good PS. I don't think people always realise how much hard, punctilious and careful work goes on behind the scenes, done by first-class civil servants like Bob Butler. His experience and skill were of particular use to me, as I had come in from outside and needed to learn quickly what the job was all about. (It is interesting that it is only the RAF Board Members who have a civil servant as private secretary, the Army and Navy both having serving officers.)

Dermot Boyle was a big man in both the physical and psychological sense: he had a great personality, was courteous to his equals and to his subordinates, and was passionately devoted to the cause of the Royal Air Force. What impressed me was how busy he was; there were enormous pressures on him, from outside as well as inside the Air Force. Above him was the political head, the Secretary of State for Air, constantly seeking guidance on the case he had to present to the Minister of Defence (Harold

Watkinson), to his fellow Ministers and to the Prime Minister. There were always meetings to be attended – of the Air Council, of the Chiefs of Staff and sometimes of the Cabinet Defence Committee – and CAS was briefed on subjects to be discussed at these meetings by papers and memoranda written by specialists in his Department, under the aegis of the various Assistant Chiefs of the Air Staff, each of them responsible for a particular field of activity – Operations, Air Defence, Intelligence, Ground Defence, Operational Requirements, Signals, Scientific Advice, Flight Safety and Defence Research. One Directorate, Air Staff Briefing, was responsible for the preparation of briefs for CAS, VCAS, DCAS and for all the committees they attended.

Working in close conjunction with the Secretary of State (Air) and CAS in the formulation of RAF policy was the head of the civil service side, the Permanent Under-Secretary of State for Air, Sir Maurice Dean. He was the latest in that distinguished line of Secretaries whose names were familiar to everyone in the RAF, if for no other reason than because they signed Air Council Instructions. Maurice Dean had become PUS in July 1955; he had been a civil servant since 1929, having been appointed Private Secretary to the Chief of Air Staff (Sir Edward Ellington) in 1934, so he knew a great deal about the Air Ministry and how RAF policy was made. He held the PUS post for eight years – longer than any of his predecessors. He was the 'Sir Humphrey' of his day to the Minister, S of S for Air, and to the CAS – the top civil servant who could give expert guidance based on his long experience of RAF policy-making. Unlike Sir Humphrey's, his advice was always well-founded. There was much paperwork generated – a stream of Air Staff papers, minutes, memoranda and briefs flowed up to CAS's office, and I was impressed by the way CAS himself and the Air Council members formulated policies on the basis of the advice they were given.

I gained a useful bonus during my time as PSO by winning the Gordon Shephard Prize Essay competition for 1960. The subject was the need for a deterrent force, and essays up to 4,000 words in length were required. An examination-style question had been set; it started off with a proposition, qualified it and asked for an analysis of its implications:

> The need for a deterrent force is well understood in the Royal Air Force. On the other hand, there is evidence from time to time to indicate that this need is not properly appreciated by the other two Services, or by a large part of the public. Discuss this problem and suggest how the Royal Air Force view should be presented to ensure a more widespread understanding of the nation's need to maintain a valid deterrent force.

The object of the competition was said to be to encourage 'original thought and good writing', so I must have produced something of both to be chosen winner by the examiners out of twenty-one entries. The essay was published in the *Journal of the Royal United Services Institution* under the title 'In Defence of a Deterrent Strategy'. I was a deterrent man then and always remained so.

What motivated the amount of paper and the number of meetings in 1959–60 was the sheer amount of business the Air Staff had to transact. There was not only the pressure resulting from the Duncan Sandys' White Paper of 1957, which I have already mentioned, one of the implications of which was a drastic reduction in the strength of the RAF – from 228,000 in 1957 to less than 150,000 by 1962; there was the problem of air defence policy, which exercised the Air Staff in 1959; there were cuts in our forces in Germany and on overseas bases; there was increased cooperation with the Americans, following their recognition of Britain's nuclear deterrent capability with the V-bomber force, on the coordination of plans and the supply of weapons; there was the deployment of Thor IRBMs (intermediate-range ballistic missiles); and there was controversy over the future strategic deterrent delivery systems – whether land-launched Blue Streak, air-launched Skybolt or under-sea launched Polaris.

There is no doubt that the Sandys' 'affair' did no good to RAF morale: the Service was annoyed with such lack of vision about what air power was all about. Recruiting was suffering. Happily the Prime Minister (Harold Macmillan) was persuaded to go to the RAF College, Cranwell, to take a specially arranged parade and to address the cadets. We all

helped with the speech but in the end it was vintage
Macmillan and it went down extremely well. It did morale a
power of good. It was circulated throughout the Royal Air
Force and helped to balance out some of the Sandys judge-
ments. But much damage had been done, and much of the
activity of CAS and his office and staff was directed at
disproving some of the wilder Sandys recommendations.
As CAS, Sir Dermot fought hard and well against Sandys
and had a large degree of success; but it was emotional and
tiring work. My own view is that he was one of the great
CASs, and the Royal Air Force owes him a large tribute for
the battles he fought in those days to make sure that lasting
damage was not done to its whole fabric.

CAS maintained his aplomb and his cheerfulness during
these difficult times, although I know he had pretty deep
feelings on certain subjects. For example, he was opposed
to the deployment of Thor on bases in Britain, as it was an
untried weapon and because it was sited in fixed positions
above ground increasing this country's vulnerability to
attack from Eastern bloc bases. However, once the Government had decided to accept Thors the RAF did a very
thorough job of manning them through its specially formed
Strategic Missile Squadrons. However, the Thor deployment (1958–63) came largely after Boyle's time as CAS: in
April 1959 it was announced that Air Chief Marshal Sir
Thomas Pike, AOC-in-C Fighter Command, was to succeed
him in January 1960.

Dermot Boyle finished off his tour as CAS with characteristic flamboyance, by visiting all his Commands. On 9
January 1959 he set off on a 20,000-mile tour of RAF units
overseas, flying himself in a Canberra. Then in the middle
of the year he visited RAF Germany, and in September all
Commands in the UK. He also went off on a trip to the
United States in November. I realised when 1959 came to an
end that I should miss him very much as CAS and he was
certainly missed in the Air Ministry: he had stamped his
own personality on the office and I found him good to work
for – he could combine being distinguished as the head of
the RAF with being friendly and at ease with everyone
he encountered. After retirement he became Assistant
Managing Director of the British Aircraft Corporation.

I found Tom Pike a very different character. By the time he arrived I had the advantage of being well versed in the duties of a PSO, the very reverse situation to my original one, that of being a new and untried PSO to an experienced CAS. Tom Pike had been a successful night-fighter pilot during the war, winning two DFCs in quick succession. In manner he was quiet and undramatic, a sound administrator rather than an outgoing personality – but tough and resilient. His Whitehall experience had been mostly in Operational Requirements, so he was particularly well equipped to deal with some of the big aircraft issues facing us. I found him interesting to work for (I was to serve him again later) and 'the office' was determined to give him the utmost possible assistance in his new and heavy responsibilities. His first months as CAS – I had about eight months as his PSO before my next appointment in September 1960 after I handed over to Wing Commander Freddie Sowrey in mid-July of that year – were marked by some dramatic events. On 13 April the Minister of Defence, Mr Harold Watkinson, announced in the Commons that Blue Streak was to be cancelled – which meant that we would be committed to a purchase of the US Skybolt ALBMs (air-launched ballistic missiles) in order to extend the operational viability of the V-bombers. Less than a month later on 1 May, the American pilot Francis Gary Powers was shot down over the USSR in a U-2, provoking an international incident of the first magnitude.

During his predecessor's term as CAS the RAF had moved into the missile age. Bloodhound air defence weapons and air-to-air Firestreaks had gone into service with Fighter Command, and Thors were being deployed by Bomber Command, the last being delivered by the USAF in March 1960. Air-to-air refuelling had been operationally verified, after long battles with the Treasury over Valiant tanker squadrons, and No 214 Squadron were making spectacular non-stop flights – leading to UK-Singapore (8,000 miles) in 1960. During 1957–58 megaton-range weapons had been successfully tested at Christmas Island, giving international proof of Britain's nuclear technology achievements. In May 1958 the Air Council had taken the unprecedented step of putting its views on future air policy

– vis-à-vis the Sandys White Paper of 1957 – before an influential cross section of public opinion at a conference code-named Prospect, held at the Royal Empire Society's premises and preceded by a 'dress rehearsal' for senior officers at Cranwell. This all caused a great furore in the press about 'revolt by the RAF'. At the Farnborough Air Display in September 1959 the marvellous Hunter formation aerobatic team of No 111 Squadron under Squadron Leader Peter Latham, the Black Arrows, had made a never-to-be-forgotten impression.

In a word, despite the buffetings of the politicians and the Treasury, the RAF which Dermot Boyle handed over to Tom Pike at the end of 1959 was in reasonably good heart and I was proud and fascinated to have seen some of the hard work which had gone on at the top, and to watch it go on under a new CAS (under whom I was later to serve in a similar capacity in a NATO appointment). When the aviation magazine *Flight* commented in its 15 January 1960 issue on his arrival as CAS, it said:

> The fifties have been a good period for the RAF. It celebrated its 40th birthday, established the V-force in Bomber Command, assumed responsibility for UK missile defence, retained control of Coastal Command and now has a new group in Transport Command with specialist responsibility for tactical airborne support operations. Sir Thomas therefore inherits a force with high commitments, but with correspondingly high morale.

During the months of 1960 when I served as his PSO the new CAS's workload in terms of Air Council and Chiefs of Staff meetings, and the preparations for them, was no less than it had been for his predecessor. Each Air Council meeting had about half a dozen new items on its agenda, ranging over the whole of RAF activities, and entire meetings were devoted to discussions of the annual defence review. However, the admirable Bob Butler was still there to advise CAS and provide continuity, and when I handed over to Freddie Sowrey before taking up my new posting I felt that my experience as PSO had been an invaluable guide to the workings of the RAF at its highest levels.

9 STATION COMMANDER, IDC, NATO – AND THE RAF CLUB

On 28 October 1960, newly promoted to Group Captain, Neil Cameron took command of RAF Abingdon. If he ever felt disappointment at being given a transport station rather than a fighter station – towards which his wartime experience must surely have pointed – he certainly never showed it. For him as a thinker about air power, aircraft were important for actually doing things; while he knew that the transport role came well down the RAF priority list the two Beverley squadrons based at Abingdon, Nos 47 and 53, had plenty of tasks to keep them occupied.

The ungainly looking Beverley had entered service in 1956, primarily in the supply dropping and freight-carrying roles, and in the days before the arrival of the Belfast and the Hercules was the RAF's main load carrier. Altogether there were five Beverley squadrons, three overseas at Khormaksar, Eastleigh and Seletar, and two at Abingdon, and one of the tasks of the home-based squadrons was to reinforce their overseas counterparts when necessary. This role, together with route missions and overseas deployment exercises with the Army, meant that Abingdon's Beverleys were often in the Mediterranean area or even further afield. They also went to Germany from time to time, where among other things they flew to Berlin in order to exercise UK rights in the air corridors. At home they were frequently required for exercises with the Parachute Brigade, practising airborne assaults and the use of forward airstrips, and with other units, for example dropping supplies. Last but not least, in emergency they would have to provide transport support for the dispersal of V-force squadrons, for in the early 1960s Bomber Command's dispersal plans were an integral part of its deterrent role.

There was therefore plenty of operational activity to keep the CO busy. While he was not permitted to fly solo, he had completed the one-month course at No 242 Operational Conversion Unit, Dishforth, before arriving at Abingdon, and – as Sir Freddie Sowrey, who succeeded him as station commander has recalled – he was immensely proud of his 'B' category as Captain. From time to time he would fly with the squadrons, partly to keep his hand in and also to give himself a chance to get to know the crews; usually these were local sorties, but occasionally he also went to Germany or the Mediterranean. For the most part, however, as CO he had to stay at home, but as one of the Flight Commanders on No 53 Squadron – Squadron Leader (later, Wing Commander) Ernie Strangeway – remembered, whenever the squadrons were going away on operations he would brief and debrief them personally. He was always at pains to explain the political implications of what they were doing; he would remind them of the need to be flexible; and he would stress the importance of doing the job well and thus safeguarding the RAF's reputation. He would insist, too, on being kept fully informed by signal of what was happening while the aircraft were deployed overseas.

Most of the real-life operations in 1961/62 were connected either with civil disturbances or flood relief in Africa, particularly Kenya, but the most important single event was Operation Vantage in July 1961. As Neil Cameron himself wrote later,

this was to prevent the threatened annexure of Kuwait by Iraq, following the cessation on 26 June 1961 of the Treaty of 1899 between the Ruler of Kuwait and Her Majesty's Government. In response to Kuwait's calls for British protection, the UK Strategic Reserve began moving into the Persian Gulf using Bahrain Island as a forward base. Many of our crews were called to readiness and began to move out to Aden to reinforce the Middle East Air Force. At that time of the year the weather in the Gulf was at its hottest, with frequent sand storms and temperatures up to 120° in the shade. Based at Khormaksar, our Beverleys soon established an intensive schedule of flights to Kuwait carrying troops, weapons, armoured fighting vehicles, and fighter bomber back-up. Within one week air transport had moved 7,000 troops and associated weapons,

LEFT. Neil Cameron at the start of his RAF career – as a sergeant, RAFVR (u/t pilot) at No 3 Initial Training Wing, Hastings.

RIGHT. Pilot Officer Neil Cameron, when with No 134 Squadron in the Hurricane Wing (No 151) at Vaenga airfield near Murmansk in 1941.

ABOVE. Crew room – Russian style. Neil Cameron is on the extreme right.

BELOW. "Soil was excavated so that the aircraft could be parked partly below ground level and the shelters were then built around them…" – No 151 Wing's dispersal area.

ABOVE. With fellow pilots of No 213 Squadron at LG172, El Hamman, on 30 October 1942. From left to right P/O 'Jock' Aitken, P/O 'Gordy' Waite, F/O Roy ——, P/O Knapton and P/A Neil Cameron.

LEFT. Flight Lieutenant Cameron in the Western Desert, 1942.

Squadron Leader Neil Cameron, OC No 258 Squadron in Burma, perched on the wing of a P-47 Thunderbolt, part of whose formidable armament (eight 0.5in machine-guns plus bombs) can be seen.

RIGHT. Outside Buckingham Palace on 11 November 1947 after the investiture when he was awarded the DSO and DFC: with his wife Patricia (now Lady Cameron), then a Section Officer, WAAF.

ABOVE. Rugby was one of Neil Cameron's abiding enthusiasms, and he is here seen (back row, next to the end on the right) as a member of the RAF Andover 1st XV in the 1948-49 season.

BELOW. As CO of London University Air Squadron, Wing Commander Cameron introducing the Principal, Sir Douglas Logan, to some of its members when he visited the UAS summer camp at RAF St Eval, Cornwall, on 1 August 1957.

ABOVE. Air Chief Marshal Sir Dermot Boyle, Chief of the Air Staff, talking with Neil Cameron at the London UAS annual dinner on 21 February 1958.

RIGHT. As Assistant Commandant (Cadets), Air Commodore Neil Cameron with Princess Alexandra when she reviewed the RAF College passing-out parade on 24 June 1965. She is here presenting the Sword of Honour to Senior Under Officer W.F.C. Tyndall.

LEFT. On his last day as Chief of the Air Staff, Air Chief Marshal Sir Neil Cameron meets the Queen and the Duke of Edinburgh at the Royal Review at RAF Finningley on 29 July 1977. Lady Cameron is on his left.

ABOVE. A word of explanation from the CAS for the Queen at the Royal Review.

ABOVE. Marshal of the RAF Sir Neil Cameron, Chief of the Defence Staff (second from the left), with the Defence Council on 13 September 1977.

BELOW. Sir Neil Cameron with crews of No 6 Tank Division, during his 1978 China visit.

ABOVE. Taking a look at the Great Wall.

BELOW. A "return visit" by the Chinese to the Ministry of Defence: on CDS's left is Yang Yung, his military equivalent in China; on his right is the Chinese Ambassador (with an interpreter behind him). Air Marshal Sir Frederick Sowrey is on the right.

Lord Cameron of Balhousie in the District of Perth and Kinross when introduced into the House of Lords on 16 March 1983 by Baroness Airey of Abingdon and Lord Flowers.

vehicles and armour plus six offensive support squadrons equipped with Hunters and Canberras into the Gulf. In the face of this the Iraqi threat to Kuwait died away, and as a result of diplomatic efforts an Arab League guarantee of Kuwait's independence was established.

Later that year, in November and December, a relief operation in Kenya and Somalia elicited a congratulatory message from the Commander East Africa to the Air Officer Commanding 38 Group which must have given great pleasure to Neil Cameron as he repeated it in his station routine orders:

The last of your aircraft which were detached to Nairobi are now on their way home. The Governor of Kenya and my AOC both personally thanked the Detachment Commander and aircrews and groundcrews of the last two Beverleys before they departed Eastleigh for the magnificent life-saving effort which they achieved here. I would like to add my own thanks and to stress particularly my admiration for the excellent co-operation which we received from your chaps in every respect. They worked long hours, maintained wonderful aircraft serviceability and their enthusiasm and morale were absolutely first rate.

Inevitably many of Neil Cameron's responsibilities at Abingdon brought him into contact with the Army – just as much of his operational flying during World War II had been in their support – and none more so than the presence of No 1 Parachute Training School (in fact the only UK-based parachute school). This conducted a wide range of courses for all three Services and generated a great many visitors, foreign as well as British, some of them very high-ranking. The CO had to devote time to meeting many of them, and occasionally he would join the OC of the School in visiting other establishments. Most important, however, he insisted on carrying out two parachute jumps into the sea off the south coast. His enthusiasm for and interest in the subject are well brought out by Group Captain Peter Hearn in his book *Parachutist* published in 1976, where he records his gratitude to Sir Neil not only for providing the Foreword and valuable guidance in the writing of it, but also for the personal encouragement given when he was Station Commander of RAF Abingdon during Hearn's formative parachuting years. As Hearn mentions, it was in 1961 that No 1 PTS's part-time display activities were formally recognised by the formation of the official RAF Parachute Display Team.

Much of Cameron's time, of course, had to be spent on the day-to-day minutiae that always concern the CO of an RAF station in peacetime, and not the least of his concerns were the living conditions of his 1,500 officers, airmen and airwomen. Knowing that he could get the best out of the personnel if he looked after them, and well aware that too many RAF units still had standards of messing and accommodation not much improved since World War II, he instituted a number of schemes to improve the catering, the barrack rooms, and the general appearance of the station. Dressed in plain clothes and driving his battered old Ford car, he would go round on his own, rather in the Paddy Bandon style,[1] so as to see for himself what was happening and what needed to be done. Much he achieved by local initiative – the 101 Club, for example, he set up as the junior ranks club, the '101' representing the sum of Nos 47 and 53 squadrons and 1 PTS. On occasion he would make himself unpopular with higher authority, for he was never afraid to speak his mind, but usually he achieved his purposes without fuss – as Freddie Sowrey recalls – by knowing where power lay and the right channels to use. As one would expect, his enthusiasm for rugby also made demands on his time, and the marked success of the station team owed much to his support.

Another of his concerns was to strengthen the ties between Abingdon and the outside community, for he regarded good relations with the local people as particularly important. Throwing himself into the local scene, he made people believe that the airfield and the town were almost synonymous, and he struck up a warm friendship with the local MP, Mr Airey Neave.[2] He and his wife were much in demand at local functions, and he would never turn down an invitation to speak at a nearby school or a civic gathering. Among other things, such occasions gave him the opportunity to answer those who were inclined to complain about some of the RAF's activities, in particular night flying. The proximity of Oxford, too, interested him: there was the Air Squadron with which he could forge closer links, and the University gave him the opportunity not only to invite speakers to address his officers in the Mess, but also to join personally in academic discussions on defence subjects and thus extend the scope of his own defence writing.

His tour of duty at Abingdon came to an end on 3 December 1962, when his former pupil, now Group Captain Freddie Sowrey, arrived to take over from him yet again. Sowrey had a difficult act to follow, for Neil Cameron had achieved a great deal in his two years and was highly respected by all. Sir Harold Martin, who had just become SASO at HQ 38 Group, remembers the AOC, Air Marshal Sir Tim Piper, commenting on the round of AOC's Inspections he had just completed: he was in no doubt that Abingdon was by far the best. Cameron himself always remembered his time there with pride, and nothing gave him greater pleasure than being invited back in 1982 to take part in Abingdon's fiftieth anniversary celebrations.

Well before the end of his time at Abingdon Neil Cameron knew that he had been selected to spend the next year (1963) as a student at the Imperial Defence College. This provided a clear indication that he was being marked out for higher things, and it would give him an ideal opportunity to advance his own military education. Air Chief Marshal Sir Lewis Hodges, who was on the same course, and was to meet Cameron again in 1964 at SHAPE, recalls that meeting and working with officers of similar rank in the other Services – many of whom one would be dealing with in later appointments – was one of the principal benefits. Another was the chance to listen to and question the many politicians, senior civil servants, high-ranking officers, and other distinguished visitors who came to Seaford House to contribute to the lecture programme. And then there were the visits that the students undertook, overseas as well as at home, all designed to broaden their interests and help them appreciate the wider world in which the Armed Services had to operate. Neil Cameron, as one would expect, took full advantage of his year away from the day-to-day pressures of command and staff work, playing a prominent part in the many discussions and also extending his interests in the defence studies field – not least with the Royal United Services Institution.

His views on current defence matters, and in particular on the role of the RAF, were well illustrated in a letter he sent to *The Scotsman* in March 1963 while at Seaford House:

Since Nassau and the questionable demise of Skybolt there have been suggestions from one or two defence correspondents (your own included) that the future existence of the Royal Air Force might be in some doubt and that now might be the time to return to the concept of two Services only, each with their own air arm. This is irresponsible thought; bad for the Country, bad for the morale and recruiting of the Royal Air Force and bad for inter-Service relations. It is also thoroughly unsound. Close inter-Service relations we must have and there is a case for some integration, but that is as far as it goes.

Trenchard won the battle for an independent Air Force against the most powerful Navy, Army, Press and political lobby imaginable. He won it on the logic of the indivisibility of air power and he defended his beliefs successfully against powerful opposition on many subsequent occasions. The Royal Air Force proved his theories during the last war and from their example the Americans created the United States Air Force as a separate service.

In the latter half of this decade, if present plans go ahead, the RAF will hand over responsibility for the main part of the British deterrent to the highly specialised Polaris submarines of the Royal Navy. I believe that this country should have a deterrent capability (as long as it is independent and effective), and whether it is mounted by the Navy, Army or Air Force is entirely immaterial. The strategic nuclear deterrent is a specialist job which should be entrusted to the available weapons system best suited to provide it. Despite this hand-over the RAF will still have a vitally important role to play in all types of war and the Trenchard philosophy of the indivisibility of air power with its inherent flexibility and adaptability is more relevant today than ever before with aircraft of very high speeds, greater ranges, and carrying weapons of catastrophic destruction.

On the introduction of Polaris it is expected that the V-bombers will phase out of the RAF order of battle in the early 1970s and what is left? As your correspondent mentions there is the TSR.2, capable of long-range, low-level penetration carrying a weapon with many times the destructive capacity of the Nagasaki bomb; this aircraft will also have the most comprehensive reconnaissance and conventional weapon capability ever known. The force will have the strike capability roughly equivalent to de Gaulle's 'force de frappe' but with greater penetration possibilities. The 1963 Statement on Defence tells us that the P.1154 fighter bomber will be developed and also a VTOL long-range transport aircraft. Britain leads the world in the VTOL field and we must keep ahead. There is also 'Space' and I am convinced (along with many others in this country) that we must get into this element in some aspect from both a defence and an industrial point of view. These developments alone go a long way beyond 'fire power in support of ground forces', and they will demand all the expertise and experience of air matters and the highest technical skill that can be mustered. It is a task for the Royal Air Force and one which will add to her already great traditions.

So let the Navy and Army get on with their basic tasks on the sea and land and let us not contemplate dismissing the RAF as a separate strategic arm. The military planners and correspondents might however take a close look at the Fleet Air Arm and the Army Air Corps in the present strategic-cum-economic climate so that they may convince the taxpayer that they are getting value for money. Would it not be more logical and economical to put all the 'air' under one central control?

Some time before he was due to finish his course Neil Cameron had a telephone message from his former 'boss' – the Chief of the Air Staff, Marshal of the RAF Sir Thomas Pike. He said that after completing his term of office as CAS he would be going to Paris as Deputy Supreme Allied Commander, Europe, and wondered if Cameron would be interested in accompanying him there as his PSO. It was a great honour to be asked. The two of them had got on well together in 1960, and Pike's suggestion illustrated the fact that a friendship made at one stage of a Service career often influences that career later on. Moreover Cameron had served in Europe only once before – for some five months at Air HQ, British Air Forces of Occupation in 1948 – and it would be useful to see something of NATO at first hand.[3] He probably felt too that he would be doing Tom Pike a service by accepting: in his new appointment, outside the

RAF, Pike would be glad of the assurance of having someone he knew and trusted working with him. So Cameron
agreed and his posting to SHAPE Headquarters was
arranged accordingly, taking effect from 20 December 1963.
Pike's own appointment dated from 31 December, so they
arrived there at about the same time.

The RAF staff at SHAPE was a small one – some thirty-
seven officers – and although he had offices in the same
Headquarters, Deputy SACEUR and his immediate staff
were quite separate from the RAF personnel there. Indeed,
his predecessor had been an Army officer, General Sir
Hugh Stockwell. The RAF element was headed by the
Deputy for Nuclear Affairs and Air Executive, Air Vice
Marshal Hodges, who had distinguished himself during
the war by his operations in support of the Special Operations Executive and had recently been with Neil Cameron
at Imperial Defence College; the UK national military
representative – the link man between the Ministry of
Defence and NATO – was Air Commodore C. B. E. Burt-
Andrews, who had been one of Cameron's colleagues on
the Bracknell Directing Staff some ten years previously.
Tom Pike was the only ex-CAS ever to become Deputy
SACEUR; he was already highly esteemed abroad and
particularly by the USAF, and his appointment sprang
out of talks he had had with SACEUR, General Lyman
Lemnitzer, during a visit the latter had made to London
early in 1963. Pike's name had been mooted as a possible
successor to Stockwell, and during conversations with
Lemnitzer he had said he would like the job – provided
there was one, because he had heard that there was not
really much to do. SACEUR had assured him that his
Deputy was indeed kept busy all day long, and on the basis
of this assurance, Pike accepted the appointment.

He was also the first airman to hold it; his British predecessors had all been soldiers. What he hoped was that he
might play an active part in the formulation of policy, but
this idea was a non-starter as SACEUR already had an
American Chief of Staff with a large staff under him, so
there was no clearly defined deputy's role. The alternative
was to become a kind of Inspector-General and go round
visiting units, but this was not what Tom Pike wished to do.

He came to the reluctant conclusion that what the British Government wanted was a representative at SHAPE to see that SACEUR did not do anything stupid or irresponsible – in other words, to hold a watching brief as part of a system of checks and balances. As far as the organisation was concerned, a Deputy was just not needed. However, the appointment had its compensations so far as its location and perquisites were concerned, and for Tom Pike it was a pleasant way to end his service in the RAF. As for Neil Cameron he found his PSO duties rewarding and interesting; they gave him, as Hodges recalls, not only a useful insight into the workings of NATO but also many personal contacts which were later to prove of great value.

He was struck by the complexity of the organisation, exemplified in its regular conferences and meetings to decide policies and the sharing of expenditure, its exercises and its constant reactions to any moves by the Warsaw Pact countries. Its governing body was the Military Committee, and its infrastructure – that is, all its fixed installations like airfields, communications equipment, radar, fuel storage and pipelines – was reviewed annually to allot costs among the member countries at an Infrastructure Conference, one of these being held in September 1964, during the year he was in Paris.

During that year two events occurred which were to have important consequences for the future, both of NATO and the RAF. The first was the French decision to leave the Organisation, for General de Gaulle was determined that France should have complete political and military independence. This meant that NATO would have to vacate its Headquarters in Paris and Fontainebleau, its airfields and all other sites on French soil, and that an assured French military contribution to the Alliance would be lost. Relations between the French and the other members had never been easy; they felt they were insufficiently represented in the top echelons of a command structure that was dominated by the Americans, and day-to-day work was made difficult by their staff officers' insistence on using French for all official business. Nevertheless, despite the impending change, the professional demeanour of the French officers remained exemplary.

The other event was the General Election in the UK which led to the return of a Labour Government in October, a change of administration which was to have important effects on British defence policy and on the RAF in particular. From the other side of the Channel the new British Government could be observed with a certain detachment, since Britain's NATO commitments were not likely to be immediately affected, if at all. On the other hand, as far as the RAF was concerned, its programme of new aircraft – particularly TSR.2 – was likely to be closely scrutinised by the Labour administration. At this time one of the major issues debated in NATO circles was the American proposal for the creation of a multilateral nuclear force (MNF), together with an alternative British scheme for an Atlantic nuclear force (ANF).

Although the duties of Deputy SACEUR were largely ceremonial and non-executive, there was still a great deal of administrative work to do – a constant flow of signal messages, from NATO and from Whitehall, to be monitored, briefs to be prepared for meetings, speeches to be written and visits to be arranged; so Cameron was kept pretty busy, and enjoyed being busy in Paris rather than in London. He and his family lived in a flat on the outskirts of Paris, and although he spoke only a smattering of French and his wife little more, they experienced few problems. His tour there, however, lasted no more than a year, for on 1 July he was promoted to Air Commodore and in mid-December Group Captain Alan Hollingsworth arrived to replace him. Tom Pike on the other hand was to soldier on until March 1967; while he felt he was not doing anything really useful, being denied any executive responsibility, he liked Lyman Lemnitzer and the SHAPE people with whom he had to work. Despite some inevitable frustration, there could have been many worse ways of finishing a distinguished Service career.

As for Cameron, the experience of being inside NATO for a short period and of working with Service representatives from other European countries and from the USA and Canada was an invaluable one which stood him in good stead in his later career, particularly as CAS and CDS. The Paris period, coming after his year at the Imperial Defence

College, had given him a refreshing change of scene and resulted in a wealth of new contacts outside the RAF; he had seen, through their varied contributions to NATO, how some other Air Forces tackled their problems; and his experience was greatly broadened, for which he had Tom Pike to thank.

It was while Neil Cameron was serving at SHAPE that he acquired another interest to which he would be committed for the rest of his life. Air Chief Marshal Sir Lewis Hodges recalls the two of them visiting the Cercle Militaire in Paris one evening, and as they were returning by car to Versailles they talked about a circular letter they had received from the RAF Club, of which both were members. It revealed an alarming state of affairs.

The Club building at 128 Piccadilly had been leased, modified and furnished in 1920 thanks to a gift of £350,000 from the late Lord Cowdray, in memory of one of his sons who had been killed while serving in the Royal Flying Corps during the First World War. Now, forty-four years later, the Club was in dire straits. It was trading at an annual deficit of some £5,000, its overdraft was over £40,000 and growing, and of its 3,800 members – only 1,500 of whom were serving officers – substantial numbers were resigning rather than pay the increased subscriptions being demanded. As Hodges and Cameron reflected on this they were struck with the contrast presented by the Cercle Militaire, a club to which every officer serving in the Paris region had to belong and whose atmosphere was so much more welcoming – not just to officers but also to the families. Might it not be possible, they asked themselves, to change the RAF Club image and require every RAF officer to join? If so, even with the most modest level of individual subscription the Club's problems would be solved.

While the Air Member for Personnel (Sir David Lee), whom Hodges approached informally soon afterwards, insisted that compulsion would not be practicable, he was nevertheless entirely sympathetic to the general idea, and Hodges and Cameron, with supporters now gathering around them, requested an Extraordinary General Meeting. This took place on 14 December 1964, when they explained their ideas and received overwhelming backing.

As a result the planned increase in subscriptions was deferred and Hodges' offer to set up a Working Party to suggest how to increase the membership was accepted. It was Neil Cameron, then at Cranwell, who became its Chairman. He and his colleagues (Group Captains I. G. Broom, F. B. Sowrey and R. A. Webster), having canvassed opinion throughout the Service, concluded that given the prospect of a new-look club and a low subscription it should be possible to attract as members a very high proportion of the officers serving in the RAF. With the consequent increase in income, coupled perhaps with a loan from the RAF Central Fund to pay off the overdraft, a long-term development scheme could then be started; in this way the Club would, the Working Party considered, both be preserved and become of benefit to the Royal Air Force as a whole, thus fulfilling the original intention behind the Cowdray bequest.

When it became clear at the March 1965 Annual General Meeting that the new scheme would go ahead, Sir Walter Pretty, the current Chairman, decided to make way for a new face, and – hardly surprisingly – Neil Cameron was chosen to succeed him. Within a very short time, on the basis of an annual subscription for serving officers of two-thirds of a day's pay, membership had risen to about 16,000, the RAF Central Fund had agreed to make an annual grant to enable a refurbishing programme to begin, and a professional manager had been appointed. So, when Neil Cameron handed over the Chairmanship to Freddie Sowrey (who else?) in November 1967, the Club had been set firmly on the road to recovery.

Neil Cameron, while retaining a close interest in the steadily improving fortunes of the Club, was not directly involved again in its activities other than as a Vice-President until he succeeded Sir Dermot Boyle as President on 1 May 1980. Sir Dermot, who had been present and strongly supportive at the critical meeting at the end of 1964 and became President in 1968, considered that the RAF Club must remain for ever indebted to him for his great contribution to its future. Indeed, had he lived, Lord Cameron – as he had by then become – would have presided over the final act in the Club's revival, for the freehold of the property was eventually purchased on 28 June 1985, just five months after his death.

Notes

1. See Chapter four, note 14.

2. MP for Abingdon from 1953 until his death in 1979 as the result of an INLA car-bomb attack, Airey Neave had distinguished himself in World War II by being one of the few Allied PoW to escape from Colditz. He was awarded the DSO and MC, served in MI9 and took part in the Nuremberg war crimes trials.

3. He had visited SHAPE while at Staff College – see Chapter six.

10 CADET COMMANDER – RAF CRANWELL

While serving as Personal Staff Officer to Deputy SACEUR, Neil Cameron had been promoted to Air Commodore, from July 1964; and at the end of that year he left Paris to go to the RAF Flying College at Manby, where he did Varsity and Jet Provost courses. In the early days of 1965 he learnt of his next appointment: to be Assistant Commandant (Department of Cadets) at the RAF College, Cranwell. This was a significant posting for him, to an institution of great importance and proud traditions – one which was in the process of being subjected to considerable changes.

The College, whose handsome white buildings dominate the Lincolnshire landscape near Sleaford, had been established under Sir Hugh Trenchard's original plans as an 'air academy' – the first in the world – to produce officers for the RAF. On 5 February 1920, thereafter known as 'Founder's Day', the first course had started; and the cadets on it had been in the vanguard of generations who reached senior ranks, though the first one to become Chief of the Air Staff had been Neil Cameron's former 'boss', Sir Dermot Boyle.

Successive generations had created traditions at Cranwell as jealously upheld as those at Dartmouth and Sandhurst. But the destructive impact of World War II on the society of the 1920s and '30s, and subsequent changes in politics, education and the economy, had had a profound effect on all three of these time-honoured Service institutions.

Another change, taking place within the Services themselves, was the planned merger of educational establishments – specifically, as far as the RAF were concerned, that of Henlow, its Technical College, with Cranwell. This was to take place at the time of Neil Cameron's posting there, and his appointment as an Assistant Commandant was one of the resultant changes in organisation.

Since 1952 Cranwell had had a Commandant of air commodore rank and a group captain Assistant Commandant: now it was to have a Commandant of Air Vice-Marshal rank and two Assistant Commandants of Air Commodore rank, who were to head specific areas of responsibility. As the *RAF College Journal* commented: 'as part of the preparation for the amalgamation of Cranwell and Henlow the College has been reorganised into Departments: the Department of Cadets under the Assistant Commandant (Cadets), responsible for all aspects of cadet training; the Department of Engineering under the Assistant Commandant (Technical)'.

Neil Cameron, appointed to fill the former of these two posts, moved to Cranwell with his family and took up his new duties in May 1965. They were to be there for fifteen months, during the time of the greatest changes which had ever occurred in the history of the College, in terms of administration, curricula and personnel.

He was fortunate in his immediate colleagues. Like him, they had entered the RAF through the pre-war Volunteer Reserve in 1939; like him, they had distinguished themselves operationally in World War II. The Commandant, Air Vice-Marshal Ian Lawson, had done eighty-nine heavy bomber sorties, on Wellingtons and Lancasters, and twice been awarded the DFC; he and Neil Cameron had first met at Old Sarum in May 1948 when they were on Exercise Pandora[1] and were to encounter each other again in the MoD when he became Assistant Chief Adviser (Personnel and Logistics) in the central Defence Staff. The Assistant Commandant (Technical), Air Commodore John Rowlands, GC, was an armament specialist who had displayed outstanding courage on bomb disposal duties, being awarded the George Cross: in post-war years he had led the RAF team working on the development of the first atomic bomb, and then commanded the Bomber Command Armament School which was responsible for introducing nuclear weapons into RAF service.

These three officers, together with the Senior Director of Studies (Dr George Tolley), formed the senior management at Cranwell, and they met frequently to discuss the College's varied activities. These meetings were characterised by 'very lively and energetic discussion', and disclosed 'a remarkable unanimity of views and an empathy between the members'.[2]

The Commandant and Neil Cameron got on well together personally; they shared similar views and were not afraid to voice those they held strongly. Recalling those days, Ian Lawson has commented that he could not have had a more loyal or hard-working Assistant: 'He was 100% behind me in the things I did; he was in his office first thing in the morning and was last to leave in the evening; and he had a first-class gift for the analysis of any problem.' Likewise Cameron and Rowlands, who had frequent meetings and informal talks to sort out both large and small problems, found that they had a similar approach and were able to cooperate in close agreement.

Sir John Rowlands recalled:

> It was always a pleasure to work with Neil. He was energetic and possessed a lively, logical and analytical mind. He was fluent both orally and on paper and always expressed his opinions directly and forcefully. He was innovative and got things done without fuss. Above all he was a leader and greatly respected by the cadets. Despite the problems and cross-currents, nothing was allowed to detract from the discipline, bearing, ceremonial, esprit de corps and efficiency of Cranwell. This applied particularly to Cadets, and Neil Cameron was largely responsible for it.

As holder of the new post of Assistant Commandant (Cadets) he had a large staff, headed by two Wing Commanders and a Wing Commander (Cadets), four Squadron Leaders commanding squadrons, each with two Flight Lieutenants (ex-Cranwell cadets), a Squadron Leader PT, a Squadron Leader (RAF Regiment) who with a Warrant Officer (Cadets) was responsible for drill and discipline, and a Station Warrant Officer. They looked after nearly 400 cadets; in November 1965 there were 367, this number increasing to 397 in February 1966. The larger total resulted from an increase of technical cadets with the Henlow merger: the November figure included twenty-four of them at Cranwell, but by February 1966 this had increased to a hundred.

The 'problems and cross-currents' referred to by Sir John Rowlands were only in part those arising from the merger and the increase in numbers. Ian Lawson and his colleagues were also running Cranwell at probably the most difficult time in the history of the College – a time of major changes in higher education generally, and of changes in the RAF organisation brought about by the pressure of the new Labour Government (in office since October 1964) on defence budgeting. There were also some powerful outside influences which, ignoring the social and educational changes which had occurred, were intent on 'putting the clock back' – perhaps in a return to the cloistered and exclusive Cranwell of pre-war days, which had produced General Duties officers who would come to occupy most of the senior posts in the RAF.

Thus there were internal and external pressures on the Commandant and his colleagues – internal as a result of the increase in size and the different courses being pursued, external as a result of different views on the academic syllabi and the authority under which Cranwell operated, whether the Air Force Board or the AOC-in-C Flying Training Command. Lawson and Cameron were not afraid to speak their minds on these matters: not having been educated as Cranwellians, they saw the importance of the College as being to produce the type of officer who would succeed where it mattered most – under operational conditions.

In keeping up the 'discipline, bearing, ceremonial, esprit de corps and efficiency' of the cadets during this time of change and reorganisation, Neil Cameron showed himself to be not only hard-working but extremely conscientious as to the wellbeing of the young men under his command. He fulfilled all his duties at the College – whether in the office, at meetings, on parades, at formal dinners, on occasional tours or when attending sports events – with enthusiasm and punctiliousness. He was invariably on the touch-line on Saturday afternoons and at church at eight o'clock on Sunday mornings. Air Vice-Marshal Lawson has recalled that he was especially good at remembering the names of the cadets, especially those on the senior course, and took personal responsibility for their behaviour away from the College on extra-mural activities – -which, by their encouragement of initiative and responsibility, were an important part of Cranwell training.

Two features of College life had always been visits and ceremonial functions. In August 1965 a party of ten officers and ninety flight cadets went off to see NATO headquarters and units, the Assistant Commandant (Cadets) leading the Paris part of the visit – a pleasant duty for him because it recalled his days as PSO to D/SACEUR there and he had come to love France. In November of that year the Flying Training and Basic Studies Wings were amalgamated with the Department of Cadets, bringing all Wings responsible for the training of flight cadets under the control of the Assistant Commandant (cadets); accordingly, a celebration to mark this event was held in the College Hall on the evening of 13 November and attended by 350 officers, their wives and senior flight cadets, making one of Cranwell's memorable occasions.

To the visitor, Cranwell must have seemed as impressive and as smoothly run as it had been since the 1920s; that it did was a tribute to the authority of the Commandant and his Assistant Commandants, all men of strong character and wide Service experience. But in fact the years 1965–66 were difficult ones for the College because of financial pressures (despite which its buildings were 'spruced up' for a Royal visit by Princess Alexandra in June 1965), dissension between the Education and Technical Branches about the curriculum, and the influence of outside academic bodies and RAF Working Parties. Thus the Holder syllabus, introduced in October 1964, had reduced the Cranwell course from three to two-and-a-half years; then the Howard-English Report, the result of a 1966 inspection to advise the Minister of Defence on the feasibility of rationalising and uniting the Service academies, had recommended that non-technical officers should spend a year at Cranwell followed by a second at the proposed Royal Defence College and then return to Cranwell. However, the results of these proposals came to fruition (or otherwise) only after Neil Cameron had left the College: during his period there the main problem was to maintain the tempo and productiveness of life at Cranwell despite a constant stream of visitors, all of whom were given an impressive welcome, while at the same time adjusting to changes which were being introduced.

The merger with Henlow was completed early in 1966 and on 2 February about fifty representatives of the national and local press came to Cranwell to hear all about it, both the Assistant Commandants briefing them. On the following day a Merger Celebration Dinner was held in College Hall, attended by the Minister (RAF), Lord Shackleton, and by Commanders-in-Chief from the Commands. But the co-location of the two Colleges brought problems of various kinds. 'Cranwell had become a very complex affair', comments its historian.[3]

> The mixing of cadets and student officers which had been viewed with such foreboding by many was now almost complete. To run the Station as a unity was the firm resolve of the Commandant, Air Vice-Marshal I. D. N. Lawson . . . and of the Assistant Commandant, Air Commodore N. Cameron. But the factors of geographical dispersion on the camp and the totally diverse nature of the principal occupations of aircrew and engineers made the process of unification extremely intractable.

It is to the great credit of the Commandant and Assistant Commandants at that time that despite all the difficulties with which they had to deal, and which were not of their making, they managed to maintain the high standards for which Cranwell had become famous among Air Force academies throughout the world.

Amid the turmoil of academic and Service reorganisation and resettlement it must have been a welcome diversion for Neil Cameron when two of his former 'bosses' – Marshals of the RAF Sir Dermot Boyle and Sir Thomas Pike – arrived at the College in mid-June to attend the annual reunion of Cranwell 'old boys', the Old Cranwellians Association. On this occasion the latter's portrait was unveiled by the Earl of Bandon.

During August the Assistant Commandant (Cadets) performed two ceremonial duties, announcing the prize-winners of No 89 Entry and promotions in No 90 Entry in the Whittle Hall on 12 August, and reviewing No 94 Entry on the Junior Mess parade ground on 9 August. Then on 26 September his term at Cranwell came to an end when he was succeeded by Air Commodore R. G. Wakeford. From that date, his thoughts turned to Whitehall, and to the duties he was to take up from the beginning of October as RAF member of the Programme Evaluation Group.

Cranwell paid a warm tribute to Neil Cameron on his departure. 'College Notes' in the January 1967 issue of the *RAF College Journal* contained the following comment:

> Just before the beginning of the Winter term, Air Commodore Neil Cameron DSO, DFC ended a regrettably short tour as Assistant Commandant (Cadets). The first to hold the post under the recent reorganisation of the College, he saw probably the greatest changes in its history, and much of the success of the merger, with the complicated planning it entailed, must be credited to him. His forcefulness and zestful approach made an impact on all who had contact with him – and not least on cadets, who will, moreover, miss his wit and warmth in after-dinner speeches on guest nights in College Hall.

It had been a difficult tour for him, but one which, with determination, hard work, and genuineness and strength of character, he had completed successfully. Whitehall was to pose far different problems.

Notes

1. Directed by Lord Tedder, its purpose was to assess the effect of scientific developments on air warfare – an analysis of RAF operations during World War II attended by wartime leaders like Coningham, Embry, Slessor, Broadhurst and Bennett. Lawson was a wing commander and Cameron an acting squadron leader, and in their subsequent careers both had commanded Transport Command stations – Lyneham and Abingdon respectively.

2. Letter to the author from AM Sir John Rowlands, 15 May 1985.

3. Group Captain E. B. Haslam, *The History of Royal Air Force Cranwell* (HMSO, 1982).

11 THE HEALEY YEARS

I had been at Cranwell for just over fifteen months when, in September 1966, I received a summons to report to the Ministry of Defence. The Secretary of State, Denis Healey, was setting up a new body, to be called the Programme Evaluation Group, and I was to be the member for the RAF. I had never met Mr Healey, and can only assume that my appointment was due to some articles I had written for defence periodicals.[1]

PEG was an inner sanctum or 'cabinet' for the Secretary of State. For nearly two years he had been seeking to refashion Britain's defences to take account of the ending of conscription, the conduct of several colonial wars, the growing escalation of weapons costs and the need to forge the three services, for the first time in history, into a single integrated weapon. He had reached the conclusion that this herculean task could not be done properly unless a small inter-Service staff was established to give him independent advice on Services' proposals and to provide more reliable data on which to base his decisions.

The crunch had come with the battle between the Navy and the Air Force over the future of aircraft carriers. The RAF had won on that occasion but it was evident that the Navy had made a poor showing in terms of advocacy. The admirals had insisted on a 60,000 ton carrier, no less, which the Air Marshals had little difficulty proving to be a bad investment by offering land-based aircraft as the better means of providing air cover in operations outside Europe. Two smaller carriers would have been cheaper, even in combination, and more effective, since warships may spend a third of their life being refitted or renovated. With one small carrier reliably on station, the Navy could in fact have provided a service well beyond the range of F-111s flying from Indian Ocean islands.

As Secretary of State, Mr Healey found himself in the position of a High Court Judge. In an inter-Service dispute, he did not expect either counsel to bend over backwards to see his opponent's point of view. The confrontation of two well-argued cases is the basis of British justice; and it is a legitimate method of arriving at the truth within the processes of government. But the judge must have access to all the facts, and he must be mindful of the interests of a third party, the citizens. He needs the facts. He needs an organisation which will frame questions so as to extract the facts with professional skill, and thus leave minimum room for evasion. This was to be the role of the Programme Evaluation Group – one of crucial importance, providing its members with great influence, but not without hazards to their own professional careers. For institutions have a way of protecting themselves and hitting back. During the next four years, first in PEG and then as Assistant Chief of Defence Staff (Policy) I could not help recalling Harry Truman's dictum: 'If you can't stand the heat, get out of the kitchen.' But the battles had to be fought, and I could not have wished for an abler man under whom to fight them than Denis Healey.

Even before he came to office, in October 1964, he had been acknowledged as one of the Western world's leading experts on defence. Born in 1917, he was christened Denis Winston Healey at the behest of his father – 'a bloody-minded Irishman' – who felt that Churchill had been badly treated over Gallipoli. It might be said of him, as of G. K. Chesterton, that 'after a brief period he began to argue'. From Bradford Grammar School a scholarship took him to Balliol College, Oxford. In that intellectual hothouse his questioning spirit flourished, and he explored every current fashion including Marxism. But the right to question is so basic to his temperament, and indeed the key to his whole career, that he soon rejected communism as alien and repugnant. He had a 'good war', rising to the rank of Major in the Royal Engineers. He was seconded to combined operations, taking part in the Anzio landing in 1944: and this experience of inter-Service cooperation was a valuable background for the future Minister of Defence. Amphibious landings had long been a weakness in British military history, owing to the excessive individualism of the three Services. That this is no longer the case today, as most recently proved by the Falklands operation – a model of inter-Service cooperation in spite of some healthy inter-Service abuse – is due perhaps mainly to three men: Macmillan, Mountbatten and Healey.

He had failed to win a safe Conservative seat in the Labour landslide of 1945 and spent the next six years furthering his political education as the official in charge of the International Department at Labour Party Headquarters. He entered Parliament in February 1952 as MP for South-East Leeds. Critics might say that when he assumed one of the largest offices of state, he had never previously run anything in his life. But the same could be said of many politicians, including President Kennedy and even Winston Churchill. What he did have was a very clear mind, a lot of charm, and an unwillingness to take no for an answer.

Healey's relations with the Chiefs of Staff were always interesting. With his considerable intellectual interests in defence and foreign policy he was clearly well ahead of them on many of the issues; and he stayed with them, as Minister of Defence, for six years. Even in the details of their own Services he was extremely expert, having to answer in the House of Commons at Question Time on quite detailed subjects. This necessitated mastering a brief and before too long beginning to get an understanding of the more detailed problems of each Service. The only Chief whom he did not overshadow, in my estimation, was Air Chief Marshal Sir Charles (Sam) Elworthy, later to become Chief of Defence Staff and a very successful one too. He and Healey had an intellectual respect for each other.

The problems which Healey faced had really come to a head with Suez. On the one hand Britain was still an immensely powerful nation, the third nuclear country in the world, with a conscript Army still policing the biggest area of any colonial power in history – the map of Africa was about as red as it had been under Queen Victoria – and engaged in more military operations than any other country including the superpowers. On the other hand its role in the world was far from clear. Suez had shown that colonialist attempts to put the clock back were liable to antagonise both superpowers at the same time. Macmillan, assuming office two months later, concluded that the Empire was no longer militarily tenable. This permitted a gradual running-down of Britain's Forces (which had been consuming over 10% of the national wealth five years earlier) and the abolition of conscription. But that was very far from the end of the matter. As with France, Britain found that her numerous colonies required military assistance not only during the transition to independence, but also afterwards. The political questions were: Would we, and could we, supply this help? Much more than sentiment was at stake; for the prospect of a political and power vacuum over large parts of the Third World was not one which appealed to the United States or our European Allies, dependent as they were on these areas of the globe for much of their liveli-hood. If, however, we were to fulfil this role of assisting and intervening on request, Suez had shown that fundamental structural changes in Britain's defence organisation were needed.

It was Macmillan who put these changes in hand, and Mountbatten who began to implement them. Both men had had intensive experience of integrated operations during World War II. In place of a system by which each of the three Services had its own minister who seldom took guidance let alone instruction from the Minister of Defence, a single Ministry was formed, under one political overlord responsible for all aspects of defence, with a single officer, the Chief of Defence Staff,[2] responsible to him alone for the programmes of the three Services. The whole was 'co-located' in the building it now occupies off Whitehall. A parallel operation took place in the field, with the more or less successful creation of unified commands in Aden, Cyprus and Singapore. It was an operation which has stood the test of time. What is more, it was conducted against a background of one of the finest decades in the whole history of Britain's armed forces.

Thus, by the time Healey took over in October 1964, inter-Service rivalries had been abolished in theory; he had to abolish them in practice. What is more, he had to do it while cutting the defence budget from 7% to 6% of the

GNP, not an objective calculated to endear him to the armed Services, each of which was determined to see that the other two did not gain at its own expense. His first problem, sticking out like a sore thumb in the extrapolation of previous Conservative budgets, was the 60,000 ton carrier. But also, sticking out like sore fingers, were the inherited aircraft procurement projects. Of these the most conspicuous was the British tactical strike and re-connaissance aircraft (TSR.2). It was fast becoming obvious that the Americans, with their far larger aircraft market, were able to supply the RAF with the equipment they needed much more effectively than British industry. But politically it was not an easy decision to take. The Labour Government concluded quite early on that the Americans could produce a much more cost-effective weapon. But while the costs of developing TSR.2 piled up, they let 'I dare not wait upon I would' for several months, and finally left the announcement of its cancellation to James Callaghan during his budget speech in April 1965. The RAF were given to understand that it would be replaced by the F-111, a much cheaper proposition thanks to the far larger American market.

The same principle was applied to the supersonic V/STOL aircraft project P.1154. This would be replaced by United States Phantoms. A limited investment would be maintained in the subsonic version, the P.1127. A third American purchase was to be a consignment of Hercules transport aircraft instead of the HS681 short take-off and landing tactical transport.

These decisions did not please British industry, but they satisfied the RAF, which was to get the latest American aircraft in larger numbers than would have been possible had the Government insisted on buying British. In one sense, therefore, it reflected well on the state of the Government's decision-making machinery. In another sense, however, it showed up a serious weakness, for there was a clear bias against V/STOL aircraft. Excuses for this bias were not wanting: against the HS681, for example, it was said that in operations outside Europe there would be no shortage of airfields, and therefore there was no case in principle for such an aircraft. Against the P.1127 the RAF complained that it was not supersonic and had insufficient payload for their purposes. These attitudes showed a lack of vision unworthy of the inventor of this revolutionary concept. Here was yet another example of a brilliant British invention running aground on the sands of conventional wisdom and bureaucratic hostility. At that time nobody foresaw the one role in which V/STOL was to prove so effective twenty years later in the Falklands – that of maritime air support. The Navy was still thinking in terms of conventional aircraft carriers, and never even raised the subject of V/STOL until it was clear that such vessels would no longer exist in the 1970s.

My own belief is that the Falklands were only the dawn of the age of the Harrier-type aircraft. We have now entered a period in which airfields are going to be intensely vulnerable. The first warning of this came as early as 1967 when the Israeli Air Force was able to knock out, in a single series of raids, not only many Egyptian aircraft but, through cratering time-bombs, the airfields from which the remainder could have flown. After that NATO contemplated neutralising Warsaw Pact airfields, in the event of war, by strategic aircraft armed with nuclear as well as conventional weapons. Against this threat, the advocates of airfields felt comparatively safe; long-range manned aircraft were becoming increasingly disadvantaged against massed surface-to-air missiles, and the use of nuclear weapons for the purpose was becoming increasingly incredible as the Soviet Union acquired parity with the West at every nuclear level.

In the 1980s, however, there exists the opportunity to neutralise airfields, and keep them permanently out of action, by medium-range conventional ballistic and cruise missiles. This is the strategy advocated by NATO's Supreme Allied Commander Europe, General Bernard Rogers, and I am convinced that it is right. To deprive an enemy of air cover in this way could be the most devastating capability imaginable, but the Soviet Union may in due course be expected to acquire the same capability. In consequence there could well be areas of any future conflict in which the only aircraft will be those which can take off vertically. Thinking strictly in terms of deterrence, I can visualise a decisive element being squadrons of aircraft capable of taking off from a forest in Germany, perhaps proceeding westwards out of range of 200-mile SAMs, turning north, and delivering stand-off missiles at Warsaw Pact targets from the North Sea or the Norwegian Sea.

Such a capability could be acquired by the West on the basis of the Harrier I and the much faster Harrier II. They would not need to be supersonic, but they would require a greater payload. Thanks to British inventiveness, the West is well ahead of the Soviet Union in this technique, even after so many years of bureaucratic delay. There is an important principle here. In my view a key to the future defence of the West, and deterrence against attack from the Warsaw Pact, lies in the far superior inventiveness of Western technologists, many of them in Britain. What is lacking in almost every defence department in the world is the receptivity to recognise that 'the man with a brown paper parcel waiting in the hall' may have something which, though it offends all traditional canons, is absolutely right. It assumes an apparatus at the centre which is strong enough and sufficiently well informed to pester, cajole and browbeat the vested interests which are always ready to resist change. Such an instrument was exactly what Denis Healey had in mind when he set up the Programme Evaluation Group in mid-1966.

In the meantime the carriers had escaped the 1965 cuts; but as the retreat from Empire went on, and pressures from the Treasury mounted, the Government developed serious doubts about its role east of Suez. On taking office Prime Minister Harold Wilson had actually advocated increasing our military presence in the Indian Ocean.[3] He talked of our role as a vital intermediary to prevent polarisation between the superpowers in the area, and reduce the dangers of 'eyeball-to-eyeball' confrontations between them. He proclaimed that Britain's frontiers were on the Himalayas. He said there was no question of an early departure from Aden. Now he began to change his tune. East of Suez was seen to be no longer sustainable in face of economic pressures. The defence review of February 1966 announced the Government's intentions to cut defence spending from 7% to 6% of the national wealth. The problem of 'overstretch' was beginning to creak audibly. Ten years earlier the average destroyer and frigate had spent only eighty-one days per year at sea; now each was spending 142 days. This mismatch between capability and commitment, and in particular the decision to cancel CVA-O1 caused a junior minister, Christopher Mayhew, and the First Sea Lord to resign. The February 1966 White Paper laid down new guidelines making it clear that we would never again undertake a major operation without allies, or without facilities provided by the host country; the CVA-O1 was sunk without trace.

This last decision was, of course, widely regarded as a victory for the RAF. But more discerning spirits concluded that the RAF might have given a hostage to fortune. If there was to be another cut, it would fall on them, as the other major equipment-using service.

This was the situation when I arrived at the Ministry of Defence: inter-Service turmoil at home against a background of fundamental strategic appraisal abroad and an alarming economic undertow which was dragging the country towards the devaluation that would take place a year later.

My colleagues were a fine group, and I subsequently valued the friendship of many of them. The armed forces were represented by Brigadier Tony Younger (Army), Commodore Colin Dunlop (Navy) and myself. The scientific representative was Professor Clifford Cornford, a distinguished member of the Defence Scientific Service who had worked closely with Solly Zuckerman when he was the MOD's Chief Scientific Adviser. The economist was David Greenwood, later Professor at Aberdeen University, who had been on my staff at Cranwell when I advised him to go academe. Frank Armstrong, a shrewd and sceptical civil servant, completed the team. We were to be Denis Healey's equivalent of Robert McNamara's 'whizz kids' in the Pentagon – Charlie Hitch, Alain Enthoven, Harry Rowen and Co. Immediately labelled as such by the Service chiefs, we had to be careful. The whizz kids had done excellent work in exposing the strategic and procurement weaknesses and flabbiness in the Pentagon's thinking, but it had not made them popular. They had introduced new methods of accounting – notably planning-programme-budgeting – without which it was difficult if not impossible to place a price tag on an overseas command. They had introduced functional management, which produced economies by cutting across Service interests. Above all they had introduced systems analysis, which asked fundamental questions about how a particular job – like invading an island or rescuing hostages – could be done most cost-effectively.

Whatever the weaknesses of the first two of these concepts, I am convinced that systems analysis must lie at the heart of any rational strategic thinking. We have seen it applied in the Nott reforms of the Royal Navy. By focusing his mind clearly on a question – 'How do you destroy enemy submarines?' – and persistently challenging the conventional wisdom, he formed the judgement that this was simply not a task which, in the age of the £150 million frigate, could any longer be left only to the surface warship. There had to be a role for other weapons systems – not only submarines but also long-range patrol aircraft and shore-based cruise missiles. I believed this to be the right way to go; it will be fundamental to NATO strategy in the coming decades. I would go further and submit that, even with these reforms, the whole concept of convoys is becoming increasingly incredible; and that the bulk of reserve supplies on the European mainland must come either from stocks prepositioned in Europe, or from independent sailings by fast and well-protected merchant ships. But an important key to determining the best solution must be the application of systems analysis.

At the time I first met Denis Healey in September 1966, systems analysis was in its infancy, and regarded with suspicion. In seeking to apply it, and to ascertain what was best for the nation's interest as opposed to those of the individual Services, we were not of course alone in the Ministry. This had been one of the primary objectives in the creation of the Defence Staff at the centre of the integrated Ministry of Defence. We worked particularly closely with two Assistant Under-Secretaries operating in the policy field. One was Frank Cooper, Assistant Under Secretary (Policy), a wartime airman who already showed the formidable administrative ability which projected him to the top of the Ministry of Defence at the time of the Falklands War. The other was Patrick Nairne, Denis Healey's Private Secretary, a highly intelligent Scotsman once described by Lord Carrington as 'the best Civil Servant of them all'; he was later a member of the Committee of Privy Councillors which produced the Franks Report on the Falklands, after a glowing career which took him to the head of the Department of Health and Social Security; he subsequently became Master of St Catherine's College, Oxford.

With these and others at the Centre we worked closely, and could always rely on their support. But the very term Centre gives a misleading impression of overlordship. As we have noted, it was Healey's job to turn the theory of integration into practice; and it was an uphill task. Their permanent Head of the Ministry, Sir James Dunnett, was heard to say: 'If you want anything done in this building, you pretty well have to do it yourself.' When asked as late as the 1970s whether the Centre was yet strong enough, Fred Mulley, then Secretary of State, ruefully replied: 'What Centre?' Things had improved a great deal by the time I became Chief of the Defence Staff. But even then, the degree of Service independence would have surprised most taxpayers. Nominally, policy was laid down in black and white by the Defence Council Ministers and top officials of the Centre overwhelmingly predominated. The extraordinary fact, however, was that the Defence Council practically never met, except for the annual photograph. A very senior colleague of mine (Admiral of the Fleet the Lord Hill-Norton) described the Ministry of Defence at that time as like a multinational company without a Board of Directors. That was after ten years of progress from the PEG days; it may be imagined what we were up against in 1966.

Healey's mandate for PEG was to help him to frame the right questions to ask the Ministry, and to see that he got the answers in good time. Nor did he want a single, homogeneous answer to any one question; he wanted at least two options laid out before him, with the reasons for and against them in terms of cost-benefit to national security. He was particularly anxious to question the value of the Services' virility symbols – the tank, the carrier, and most immediately the long-range strike aircraft. For his purpose he souped up the somewhat parochial Defence Operational Analysis Establishment at West Byfleet. This had previously been an Army Unit, war-gaming the problems of military tactics. Healey promoted it into a machine which could ask fundamental strategic questions about the air/land battle.

Another question which deeply concerned Healey was that of the education of the armed services. The structure of Britain's war machine, by long tradition, ordained that the 'leaders of men' produced by the armed forces would in due course become responsible for the creation of defence policy. In fact 'in due course' is putting it generously; often enough policy initiatives originated from well down the ladder. It is not unreasonable, though unorthodox, to ask whether a leader of men is by definition the best person to grapple with complex intellectual issues. Quite often he is; men like Marshal of the Royal Air Force 'Sam' Elworthy (a barrister) or General Sir John Hackett (a classical scholar) are just what is needed. Nevertheless it might be suggested that the system in principle is not automatically sound. But on the equal hypothesis that any other system would be just as fallible, the urgent task is to educate the men of action into the increasing complexities of defence decision-making – which of course includes broadening their horizons to encompass the points of view of the other two Services. This last problem was approached from the other end by Lord Mountbatten in the early 1960s, when a celebrated Report by Generals Jacob and Ismay envisaged the creation of a single list for all servicemen over one-star level. Many people still think this is the right way to go. But for lack of it, service education must be fundamental to the promotion of defence policies which reflect the needs of the nation as a whole.

Healey took an intense personal interest in service education, and would lecture to staff and defence colleges at every opportunity. The Joint Services Staff College at Latimer for middle-level officers enjoyed his lectures for twelve years in succession. I too was a frequent visitor; and Healey and myself, together with General Al Haig, were probably the only honorary members of Latimer who were never on a course there.

More grandiose proposals for Service education were put forward, such as the Howard-English Report; but the cost of its proposals under which the individual service cadet colleges would have been merged into a Service University, proved prohibitive, and the precise curricula were never very clearly spelt out.[4] My own view is much more in sympathy with that of the Duke of Edinburgh, who has argued that there is an overwhelming case for a degree in Military Studies at the start of a serviceman's career. As he has put it, the armed services are at present almost the only major profession without such a degree course. It is true that all three Services now offer degree courses to their cadet officers, but the subject areas are wide and the universities have been slow to perceive that there really is a deep intellectual content in Military Studies.

The Howard-English Report caused a good deal of hostility among the armed forces, who spoke darkly about 'Healey and his academics' – but not nearly so much as the Geraghty Report, which proposed a further restructuring of the Ministry of Defence. This would have enhanced the power of civilian officials against their service counterparts; and it was compellingly argued. However, close analysis revealed that this would have been its only gain; it offered no saving in money or jobs to compensate for the sacrifices asked of the armed forces. The Service chiefs were able to exposed this rather fundamental weakness, and the Report was consigned to the wastepaper basket.

But the biggest battle of all, brought on by the worsening economic situation, was the future of the F-111. In seeking to grapple with this, as with other problems, we faced the opposition of all the Chiefs, who objected to PEG in principle; they saw it gaining too much power with the Minister and giving advice without responsibility. They successfully sought to deprive us of the information which was essential to a proper briefing of the Secretary of State. Having done so, they were able to ridicule some of our findings, and did not hesitate to quote them contemptuously out of context. The difficulty was that constitutionally our responsibility lay to the Chiefs; they had insisted on that when PEG was appointed. But in practice the whole object of the exercise would have been nullified if we had not informally main-

tained close contact with Mr Healey. It was a highly unsatisfactory – indeed contradictory – situation; and clearly the
very existence of PEG was at stake. On the other hand I had
a good personal relationship not only with Sam Elworthy
but also with many members of the Air Staff; on the whole I
persuaded them that it would be to the benefit of the
Service if I was fully briefed.

For us serving officers, there was a further dilemma. This
was a theoretical conflict of loyalties between the Service
which we had joined and the government of the country.
None of us had any doubt that even to question the wisdom
of the policies of one's own Service was to jeopardise one's
career. To go further and reach conclusions in conflict with
those policies might well be asking for real trouble. We
were in fact antagonising the men who were writing our
confidential reports, and risking the charge of being called
insubordinate or even subversive. Nor could we blame
them if they regarded themselves as more patriotic than a
Labour government which was cutting Britain's defences
and depriving the Forces of equipment they believed to be
essential.

So in theory there was a dilemma. In practice I can
honestly say that I never gave it a thought. My loyalty was
to my country, come what may. I believe this would have
been the view of any Serviceman placed in my position.[5] In
taking this unambiguous stand, however, I did indeed
jeopardise my career, for when Healey left office in the
summer of 1970 I was shunted abruptly out of the Ministry
of Defence into a form of oblivion. At that moment the odds
were heavily against my rising above the rank of Air
Vice-Marshal.

But I must return to PEG, where the impending with-
drawals from east of Suez were focusing our attention
increasingly on Europe. The intention was to reduce force
levels to some extent but to redeploy most of the returning
legions on the European continent, in Britain, and on the
seas within the NATO area. This reorientation was one of
the factors prompting a major reappraisal of NATO's
strategy. A great deal of thinking had already been done in
Washington about the need to replace the doctrine of
'massive nuclear retaliation' as the principal means of

checking any Warsaw Pact invasion. The problem was that, since Sputnik had first girdled the earth in 1957, it was clear that the Russians were on their way to possessing the means to cancel out America's capability of massive retaliation. This left the West in a perplexing position, since it had never, from the birth of NATO, been able to match the Warsaw Pact at a conventional level. De Gaulle, observing this dilemma, simply pulled the French out of the NATO military command. For America's other allies the question remained: what form of nuclear reply were the Americans prepared to make in the event of a Soviet invasion? This led to the doctrine of 'Flexible Response' evolved under Robert McNamara, the US Defence Secretary, though I maintain that Denis Healey had been propounding the theory for some years previously. This meant that low-yield tactical nuclear weapons would be deployed in Western Europe and inserted into the West's defence spectrum between the conventional and strategic levels. Later, when the Warsaw Pact caught up with the West at every level of nuclear capability, this doctrine too had to be considered out of date; on this account the West seemed to me to have no alternative but to build up its conventional defences.

In the mid-1960s, however, the doctrine of flexible response held sway: it was important not to allow the Warsaw Pact to think that the West would never use nuclear weapons, and the doctrine gave a plausible rationale for believing that they might be used at a tactical level. However, the Europeans naturally wanted to know something about the Americans' intentions in terms of target planning, and in December 1966 the NATO Council of Ministers agreed to set up a Nuclear Planning Group. In this, Healey was far and away the most dominant European figure. As one of the founders of the Institute for Strategic Studies, he had followed the strategic arguments of such men as Schelling, Wohlstetter and Herman Kahn through every twist and turn of their complicated theology. He understood the complex doctrine of Mutually Assured Destruction, with its dependence on mobility and survivability as much as on numbers. The NPG was in fact set up on his initiative. McNamara agreed to it as a way of taking the Europeans into his confidence without deferring overmuch to their

opinions. In point of fact these opinions were never particularly sophisticated. In most European countries, defence is
not considered an important political job, and Ministers
seldom hold the portfolio long enough to make an impact.
Helmut Schmidt had not yet arrived on the scene as
German Minister of Defence. In consequence, meetings
of the NPG (which I attended) tended to develop into
fascinating dialogues between Healey and McNamara.

There is no doubt that Britain did succeed in exerting
some influence on American policy, edging it away from
the 'tripwire' strategy of massive retaliation. This helped to
clarify American defence thinking, which was not always
logical and was frequently disunited. For example, Flexible
Response was emerging as a doctrine by which NATO
reserved the right to undertake the first use of nuclear
weapons if the conventional battle was going against it. But
this was clearly only at battlefield level. It certainly did not
give *carte blanche* to Strategic Air Command to launch a first
strike against Soviet strategic targets. Yet McNamara subsequently revealed a document from the US Air Staff strongly
advocating just that. He also revealed that, even at that
time, he himself would never have recommended the first
use of any nuclear weapons in any circumstances. This was
certainly not the message he left with his NATO colleagues
in the mid-1960s when selling flexible response.

The heart of the dilemma was the danger of uncontrolled
nuclear escalation. With this in mind, the NPG evolved the
notion of the demonstrative use of one or more nuclear
weapons, as for instance over the Baltic Sea, or possibly
over a purely military target. These discussions always
ended inconclusively. The fact is that, even at this time of
American nuclear superiority, the West's nuclear doctrine
was never clear. It rested on the perfectly sensible but
somewhat imprecise proposition that in one way or another
the Soviet Union would suffer quite unacceptable damage if
it chose to trifle with the NATO Alliance.

This proposition has subsequently survived but I think
could become hazardous in the future. The danger of war is
the danger of a Soviet miscalculation; and this can only
have grown in recent years with the increasing strength of
the Warsaw Pact at both the nuclear and conventional

levels. However, there is a way to head off this danger of miscalculation: it is offered by the new electronic technology which can vastly enhance the surveillance and destructive capability of NATO's conventional forces. We should make greater use of it while believing strongly in the ultimate value of the nuclear deterrent. I considered it something which needed constantly to be kept up to date.

Meanwhile, at home the Air/Sea 'battle' continued unabated. As the need for further economies intensified, PEG was asked to consider whether there was really any operational requirement for a long-range strike aircraft. For practical purposes this meant the F-111. The Chiefs of Staff had reported back in glowing terms on the performance of this aircraft after a visit to Washington. We concluded however, having in mind the considerable equipment programme already in hand for the RAF, that there was no requirement for it. Another major fact behind this conclusion was the impending reduction of our commitments outside Europe; these envisaged complete withdrawal from Singapore and Malaysia in the mid-1970s, departure from South Arabia and Aden in January 1968, the phasing-out of all aircraft carriers by the mid-1970s, and the regrouping of many of the troops withdrawn into a new Army Strategic Command. Such was the climax of what had in effect been a three-year review, whose results were announced in July 1967. The announcement made no mention of the F-111. But it was fairly clear that its days were numbered – its acquisition was in fact cancelled the following January – and PEG's recommendations were well known.

It was thus no wonder that opposition to PEG boiled over to the point at which Healey could no longer defend it. It was always a vulnerable body, with a much weaker structural foundation than its equivalent in Washington. Arguably, Healey might have given it more support. But by this time, his own job was at stake, and many were demanding his resignation, so instead he settled for a compromise with the Chiefs of Staff which conceded their right to a greater say in policy management in future, and incidentally preserved my own central part in it. This was the creation of the Defence Policy Staff; and one of Healey's conditions for its creation was that I should be head of it, with the appointment of Assistant Chief of the Defence Staff (Policy).

The new arrangement was an important innovation. A Joint Planning Staff already existed in the Ministry of Defence, but at a less exalted level than now envisaged. Its Chairman did not have access to the Secretary of State. Nor was it concerned with questions of strategic forward planning. Its main task had been to respond to questions from the Chiefs of Staff about particular problems, such as Belize or Simonstown. The purpose of the new Policy Staff was to provide a much wider and longer-term strategic view. In return, Healey surrendered *de facto* control to the Chiefs of Staff and relinquished his claim to a personal 'cabinet'. The new body was to answer neither to the Secretary of State nor to its members' own services, but the Chiefs.

It was my job to set up the Policy Staff. I decided to break up our enormous remit by forming five teams to handle different aspects of it. Team A, responsible for Global Strategy, was run by Commodore Dunlop, formerly of PEG. Team B was concerned with the Future of NATO, and was headed by Brigadier David Fraser, later to be Britain's military representative at NATO, and one of the sharpest brains in the Army. Team C, led by my old friend Freddie Sowrey, dealt with the world outside the NATO area. Team D dealt with a wide variety of policy questions, including arms control, and had a mandate to raise troublesome issues and play the devil's advocate; this was in due course headed by Michael Quinlan. Team E covered scientific matters, and was headed by Dr Eddy Benn, whom I had first met at SHAPE as the Deputy Scientific Adviser under Dr Harold Agnew, a distinguished American scientist.

Contemplating this comprehensive carve-up, the layman might at this point wonder what was left in security policy-making for the Foreign Office: a fair question. Mr Healey had actually stated, in a White Paper, that defence was the servant of foreign policy; so one might have expected constant surveillance of our work from across the road in Downing Street. The Defence and Overseas Policy Committee of the Cabinet, which included the Foreign

Secretary, certainly retained the power of ultimate decision in the deployment of the armed forces. But the Foreign Office have seldom concerned themselves closely with defence policy-making. The Defence White Paper, opening with a statement of British security interests overseas, is not normally seen in the Foreign Office until it has reached the galley stage. There is indeed a Defence Department in the Foreign Office; but its members rotate too rapidly to acquire anything like the expertise of their opposite numbers in the MoD, and they tend to concentrate on such peripheral defence questions as the political impact of arms sales.

Relations between the two departments are normally healthy. The weakness in the arrangement is that the Foreign Office tends to demand action at such short notice that it is either impossible or very difficult to provide. As one permanent head of the Ministry of Defence observed, 'Ambassadors seem to expect a frigate over every horizon.' He meant that if that was what they wanted, they should say so, preferably ten years in advance, which is the approximate lead time of a frigate from blueprint to commissioning. Many of our defence problems spring from the fact that, while the Ministry of Defence has permanently to think ten years ahead, the Foreign Office does not even possess the planning machinery for doing so. Thus, so far from duplicating anybody else's work, the new Defence Policy Staff was really filling a vacuum right in the heart of Whitehall.

From the first, it was clear that retrenchment was to be the order of the day. The Government had devalued in November 1967, two months before my appointment as ACDS(Pol); and the consequences for defence were apparent in the cuts announced in January. All forces were now to be withdrawn from the Far East, except Hong Kong, by 1971 – not the mid-1970s as earlier envisaged. The armed forces as a whole were to suffer a further cut of 75,000 men. Our aircraft carrier force would be phased out as soon as the withdrawal from Malaysia, Singapore and the Gulf was completed. The F-111s were cancelled, a decision which I blame on the Treasury and a weak Cabinet.

This was the one issue on which Healey nearly resigned. He had agreed with the Services that Britain needed the

F-111 and felt that he had given his word to them when they had accepted the cancellation of the TSR.2. He felt, and was made to feel, that his good faith was at stake. This was the period when his enemies were thumbing through the files of his pre-war membership of the Communist Party. Yet, as I shall show, the extraordinary fact about his six-year stewardship, at this most controversial period in the history of Britain's defences, is that on assuming office, the Conservative Party accepted over 95% of the decisions he had taken.

Meanwhile we got the Policy dynamo humming. I had a seat 'in attendance' at the Chiefs of Staff Committee, and reported to them every Tuesday and Thursday. The Staff, which included the pick of all three services, produced some first-class papers. In a major review we studied the consequences of leaving the Indian Ocean and redeploying in Europe, which entailed asking what this would mean in terms of equipment. We were being urged by the Government to form closer links with Europe. And we took a stage further the implications of the new strategy of Flexible Response in Europe.

I started a series of staff talks with my opposite numbers in other NATO countries, notably France, Germany, Italy and the United States. In the latter, this gave me a very close link with the Joint Chiefs of Staff Committee. In France I worked with General Jacques Mitterand, whose brother became President. With him, there was much talk of an Anglo/French nuclear deterrent, which I never thought possible, because of the close US/UK agreements, but which reflected European concern about the reliability of the American nuclear umbrella.

Healey instituted 'Euro-dinners', in order to get European Ministers talking together informally about equipment. These took place on the eve of the NATO Defence Policy Committee meetings in Brussels; Healey wanted a forum for more purposeful discussion beforehand. Inevitably there were objections from excluded members, but the practice became successfully formalised into the Euro-Group, of which France was a member; this was valuable because of her withdrawal in 1966 from the NATO military command system.

The Nuclear Planning Group developed remarkably well. Composed of the United States, five permanent European members and two rotating members, its meetings always started with a briefing by the American Secretary of Defence on strategic nuclear developments. These helped to alleviate European fears that the deterrent would not be available when it was needed. Some European members travelled to targeting briefings at Strategic Air Command in Omaha. Papers were produced on 'Flexible Response' and 'Demonstrative Use'.

This was a job of enormous opportunity and challenge. I frequently worked till midnight, particularly when it was necessary to get an agreed paper to the Chiefs of Staff the following day. One subject we became involved in was the Multi-role Combat Aircraft (MRCA), to which the Air Staff had been devoting a great deal of time: Brigadier Fraser and I were asked to estimate the number of aircraft which would be required in aggregate by the three producing nations – Germany, Italy and Britain. Working on the back of an envelope, we arrived at the figure of 385 for the UK requirement; and though the name changed – it is of course now called the Tornado – the figure remained exactly as we worked it out that evening in 1968. Not perhaps the best way to do business, but effective as it turned out. The first squadrons were not operational until 1983, which gives some idea of the lead time for joint national projects.

Among all our other tasks, we took very seriously the education of the British public. Healey's White Papers were always far more generous with information than anything seen before. The public was being given basic facts about defence for the first time; the question was whether it could digest them. In this context Press briefings were more frequently held than before. Defence lectureships were set up at universities, and promising servicemen were encouraged to study special subjects – such as the case for conscription, or the merits of United Nations peace-keeping.

The sober portals of the Royal United Services Institution were given a new look. Impressed by the example of the Institute for Strategic Studies on the international front, we wanted to open the windows of the RUSI to provide the basis of a wider debate on purely national defence issues. Without Healey's support this organisation, which now flourishes, would have gone to the wall. To promote this object I worked with Brigadier Kenneth Hunt and Admiral Louis Le Bailly on a scheme to finance a new regime of seminars and research, which would provide an independent source of advice to the Minister of Defence as well as an outlet for public education. Some questioned whether such an organisation, financed by a Government Department twenty-five yards away, could ever be independent; and I particularly remember scepticism being expressed by the then defence correspondent of *The Times*, Charles Douglas-Home. But twelve months later, after he himself had produced the new regime's first defence paper on UK Reserve Forces, which staggered the Ministry by its audacity, no one could be in any doubt about the Institution's independence. At one point Healey invited me to be its first director; but I felt that I was happier at the centre of events.

The Defence Policy Staff were also asked by the Chiefs to look at staff training at various levels. Together with Air Vice-Marshal Lawson[6] I wrote a report on Staff Training for Senior Officers; and I held out strongly and successfully for the reconstruction of Latimer as a National Defence College where the three British armed forces could talk to each other frankly and informally without inhibitions. There was much opposition to this. We also covered the rejuvenation of the Imperial Defence College (one of the last institutions in Britain to retain the term 'Imperial'). The course in Belgrave Square had become something of a sabbatical for high-flying officers and diplomats. It is said that they went 'hunting on Thursdays'; and though this may have been a slight exaggeration, nobody pretended that the IDC was anything but a rest cure. It was my idea to revolutionise the establishment by appointing as Commandant a civilian from outside Whitehall, in the person of Alastair Buchan. Healey strongly supported me. He had backed Buchan as first Director of the Institute for Strategic Studies, and Buchan had fully justified his choice by showing a rare combination of administrative ability, integrity, modesty and phenomenal contacts. Buchan simply set these high-powered students to work; and in doing so he saw himself on a form of kamikaze mission, 'I'm the last civilian they will have as Commandant here,' he growled. But the best of them loved it; they knuckled down to lectures and seminars five days a week, with overtime, and each was made to produce his own thesis. I remember Michael Gow, later General Sir Michael, taking his subject 'The Generation Gap' particularly seriously, and disguising himself as a hippy to take part in a rally in the Isle of Wight. Thus were minds broadened; and – under the new title 'Royal College of Defence Studies' – Buchan's experiment was to last.

Much else was to endure from Healey's reforms; and since Ministers of Defence seldom get either the credit or blame which is their due, if only because the harvest takes so long to come up, it is worth recapitulating the legacy of the Healey years. Perhaps the most far-reaching, albeit the most intangible, legacy lay in the realm of public education. Whatever may be thought of the current peace debate, I believe it to be salutary and essential to the health of an adult democracy; and it had its roots in his period. It is quite true, and extraordinary, that for nearly ten years after Healey's departure, the House of Commons never held a single debate on nuclear matters; but all the time public interest was growing through the RUSI, the ISS, confidential briefings, the development of peripheral defence groups – particularly in the universities, and above all the creation of Select Committees in the House of Commons towards the end of the 1970s. The public debate was explosive when it came; but it could have been even more so if Healey had not previously opened the safety valves, so that the basic principles of British defence policy, particularly towards NATO, were understood by a large body of opinion-makers. Thus, when the battle was joined, reason soon prevailed; and the British public – sensible as ever once it is informed – aligned itself overwhelmingly behind NATO.

Among other enduring legacies I would put the structural changes in the Ministry of Defence – nearly all of which were approved by the incoming Conservative administration; the strengthening of the Centre, a process still to be completed; administrative techniques such as functional budgeting and systems analysis; and highly successful items of equipment, particularly the Tornado and the Harrier. That is a remarkable record. Healey's own regret is that in his view he stayed a year too long. During that time battles with the Services did not abate; and he lost two more. One was over the RAF's plan to convert the island of Aldabra into a major Indian Ocean air base. The other was over the Navy's pressure for a through-deck aircraft carrier. In view of the success of HMS *Invincible* in the Falklands, the Navy's case might seem to have been vindicated; but subsequently Healey was convinced that *Invincible* was phenomenally lucky to survive.

Perhaps a more objective criterion for assessing the Healey years lies in the attitude of the incoming Conservative administration. Any expectation among servicemen that 'now we can get back to where we were before' was falsified from the word go. Practically the only structural change made by the new Minister, Lord Carrington, was the revival of the individual Service Ministers; and even this was reversed before he left office. Even the Tories' East of Suez policy turned out to be not all that far away from that of Labour. Labour had said that after 1971 it would maintain a general capability for reinforcing the area, seven major units in Hong Kong, frequent exercises, membership of SEATO, support for our remaining colonies, and maintenance of the Tri-service Jungle Warfare School at Kota Tinggi in Malaysia. The Tories accepted all this; and they positively rejected a military ground presence, apart from the Gurkhas in Hong Kong. They reasonably criticised the *pace* of the decisions on both the Gulf and the Far East in 1967/1968; this was precipitate and ill-mannered, and there is no doubt that it angered many of our allies in the area. But the Conservatives showed no inclination to reverse it. This was really not surprising; our departure was in large measure due to the logic of all-volunteer forces, which had been the creation of an earlier Conservative Government.

Lord Carrington, reviewing the whole scene in 1971, said that East of Suez was 'the main area of disagreement with Labour. But there is much more with which we are agreed.' He commended Healey's administrative ability.

On the size of the Ministry, its record in recent years has been a good one – indeed notably so when contrasted with the expansion of most Whitehall departments. Here I am very happy to pay tribute to the work of my predecessor. There is always the initial risk that the creation of a large department will lead to an increase in staff, and I think this could have been particularly real in defence if a central staff had been allowed to grow up which merely duplicated and added a fourth star to that of the three Service departments. This has been very largely avoided by controlling rigorously the numbers of additional military staffs needed for the Centre, and by integrating the various civilian experts in the old Service Departments to form, for example, unified Directorates of Accounts, Contracts, Statistics and so on . . . I am determined that this process will continue.

This testimony, and the acceptance of 95% of Healey's other reforms, is a remarkable tribute; and I was happy to have played a part in the formulation of some of the decisions in those exciting years. But to have been involved at the centre of such controversies, both in PEG and as ACDS (Pol), did my career no good. I was moved to a series of interesting but peripheral appointments at the same rank and given the clear feeling that 'somebody up there doesn't love me'. By 1972 I was seriously thinking of leaving the Service and trying my hand elsewhere. But times change, and when Air Chief Marshal Sir Andrew Humphrey took over as Chief of the Air Staff my fortunes changed dramatically for the better.

Notes

1. Since 1959 Neil Cameron had contributed articles on defence policy to the *RAF Quarterly* and the *Journal of the RUSI*. Mr Healey's recollection, however, is that they first met at interview after Cameron's name had been short-listed for appointment (conversation with Head of AHB, 6 January 86).

2. Mountbatten was Chief of the Defence Staff from 1959 to 1965; the appointment had first been filled by MRAF Sir William Dickson.

3. In 1964 and 1965 the Indonesian Confrontation campaign, a particularly successful operation, was at its height.

4. See Chapter nine.

5. Lord Elworthy who was Chief of the Air Staff from 1963 to 1967 and then Chief of the Defence Staff, recalls that, while he had a good relationship with Mr Healey and enjoyed working with him, he saw serious dangers in his providing himself with his own policy staff, not least because the officers concerned would face a conflict of loyalties. Elworthy is sure however that Cameron treated him with complete loyalty, though he accepts that many RAF officers of equivalent or slightly junior rank regarded him with suspicion (interview with Head of AHB and Mr Wynn, 10 July 1985). Marshal of the RAF Sir John Grandy, who succeeded Lord Elworthy as CAS, takes very much the same view: Cameron had been given a new and important job as Assistant Chief of Defence Staff (Policy) and did it well (interview, 5 September 1985).

6. Lawson had been Commandant of the RAF College, Cranwell, when Neil Cameron was Assistant Commandant (Cadets): see Chapter nine.

12 THE AFTERMATH – THE PENALTY OF TAKING A DEFENCE VIEW

The 'two interesting but peripheral appointments' to which Neil Cameron was moved 'at the same rank' after he had been head of the Defence Policy Staff and where he considered his 'policy experience was wasted'[1] were those of Senior Air Staff Officer at Air Support Command HQ (September 1970 to December 1972) and Deputy Commander, RAF Germany (December 1972 to November 1973). While he was at ASC it was merged into Strike Command (in September 1972) as No 46 Group, of which he became Chief of Staff in 1974. In these appointments he was still an air vice-marshal, as he had been when Assistant Chief of Defence Staff (Policy), thus staying at the same rank for nearly six years. As Lord Elworthy has commented, he had certainly been passed over several times, and it was this lack of promotion which led him to consider leaving the RAF for another sphere of activity. Air Marshal Sir Harry Burton, who was his AOC-in-C for most of his time at Air Support Command, remembered discussing this possibility informally with him on one occasion and strongly urging him not to resign; Burton felt that his departure would be a serious loss to the RAF and hoped that he would still be advanced in the Service, a view which he relayed to Sir Andrew Humphrey when the latter was at Strike Command.

Cameron's service at Air Support Command, which controlled all the RAF transport forces, was a logical extension of his experience ten years previously when he had commanded Abingdon with its two Beverley heavy-lift squadrons. At Upavon, the famous old RAF Station on Salisbury Plain where ASC had its headquarters, he was far removed from the political conflicts of Whitehall; nor was the Command in which he was serving likely to be involved in controversy except when its operations took it to diplomatically sensitive areas, and then only if something unforeseen occurred. In fact one of the first matters with which he had to deal was the return of Arab terrorists (including Miss Leila Khalid) to Cairo by ASC Comet at the end of September 1970 following the hijacking and destruction of a BOAC VC10 at Dawson's Field, Jordan. ASC had inherited the roles of the former Transport Command, whose title had been changed in 1968. Its AOC-in-C when the new SASO arrived was Air Marshal Sir Lewis Hodges, who was nearing the end of his tour; he was succeeded, only a month later, by Sir Harry Burton. Soon after arriving at Air Support Command, Neil Cameron was appointed a Companion of the Order of the Bath in the 1971 New Year Honours, a reflection of his sterling work during his time at the centre.

ASC's role however was wider than that of its wartime and post-war predecessor: not only was it responsible for all RAF airlift capability, but also for offensive close support. Its transport tasks were both strategic and tactical. The strategic task involved the provision of a reliable passenger and freight transport service to any part of the world, backing-up the deployment of squadrons overseas and supporting British forces wherever they might be required to operate in a conventional war or peacekeeping capacity. These strategic functions, which were of particular significance while Britain still had bases east of Suez, were fulfilled by the Command's VC10s, Britannias, Belfasts and Comets which operated worldwide and maintained a high reputation for safety and reliability.

ASC's tactical role – one with which Neil Cameron had particular sympathy because of his long experience in Army-RAF cooperation – involved the close support of troops in battlefield areas, with STOL (short take-off and landing) transports and with fighter aircraft. This task was fulfilled by No 38 Group with Argosy and Hercules transports and Wessex helicopters, supported by ASC's Phantom and V/STOL Harriers with their ground-attack capability.

All these operational activities, plus the training of parachutists and administration of The Queen's Flight, were ultimately controlled from ASC's three-storey glass-fronted HQ building looking out over Upavon's historic grass airfield – Neil Cameron's 'business address' from September 1970 to the end of 1972. Sir Harry Burton found him an ideal 'anchor man'; Burton himself had to be away very frequently, so Cameron spent most of his time in the headquarters, where the two of them had a happy working relationship, with Cameron's Whitehall expertise proving of particular value. As Sir Harry recalls:[2]

> Neil was fully occupied at Upavon in supervising the operations of the Command. There were frequent minor crises with transport aircraft operating throughout the world (at any one time an average of about 40 aircraft would be overseas), and more major activities such as the reinforcement of Belize when under threat of attack. He also took a leading part in furthering the development of ground attack techniques in bad weather and at night. We had several discussions and a seminar with RAF Germany and 38 Group on this subject. We also worked closely with UK Land Forces and the Fleet through my membership and sometime Chairmanship of the Commander-in-Chiefs' Committee (West) in which we were responsible for contingency planning outside Europe. Neil's background of working with the Army was invaluable in this context.

Sir Harry makes it quite clear that, whatever Neil Cameron and others may have thought about the status of his post at Upavon, he worked very hard, devoting many long hours to the job, was popular with the staff, and got on well with his colleagues both in the other Services and in Whitehall.

The integration of ASC with Strike Command in September 1972, 'to create a single multi-role operational command', meant that it was down-graded to group status as No 46 Group (an all-transport formation without any close-support element), Neil Cameron becoming Chief of Staff. This change also meant that he came for the first time, briefly, under the aegis of the man who was to have a major influence on his future career – Air Chief Marshal Sir Andrew Humphrey, AOC-in-C Strike Command – and also of its Deputy Commander, Air Marshal

N. M. Maynard, whom he was soon to meet again in his next appointment.

His time as Chief of Staff was short: in early December 1972 he went to RAF Germany as Deputy Commander. Sir John Barraclough, who was Air Secretary at the time, observes that this was intended to give him experience of front-line operational command, and it had the special merit of being in the Central Region of whose importance Cameron was so strongly persuaded. The post entailed responsibility for day-to-day running of the Command and the efficiency of its stations and supporting services, while the Commander-in-Chief was involved for most of his time with the wider and more political responsibilities of his NATO appointment as Commander of the 2nd Allied Tactical Air Force.

At the time of Neil Cameron's move to Germany the C-in-C was Air Marshal Sir Harold Martin – 'Mickey' Martin the famous bomber pilot who had taken part in the Dambusters' raid, whom he was to succeed as Air Member for Personnel less than two years later. Martin has recalled[3] that when the Camerons arrived the weather was bitterly cold and the lakes in the area were frozen hard enough to skate on. It was typical of his enthusiasm for new places that he should want to try the local food, drink, sport and so on. In this case, however, he was already something of an expert – skating had been a popular pastime during his boyhood in Scotland. Just down the road from the house at Wegberg there was a small lake surrounded on three sides by fir trees and on the fourth by a beer keller. Clearly the idea was to spend an hour or so on the ice and then to repair to the bar for a glass of German beer before lunch. For a few days this regime seemed to work out very well and it was clear that he had lost little of his expertise on the ice. One of the hazards of outdoor skating is the pieces of wood and other debris which get frozen into the surface of the lake. On the day before Christmas Eve, skating around at considerable speed, he caught one of his skates on a piece of wood and fell very heavily on one knee. The crack seemed to echo round the lake but he refused to cut short the outing and not only continued to try to skate but insisted on walking home. During the course of lunch his knee swelled up badly and he was finally persuaded to go over to the RAF Hospital at Wegberg, just the other side of a playing field. The result was Christmas spent in hospital having his knee cap removed – according to him it had been smashed into so many pieces that it was kept in a bottle for teaching purposes. The doctors predicted a stay of several weeks in hospital but his response was to take on a bet with them that he would be on his feet and out again in ten days. With characteristic determination he worked so hard at the exercises prescribed by the physiotherapist that he won the bet easily.

The C-in-C had no doubts about his background experience and his ability to do the job, knowing that he would hold together the Command's administration and morale, and feeling confident that his wartime fighter squadron achievements were an assurance of his character and leadership qualities. Thus a good liaison was established between the two men, both of whom had achieved marked distinction operationally; but it was unfortunately only to last for about three months: 'Mickey' Martin left RAF Germany in March 1973, on the expiration of his tour, to join the Air Force Board as Air Member for Personnel.

Martin's successor as Commander-in-chief was to be Air Marshal Sir Nigel Maynard, Deputy Commander, Strike Command, who recalls that they formed a good working partnership in Germany; he was particularly grateful for the care taken by Cameron to help him into a complicated scene. The two of them continued to divide their responsibilities along the same lines as during Martin's time, with Cameron concentrating mainly on the day-to-day running of RAF Germany while Maynard looked after the NATO and international side of affairs. Maynard had a high opinion of Cameron's ability.

RAF Germany in 1973, when Neil Cameron was Deputy Commander, had benefited operationally from the introduction of three new types of aircraft – Harriers, Phantoms and Buccaneers. This re-equipment programme, largely stimulated by the Soviet takeover of Czechoslovakia in 1968 and involving some airfield improvements, had been completed during 1972.[4] As a result, the Command now had three squadrons of Harriers at Wildenrath, three of Phantoms at Bruggen, two of Buccaneers (in a strike role) at Laarbruch, and two of Lightnings, plus a squadron of Wessex helicopters, at Gutersloh. The 'clutch' airfields – Bruggen, Laarbruch and Wildenrath – were protected by Bloodhound surface-to-air missile squadrons, supplementing the Bofors anti-aircraft units.

'Whether such a comprehensive programme would have been carried out if the Czechoslovak incident had not taken place, it is hard to say', the historian of RAF Germany commented, 'but it is at least unlikely that it would have been achieved so quickly. One must, therefore, conclude that Russia's precipitate action in 1968 had a most salutary effect in sharpening the teeth of the NATO alliance.'

As Deputy Commander, one of Neil Cameron's responsibilities was to see that readiness and efficiency standards were maintained on the stations – standards which were tested regularly, on a no-notice basis, by multinational NATO tactical evaluation teams, varying in size according to the role of the station: strike/attack bases like Bruggen or Laarbruch received visits from seventy-five-member teams, air defence bases visits from fifty-four-member teams. TACEVAL, as these inspections were called, involving every aspect of a station's role and beginning when a team descended on it at any hour of the day or night, dominated the lives of the stations, and they always reacted well.

By November 1973, however, Cameron was back in the UK: he was posted to No 46 Group in December, this time as AOC, with promotion to Air Marshal. It was an appointment he may have viewed with mixed feelings, as one which did not offer any new challenge to his abilities or experience; he was already familiar with the long-range transport role from his previous service at Upavon, and he was still not back in the centre – in Whitehall. Sir John Barraclough, however, says that he was overjoyed at the prospect; some further heart problems had been causing doubt about his suitability for promotion but when asked to promise never to pilot an aircraft other than 'in the air' (i.e. not while taking off or landing) he readily accepted the limitation and his new appointment went ahead.

Now back at 46 Group he was once again within the aegis

of the AOC-in-C Strike Command, ACM Sir Andrew Humphrey, who in four months was to become Chief of the Air Staff. The shortness of his tour in RAF Germany had not been accidental, nor was his posting fortuitous. A thinker himself, Andrew Humphrey wanted more men in the RAF to be thinking about their Service and the way in which it should go, and in Neil Cameron he recognised an outstandingly clear thinker on Defence matters. Although they had never served together, nor been personal friends, he knew of Cameron's abilities[5] and had a high regard for his character. He was also looking ahead to the future, to the time when he himself would become CAS and would need to consider possible successors.

Cameron's move to 46 Group, therefore, although it might not have appeared remarkable to his contemporaries – indeed it could well have looked to be his last appointment in the RAF – was in the event an important move, not in terms of the post itself but of its long-term implications.

His 'second tour' at Upavon lasted only ten months. The Group at this time still controlled the RAF strategic transport forces and its communications squadrons, parachute training and The Queen's Flight. Ironically, it was to be the hardest hit of any individual RAF formation by the cuts he was compelled to announce when he became Air Member for Personnel, as will be seen subsequently.

The new CAS, who took up his appointment on 1 April 1974, had asked some of his predecessors for advice on those officers considered suitable for promotion to the most senior posts. Lord Elworthy has recalled[6] that he recommended Cameron, and that this reinforced Humphrey's own view. As a result Cameron was soon to take a major step in his career, from Salisbury Plain back to Whitehall. In September 1974 his appointment to the Air Force Board was announced, as Air Member for Personnel in succession to 'Mickey' Martin. He was then fifty-four and his years in the wilderness were over; he was soon to be back 'in the midst of things'.

Notes

1. Air Chief Marshal Sir John Barraclough recalls that he had hoped to be appointed Commandant of the RAF Staff College (interview with Head of AHB, 8 October 1985).

2. Letter to Head of AHB, dated 15 September 1985.

3. Interview with the Head of the Air Historical Branch, 29 May 1985.

4. See ACM Sir David Lee, *The Royal Air Force in Germany 1945–1978* (AHB, 1979).

5. Denis Healey, who had been told by Cameron that he was thinking of leaving the Service, recalls urging Humphrey not to allow this to happen (conversation with Head of AHB, 6 January 1986).

6. Interview, 10 July 1985.

13   HEAD OF RAF PERSONNEL –
FORCE REDUCTIONS

'The appointment of AMP is a graveyard for the career of promising officers.' Lord Trenchard's blunt opinion, in a letter to Sir John Slessor when he was appointed Air Member for Personnel in 1945, was quoted by Neil Cameron at a farewell gathering to thank his staff when he relinquished this appointment in June 1976. Certainly for Slessor it had not been a graveyard; nor was it for Cameron – he was going on to become CAS and later (though he could not have foreseen it at the time) CDS.

Later in life, looking back on his career, he said he had 'never thought of joining the Air Force Board or of becoming AMP'.[1] However, when the post was offered to him by Andrew Humphrey – who wanted him in that job – he took it, and made a success of it, at a very difficult time. Modestly and typically, in a valedictory speech he said, 'I can only believe my staff have saved me'; though as Head of a large Department he had had to provide the impetus to decision-making, and also had to present to the Air Force Board the decisions made. He confessed that he had found the task of being AMP both 'fascinating and satisfying'. With a Gilbertian touch of wit he referred to the wide span of interests covered – medical, dental, gastronomical, legal, moral, intellectual, financial, musical and sartorial – as having a 'cradle to the grave' touch about it, and the responsibility for nearly 4,000 WRAF personnel had worried him (he had 'innocently described' the WRAF at the last AFB meeting as an important 'manning regulator').

Referring to 'what had been achieved in eighteen months' and paying tribute to 'our Civil Service colleagues'[2] who had been 'worked to death' – he considered the liaison between the RAF and the Civil Service to have been 'excellent' – he underlined the three Rs: 'reductions, redundancy, resettlement programme'. There had been thirty-two AFB papers ('a record in time'); they had 'had a good look at' the GD Branch structure, Airmen Engagement Policy, Times versus Merit Promotion, and at the Medical and Education Branches, and had formed the Administrative Branch.

He went on to mention other achievements and to refer to his favourite theme of Air Power and the part the RAF had to play; but 'having said that', he went on,

> I come back to personnel. It's like building on sand without the resolve of people – and these are a new type of people we are dealing with: we must remember this and adjust accordingly. People have feelings and people have morale – RAF morale has held up in bad times – and this is what AMP's Department is all about.

The AMP appointment, Sir Frank Cooper later commented,[3] had an enormous influence on him – 'he was really feeling responsible for people'. It affected his approach as CAS.

Then fifty-four, he could hardly have taken over as Air Member for Personnel – on 5 October 1974 – at a more testing time. But all his capabilities, his character and his experience – especially his knowledge of the workings of Whitehall, gained in his previous appointments there – made him eminently suitable for the job. Others beside Andrew Humphrey had recognised his ability – notably Roy Mason, the new Minister of Defence, with whose approval he had been brought back into 'the midst of things'. There was a particular empathy between the CAS and the new AMP which helped Neil Cameron in his new role: Andrew Humphrey's confidence in him, in wishing to have him on the Air Force Board, was to be amply vindicated; there was mutual trust and understanding between them.

In March 1974 the Labour Government which had recently been returned to power had instituted a Defence Review aimed at giving effect to its election pledge 'to achieve savings on defence expenditure of several hundred

million pounds per annum . . . while maintaining a
modern and effective defence system'.[4]

As far as the RAF were concerned, the implications were
that by 1979 manpower strength was to be cut from 100,000
in 1974 to 82,000 – a reduction of 18% (greater than that of
the other Services – Army 8%, Royal Navy 6%). As far as
possible, this was to be achieved by normal wastage and by
adjustment of recruiting; but some redundancies were
unavoidable: the number being made redundant in the
RAF would be approximately 4,000, including 800 officers.
This redundancy would be largely compulsory, though
there would be a voluntary element in it, with provision for
appeal against compulsory selection. Other implications
were that by early 1976 the fixed-wing transport fleet was to
be reduced by 50%: the Comet and Britannia squadrons
and the Andover tactical transport force were to be disbanded and the number of VC10s and Hercules reduced by
a quarter. The Nimrod maritime patrol force was also to be
reduced by a quarter. The RAF Regiment was to be reduced
in size and twelve stations were to be closed.

This was a daunting task – a substantial reduction in the
size of the Air Force – which Neil Cameron took over from
'Mickey' Martin in the autumn of 1974, in addition to his
many other duties as AMP.[5] It was, as he recalled later,[6] 'a
very difficult time'. Decisions on the redundancy programme had to be made after much thought. 'We knew we
would have to cut stations and personnel, and that the
sooner we did it, the sooner the scars would heal.' Of
paramount importance, he believed, was the need for
communication about the decisions which had to be taken –
to keep all personnel informed about what was going on
and how each member of the Service would personally be
affected.

At Air Force Board level, RAF affairs were intermingled
with politics: the members had daily contact with Ministers, and Brynmor John MP who as Under-Secretary of
State (RAF) welcomed Neil Cameron to his first meeting as
AMP on 21 October 1974 has recalled[7] that 'the fight had
been on' to 'get him out of the wilderness' and that had it
not been for Roy Mason he might never have got beyond
No 46 Group.

Brynmor John has admirably summed-up Neil Cameron's character and capabilities at this crucial stage in his career, when he had reached an important plateau, though at that time it could not have been foreseen that within two years he would be CAS and a year later CDS:

His quality was apparent; he had a breadth of imagination but was also sensitive to the operational and personal implications of personnel decisions. He was his own man – decisive and logical, tough but fair. You could persuade him to the contrary, but in order to do so you had to hold up your end in argument. He was an extremely good AMP – he knew his brief. In character he was the essence of a Scots Covenanter – morally erect, of good standing; perhaps difficult to get to know, but a nice man.

James Wellbeloved, who succeeded Brynmor John as US of S(RAF) in April 1976 and saw Neil Cameron in action both as AMP and as CAS, has recalled[8] that he shared the Ministerial view that if cuts had to be made, it was best to get them over with as quickly as possible. He had 'a deep love for the RAF'; he was much concerned about pay and conditions for its personnel. But although a military officer in the best sense, he was also loyal to whatever Government had been democratically elected.

In retrospect, James Wellbeloved considers that Neil Cameron paid a heavy price for the years he had spent working for Denis Healey: 'he felt he'd been shuffled off' – it was only with the appointment of Brynmor John that he came back. The key to his attitude was, quite simply, his political loyalty despite his professional sympathies. Regarded in personal terms as a Board member and a colleague, he was 'tough but not malicious – not afraid to take hard decisions. He had clear, well-thought-out views; he was deeply compassionate and considerate, a nice man to work with'. He was a good listener and easy to talk with: 'one could talk to him at any time with all frankness', T. C. G. James has recalled; 'in no way did he ever discourage an honest expression of views'.[9]

Just how hard he worked, and how he formed his views,

becomes clear from the recollections of Roger Palin who was his Personal Staff Officer during his first three months as AMP:[10]

> He was very regular in his working habits – would arrive at his office at ten to nine every morning. The first thing he would do was to fire half-a-dozen quick questions at his PSO – about things which were on his mind, or queries arising out of the work he had taken home the night before. He was very thorough: each day he would produce blue slips of paper – on which he'd written reminders to himself of things he had to do – and carefully laid them on his desk, so that he didn't forget anything.

In Palin's view, Neil Cameron was a 'Whitehall warrior' – he knew his way round the system, from previous experiences,[11] and because of this knowledge was better placed than an officer who had come to Whitehall straight from a series of operational commands. He was also, in the best sense of the term, a 'wheeler dealer' – he would consult with people to get their views, and never committed himself to paper until after such consultations – until he was quite sure of his ground.[12]

He worked extremely hard. When in the office, and not away on the many visits which fell to the lot of AMP through his honorary appointments, his day went on until he left the Ministry of Defence headquarters at ten to seven with a briefcase full of papers to be studied that evening – on which he would invariably have a series of questions to ask the following morning.

Neil Cameron was especially good, Palin recalls, at talking with groups of people – he was excellent at the give-and-take of question-and-answer sessions and was in his element at RAF stations with an audience of a hundred or so, talking, listening and answering.

One particular issue which showed how he acted when there was a disagreement to be resolved concerned the use of the Scottish Aviation T. Mk 1 twin-turboprop aircraft ordered by the RAF in 1972 for multi-engine flying training. As the then Director-General of RAF Training and AUS (P) have recalled,[13] Andrew Humphrey and Neil Cameron had to be persuaded of the need to retain it for this purpose. The latter was convinced that twin-engined flying training, for both the RAF and the Royal Navy, should be done on civil contract at Hamble. DGT and AUS (P) were worried that the trainees would thus be outside Service influence at a key stage in their careers; there was 'widespread concern' at AMP's view – he was after financial economy – and DGT and AUS (P) felt that they had to confront him on this issue. They were successful in persuading him of their opinion and then ran up against Andrew Humphrey, who also had to be persuaded. 'Once Neil Cameron was convinced that we had done our homework properly', they recall, 'he was prepared to change his mind and bear no malice.'

In their recollection of those days, they considered that there were two members of the Air Force Board who were never prepared to fudge an issue – CAS and AMP, who both considered that if unpleasant things had to be done, it was best to get on with them. Neil Cameron 'could be quite ruthless on occasion' – he was well-prepared to take difficult decisions when necessary.

During his fifteen-month period as AMP (October 1974 to May 1976) he attended eighteen Air Force Board meetings – being listed as Sir Neil Cameron for the first time at the 16 January 1975 meeting – and spoke at all but two of them: although, in Brynmor John's view, there was never a 'genuine dialogue' at these meetings – the arguing had been done at the Standing Committee stage – papers had to be presented and a case made, and Neil Cameron spoke with directness and economy.

The human implications of the RAF redundancy programme, for which AMP had the prime responsibility, were to affect Neil Cameron for the rest of his Service career – indeed for the rest of his life.[14] His first statement on it was made on 2 December 1974, when he reported that 'detailed work was now in hand' on it. The intention was that 'all those who would be affected should as far as possible be treated as individuals'. He added that the redundancy terms 'could be described as reasonably fair'. His view in retrospect[15] was that the RAF had a more difficult problem than the other Services: that the Navy had 'no real problem because they were heavily undermanned', and that the Army believed that the problem would go away with time and a change of Government.

The officers responsible for personnel in all three Services shared a common forum for discussion in the Principal Personnel Officers' Committee – attending whose meetings was one of AMP's 'many other duties'. Neil Cameron went to his first on 16 October 1974: they were held monthly and discussed problems of mutual interest – particularly Services' pay (a matter which he was to take up strongly in his subsequent appointments as CAS and CDS), redundancy, recruiting, living conditions and allowances, and higher defence training – a review of which he considered to be 'important and timely'. The ability to 'deploy the military case in Whitehall' was in his view 'very important'. When, in February 1976, the committee received the Chief Public Relations Officers' periodic report he urged that there should be a 'PR offensive' aimed at influencing attitudes to defence.

When, at the first meeting he attended, redundancy was discussed and the PPOs considered a draft Ministerial announcement, he said that the RAF figures were for approximately 5,000 redundancies in a total reduction of 17,000. Having taken stock of the manpower situation and of what he had to do, he circulated an 'Informatory Note' on officer manning six weeks after he had taken over, setting out the implications of the Defence Review and suggesting to his colleagues how officer redundancy might be handled and in what timescale. He suggested that, as there would not be a Standing Committee meeting for some time, he would find it extremely helpful to have an informal discussion with the Note's addressees – AMSO, CA, VCAS and DUS (Air). In a long and detailed note he said that he saw the need for a redundancy programme involving some 600 GD and up to 200 ground branch officers – a programme that could not begin before 1 October 1975 and should end by 1 April 1977. As far as a compulsory or a voluntary scheme was concerned, he was in favour of the former: 'I hold the view that . . . the balance of advantage, for the good of the Service, is with a compulsory scheme – certainly for the GD Branch.' By this means the RAF would decide who should leave; otherwise, too many of the best men would probably go.

The information was circulated throughout the RAF by the end of 1974, the Service being told that the total officer requirement was expected to come down from 16,200 to an estimated 13,700 by 1 April 1977, that much of the 2,500 reduction would be brought about by some limitation in intakes and other manning regulators, and that the probable redundancy figures were 600 GD and up to 200 ground branch officers. The total ground trades requirement was expected to come down from 73,500 on 1 April 1975 to 56,300 by 1 April 1978: much of this would be brought about by normal wastage and some limitation in the recruit intake; the redundancy figure would be about 3,000 and would be centred principally on the engineering trades, probably requiring about 2,400 SNCOs to leave on redundancy terms. The signal added that the Secretary of State had promised in his Parliamentary statement that redundancy terms would be 'fair and reasonable'.

The closing-down of squadrons and stations (a matter primarily for AMSO) was, in a similar way, conveyed to the whole Service in an announcement to all personnel on 19 March 1975. This said that the Comet and Britannia squadrons and No 46 Squadron (Andovers) would be disbanded and the VC10 and Hercules fleets reduced. Largely as a result of being able to concentrate the smaller transport force on major flying stations, twelve stations in the United Kingdom would be vacated by the RAF.

The matter of redundancy was to run like a counterpoint to all the themes discussed at AFB meetings while Neil Cameron was AMP – it was a nettle which he had to grasp, and he grasped it firmly. The RAF could not have picked a more suitable man as AMP at that time: he was a humanitarian, who had been brought up in severe and humble surroundings; he had never lost his social conscience and his concern for his fellow men. He was also a good communicator: he recommended, in a memorandum to the Air Staff on 8 January 1975, that 'as much information as possible on redundancy should be made known to officers and airmen likely to be affected'.

He didn't like having to cut short the Service careers of so many men who had trained so long to reach their standards of skill, and to the end of his days he regretted the action which had to be taken: he thought of redundancy very much in personal terms. However, he had been called to the Air Force Board to do a particular job; and being Neil Cameron, he did it loyally and efficiently, but with as much regard as possible for the personnel who were affected by the cuts in expenditure.

As AMP, he had a very wide field of responsibilities, covering all aspects of the lives of personnel – the nerves and sinew of any military Service – in the RAF. Thus he spoke, and presented papers on, subjects as diverse as forthcoming Royal visits to the RAF and its participation in public events during 1975; the St Clement Danes Appeal (he was Chairman of the church's Executive Committee); the future of the *Royal Air Force Quarterly*; the officer branch structure; a review of the Education Branch; the future of the Red Arrows aerobatic display team; plans for the Queen's Silver Jubilee celebrations in 1977 (the RAF part in which – at Finningley – was to be his 'swan song' when he was Chief of the Air Staff); the MRCA (multi-role combat aircraft – subsequently named Tornado) and tri-national joint operational training. AMP had to be particularly versatile, and to know his brief on every subject for which he was responsible.

During his first period of service on the Air Force Board, Neil Cameron proved himself to be an able and clear-minded administrator. But an even greater responsibility lay ahead. At the meeting on 20 May 1976 the Chairman, Mr James Wellbeloved, said that the Board would be saying farewell to Air Chief Marshal Sir Neil Cameron as AMP but would be welcoming him back in another role.

Notes

1. Interview with Air Cdre R. A. Mason at the RAF Staff College, Bracknell, 23 July 1980.

2. Naming particularly J. H. Nelson and his successor as AUS(P), T. C. G. James.

3. Interview at AHB, 29 July 1985.

4. *Statement on the Defence Estimates 1975* (Cmnd 5976). There was no Defence Statement in 1974 because of the General Election.

5. His Department had a staff of some 355 officers and covered in addition to all aspects of Personnel, Personal Services, WRAF, Sport and Recreation, Provost Marshal, Training (Ground and Flying), PT, Nursing, Chaplaincy, Medical and Dental Branches, Educational and Legal Services, the Air Secretary's Branch and Resettlement.

6. Interview with Air Cdre Mason, RAF Staff College, Bracknell, 23 July 1980.

7. Interview with the writer, 16 May 1985.

8. Interview with the writer, 17 May 1985.

9. Interview at AHB, 21 August 1985.

10. Interview with Air Cdre R. H. Palin on 13 May 1985.

11. As PSO to CAS as a Wing Commander, and with the Programme Evaluation Group and Defence Policy Staff as an Air Vice-Marshal.

12. His predecessor as AMP, Sir Harold Martin, has recalled that he advised his successor to 'go round the staffs before arguing round the table' – to prepare the ground and condition people – advice which was evidently well-heeded.

13. Air Marshal Sir Frederick Sowrey and T. C. G. James, interview with the Head of AHB, 21 August 1985.

14. In one of the writer's meetings with him, on 13 September 1984, Lord Cameron referred to the number of Chief Technicians he had 'had to get rid of' as AMP under the 1975–77 redundancy programme. Clearly the loss to the RAF of so many skilled and experienced men, and the social and personal implications of making them redundant weighed on his mind long after he had ended his Service career.

15. Interview with Air Cdre R. A. Mason, RAF Staff College, Bracknell, 23 July 1980.

14   CHIEF OF THE AIR STAFF

Neil Cameron took up his appointment as CAS on 7 August 1976. He was then fifty-six and brought to the post all those attributes of character and experience which might have been written into a 'job specification' for the head of the RAF: good looks and an attractive, energetic and open personality; an outstanding operational record and proven powers of leadership; command in the field, as Deputy Commander in Germany and AOC at Upavon; knowledge of the ways of Whitehall, from his PSO/CAS days through to his time as ACDS (Pol); experience on the Air Force Board and of RAF manpower/personnel problems as AMP; familiarity with, and the respect of the Ministers and civil servants with whom he had to deal; and a reputation for honesty and integrity in all his actions – although the forthrightness with which he expressed his views might not be to everyone's liking.

Such characteristics and achievements would not, however, have qualified him automatically for the top post in the RAF. When such an appointment is decided on, the reigning incumbent has an influential say in the choice of his successor and the Secretary of State relies very much on his recommendation. In Neil Cameron's case, Andrew Humphrey had decided that he would be the next CAS, having taken advice from former holders of the post:[1] hence the move from AOC No 46 Group, where he had been within Humphrey's aegis as AOC-in-C Strike Command, after a mere ten months to the Air Force Board as AMP, when Humphrey had become CAS. He was 'the chosen son' indeed, and Humphrey's choice was to be fully justified in the leadership that Neil Cameron gave to the RAF.

He himself was fully conscious of the debt he owed to

Andrew Humphrey; when, as Chief of the Defence Staff, he visited Cranwell on 19 December 1977 to unveil a portrait of his predecessor he said: 'This is the man to whom I owe everything.'[2]

Neil Cameron was to hold the post of CAS for less than a year – a shorter time than any of his predecessors, apart from Major-General Sykes and Sir Geoffrey Salmond[3] – because in July 1977 he was appointed Chief of the Defence Staff. But in his short period as head of the RAF he made a distinctive contribution to its activities, notably in the sphere of communications, following the pattern set by his immediate predecessor.

His forum for final decisions on RAF policy was the Air Force Board of which he had been a member as AMP. It was normally chaired by the Parliamentary Under-Secretary for State for Defence for the RAF (James Wellbeloved, MP) and the new CAS's RAF colleagues were Air Chief Marshal Sir John Aiken, his successor as AMP; Air Chief Marshal Sir Douglas Lowe, Controller of Aircraft; Air Marshals Sir Alasdair Steedman and D. G. Evans, respectively Air Member for Supply and Organisation and Vice-Chief of the Air Staff; and W. J. Charnley, Chief Scientist (RAF). DUS (Air) was P. J. Hudson and 2nd DUS Sir William Geraghty. James Wellbeloved has recalled[4] that there was 'not a lot of argument' at the Air Force Board meetings – matters had generally been thrashed out in the Standing Committee; and Brynmor John, his predecessor, confirmed[5] this view, feeling that there was never 'a genuine dialogue' on these occasions. Early in his period of office Neil Cameron took the opportunity, at the AFB meeting on 18 November 1976,[6] to draw a clear distinction between the functions of the Standing Committee and the Board, speaking at some length on this subject. It was the former's task, he said, 'to consider items not important enough to be put to the Board, or subjects which would benefit from a preliminary discussion before the Board considered them'.

It was at the 2 December meeting that the decision was made to issue what was referred to as a 'Commanders' briefing sheet' – later known as the 'Commanders' Brief', the first of which was issued in January 1977 and which will be referred to later as part of the deliberate effort Neil

Cameron made to sharpen-up communications within the Service.

The Board, whose deliberations gave the CAS and its members an overview of all matters pertaining to the RAF, also discussed during his short term of office the 1977–78 Estimates and 1977 Long-term Costings, RAF publicity, the long-term rates of flying effort for front-line units, the rationalisation of basic helicopter pilot training, the maintenance of the Harrier force, MRCA (multi-role combat aircraft) costings, the redevelopment of Bentley Priory and the air defence of the United Kingdom, redundancy in the ground trades (a subject which the CAS knew a great deal about from his experience as AMP), deployment of the Tornado IDS Force, NATO force goals for 1977–82, progress of the 1978/9 Cuts Exercise, air-to-air missile requirements for Phantoms, the Battle of Britain Memorial Flight and RAF Publicity – in other words, as wide a spectrum of subjects as those with which the Board's predecessor, the Air Council, had had to deal.

One subject on which the CAS showed particular concern was the Tornado MRCA. He told the Board at their 19 May 1977 meeting that when he had met the German and Italian Chiefs of Staff on the previous day they had

> agreed that Ministerial authority would be sought for the placing of the next order for 110 Tornados to add to the 40 already ordered.[7] A Press release had gone to Ministers for endorsement indicating that the three Chiefs of Staff were entirely content with the way the programme was going.

Because of controversy about this programme, Neil Cameron decided to experience Tornado at first hand, and on 22 June 1977 went up to British Aerospace Warton Division to fly in one of the development aircraft. At the AFB meeting on the following day US of S (RAF) (James Wellbeloved, MP) said that he was to be congratulated on his successful flight and on the Independent Television News treatment of this. The impression made, he said 'would go a long way to counteract criticisms of the aircraft which had received some publicity in recent months'.

Neil Cameron's appointment as CAS also conferred

membership of the Defence Council – on which, as in the COS Committee, he encountered his fellow Chiefs of Staff – Admiral Sir Edward Ashmore, CNS, and General Sir Roland Gibbs, CGS. The Council, which had about a dozen members, represented the whole of the British defence establishment – military, political, civil service and scientific. Neil Cameron only attended two meetings of the Defence Council as CAS, but he was to have a considerable influence on its discussion when CDS.

He attended twenty-one COS meetings, however, during his time as CAS – and Defence Budget reductions loomed large on the agenda. On 21 December 1976 the Chiefs had before them a draft of the 1977 Defence White Paper, and at four meetings in the early months of 1977 discussed cuts in the 1978/79 Defence Budget. Services' pay – an award was due on 1 April 1977 – and conditions of service were under discussion in January and February, Neil Cameron raising at the meeting on the last day of February the situation regarding accommodation charges. Clearly recalling his experiences as AMP, he was worried at the prospect of a cynically dubbed 'Irishman's rise'.

But the subject which came up most often in COS discussions, especially at the last five meetings he attended as CAS, was a foreign one – the crisis situation in Belize, which had originally arisen in 1975 with the threat of an invasion by neighbouring Guatemala. At their June-July 1977 meetings the Chiefs discussed the reinforcement of the garrison there, which took place at about that time and included the deployment of Harriers.

The COS meetings of the winter of 1976–77 were particularly saddened for Neil Cameron by the sudden illness and death of Andrew Humphrey, who had been such a significant influence in his career and who had had so brief a time as Chief of the Defence Staff, taking the Chair at a COS meeting only three times. On 11 January 1977 Sir Edward Ashmore took his place as Acting CDS, and on 1 February the Chiefs paid their formal farewell tribute to him. During his time on the COS Committee under Ashmore's chairmanship Neil Cameron would have learnt a great deal, for Ashmore was a strong CDS, always prepared to give a lead.[8]

Some three months after becoming CAS Neil Cameron had told an audience at the RAF Staff College, Bracknell, that he had set himself five objectives: to get air power thinking going again at all levels throughout the Service; to keep on warning people about the Soviet air threat to the United Kingdom and to NATO; to fight for the RAF share of the Defence 'cake'; to sharpen-up communications, both within the Service and in its external relations with the public; and to rebuild the confidence of the Royal Air Force after the various Defence Reviews and the reductions in its strength.

How well did he achieve those objectives during his short period as CAS – an office which he had expected to hold for three and a half years?

For a long time during his post-war career he had done his best to stimulate the study of air power, by writing and speaking on it. Since 1959 he had published articles on deterrent strategy, air power and Britain's future world role, the strategic balance, the UK Mobile Force and the effects of technological development on air power. He had also lectured on numerous occasions to Service and civilian audiences – some forty lecture scripts are preserved in his personal papers and there was nothing he liked more than the give-and-take of question-and-answer sessions. He would challenge his listeners with the question: 'Where are the Trenchards, the Mitchells, the Douhets, the Arnolds, the Slessors of today?'[9]

When he attended a symposium on air power at Southampton University in April 1977 he observed that while there had been little original thinking about the doctrine of air power in Britain since Slessor's day, there had been enormous changes in the technical and strategic situation.

Even after so short a period as CAS he was able to point to developments during his time in office which would help to remedy this imbalance in the UK between thinking about air power and the technological and strategic changes which had affected it: a new post, Director of Defence Studies, had been established at the Staff College at Bracknell; the course there had been lengthened to nine months; and the universities – Southampton, Lancaster, Edinburgh and King's College London, for example – had shown an increased interest in air power studies.

His warnings about the Soviet air threat – a fundamental aspect of Neil Cameron's own thinking about air power – were conveyed on numerous occasions to a variety of audiences. He would stress what he saw as the unchanging aims of the Soviet Union – a steady increase in military expenditure and major developments, both quantitative and qualitative, in the nature of the threat posed. As a corollary, he stressed the pattern of advancing technology at present and in the future, and the impact of this on both Russian and British air power. He would invite his audiences to consider such questions as the development of precision conventional weapons, the need for better command and control techniques, AEW (airborne early warning) aircraft, the use of missiles for most of the terminal work,[10] the inevitability of cruise missiles, the role of the air in anti-submarine warfare and a re-examination of the tanker role.[11]

Whatever the precise subject under discussion, wherever the forum, the fundamental message was always the same – the seriousness and magnitude of the Soviet threat. In common with Alexander Solzhenitsyn, whom he often quoted, he believed that there were all too many parallels with the Munich years.

His third objective, that of fighting for the RAF's share of the defence 'cake', was not one that he could discuss much in public – though it was undoubtedly a major preoccupation with him. Not only was there the question of adequate funding for the Service, but also of its independence. There were still those in influential positions who considered that Britain could do with just an Army and a Navy: this was a challenge that Neil Cameron, like some of his predecessors, had to face. Thus in March 1977 he took the opportunity of assuring his audience at the RAF Dinner Club that the RAF was not just a tactical air force and that its amalgamation with the Army would be both ill-considered and naive. However, on many matters he and his Chiefs of Staff colleagues were at one, and not least when they exercised their right of direct access to the Prime Minister over the defence cuts in early 1977. This right was also to be exercised later, when Neil Cameron was Chief of the Defence Staff, on the question of Forces' pay.

When it came to sharpening-up communications, within and outside the Service, this was done both orally and in written form. As in his days as AMP, Neil Cameron was a great one for speaking directly to all ranks in the RAF. Recalling a visit he made to RAF Germany in 1976, Sir Michael Beetham remembers[12] that he asked, on going to each station, to talk to all personnel – officers, SNCOs, airmen and airwomen – about what the Air Force Board was doing. This practice was extended throughout the whole of the Air Force, and as he was unable to go everywhere himself, his AFB colleagues were required to join in. As a result he was able to claim, when speaking at an Air Marshals' Club luncheon in April 1977, that by then 60,000 out of the 90,00 men and women in the Service had been addressed directly by one or other of the Board Members.

On the same occasion he referred to the new Commanders' Brief, the first of which had been issued in January of that year, as a result of the AFB decision taken on 2 December 1976 when communications within the Service had been discussed. The overall purpose was 'to keep those responsible for implementing policy aware of important decisions and the underlying reasons for them', not only through RAF publications but additionally through a briefing sheet, issued for the personal information and guidance of Station Commanders. These Commanders' Briefs were published at two-monthly intervals: their contents reflected current topics. Thus the January 1977 issue led off (almost inevitably) with an item on cuts in Defence expenditure; it described the part the RAF would play in Offshore Tapestry operations, referred to plans for the Battle of Britain Museum and for the Royal Review of the RAF at Finningley on 29 July 1977, and in mentioning future types of equipment described AEW developments, MRCA progress and deliveries of the first Hawks to the RAF in October/November 1976. The second issue (March 1977) also referred to cuts in Defence expenditure, published in the White Paper at the end of February, to Offshore Tapestry diplomatic complications and to AEW developments; it went on to mention further purchases of Harriers and the introduction of Sea King helicopters to replace Whirlwinds, among many other items of topical information. Thus a real effort was being made to keep those in senior positions informed of what was being done, so that through them the RAF at large would be aware of present problems and future plans.

Nevertheless Neil Cameron remained dissatisfied with the results of these efforts: in valedictory addresses to officers at Strike and Support Command Headquarters in July 1977 he observed that communications were still breaking down at station level and that station commanders would have to make greater efforts. He himself would undoubtedly have liked to continue his campaign, which had its roots in his wartime experience of high commanders visiting their units in the field, to explain strategy and raise morale.

The exercise in improving communications was, of course, a corollary to his final objective – the rebuilding of confidence throughout the RAF after the Defence cuts had reduced its strength and damaged morale. To achieve this, the importance of the Service and its current achievements had to be fully recognised. It was also necessary to be able to point to a challenging future. Thus, as CAS, Neil Cameron was at pains to stress the significance of new aircraft like the Tornado, to emphasise the continuing roles of manned aircraft and to underline the capabilities of a new generation of weapons. But he fully realised that, however important the 'hardware', personnel were equally important. From his experiences in positions of command and as AMP, he appreciated that conditions of service had to be right. He recognised the fundamental need to resolve the pay issue, on which he fought very hard with his fellow Chiefs of Staff, particularly after becoming CDS.

It was Andrew Humphrey who had been such a good communicator and who saw in Neil Cameron someone who could succeed him in that role. His hopes were fully justified, but for Cameron it was his experience as AMP which was probably most influential in shaping his outlook as CAS and subsequently as CDS. Someone who worked closely with him during these periods[13] has observed that his time as AMP had had 'an enormous influence' on him –

he really felt responsible for people in the Service – and this 'carried over' to his period as CAS, especially in the matters of pay and conditions. Always keen to change things, he was particularly enthusiastic about training and education, and he felt frustrated at not being able to do some of the things he wanted to do. This probably resulted from the fact that the system within which he had to work, by its very nature cautious and conservative, put the brakes on his enthusiasm. The civil servants with whom he worked liked him personally, but thought him overenthusiastic; and his own Service colleagues considered him something of a reforming radical – he would 'rush in where angels feared to tread' when a cause was dear to his heart.

One reason why he was unable to achieve some of the objectives which he had set himself was the shortness of his time in office. He told the officers of Strike and Support Command HQs when bidding them farewell that he had expected to serve as Chief of the Air Staff for three and a half years. The fact that he was being moved on to become Chief of the Defence Staff just over a year after becoming CAS was due to the untimely death of MRAF Sir Andrew Humphrey in January 1977 and followed the interim appointment of Admiral of the Fleet Sir Edward Ashmore as CDS. For Neil Cameron himself a pattern was being repeated as, curiously, all his senior appointments up to that time had been of short duration (a year at ASC/46 Group as SASO/Chief of Staff, less than a year in RAF Germany as Deputy Commander, ten months as AOC 46 Group and fifteen months as AMP) – his rise to the top had been swift indeed.

His period of Service as Chief of the Air Staff ended on a high note, when with other AFB members he welcomed the Queen to the Royal Review of the RAF at Finningley on 29 July 1977, a great occasion which gave him justifiable pride in the Service of which he had proved himself such a strong and determined leader.

He would probably have been content to fulfil his term as CAS, to complete the tasks to which he had set his hand; in fact he was disappointed not to be able to do so. The decision to appoint him Chief of the Defence Staff came as a surprise to him – as Sir Michael Beetham, his successor as

CAS, has recalled.[14] But, if the tri-Service sequence of appointment to the CDS post was to be followed, Neil Cameron was obviously the right choice; and he enjoyed the total confidence of the senior ranks of the RAF. His experience of high-level policy, his acceptability to both Ministers and his Service colleagues, his knowledge of the workings of Whitehall, his open and determined character and his record as a writer and speaker on Defence matters, made it almost inevitable that the RAF should provide the successor to Sir Andrew Humphrey and so complete the normal turn in the CDS post. But Neil Cameron was to find the environment quite different from the familiar one in which he had previously served, and in some respects a dangerous and more difficult one. Nevertheless he was well equipped, experienced and ready, to accept the wider opportunities and challenges now being offered to him.

Notes

1. Lord Elworthy, former CDS, was one of those consulted by Andrew Humphrey after he became CAS as to which officers should fill the top posts (interview with the Head of AHB and the writer, 10 July 1985).

2. Interview with Lady Humphrey by the Head of the AHB and the writer, 13 June 1985.

3. Sykes was CAS from 13 April 1918 to 31 March 1919; Salmond was appointed on 1 April 1933 but died on 27 April 1933.

4. Interview with the writer, 17 May 1985.

5. Interview with the writer, 16 May 1985.

6. Air Force Board Conclusions 7(76).

7. An initial production batch of forty aircraft had been authorised on 29 July 1976, just before Neil Cameron became CAS.

8. Interview with Lord Mulley, former Minister of Defence, by the Head of AHB, 31 July 1985.

9. Group Captain J. A. G. Slessor remembers that, when he was CAS, Sir Neil visited MRAF Sir John Slessor two or three times – the only CAS to have done so (conversation with Head of AHB, 6 January 1986).

10. His own term – presumably referring to accuracy of impact on targets.

11. One which proved to be crucial in the Falklands operation.

12. Interview with the Head of AHB, 17 July 1985.

13. Sir Frank Cooper, formerly PUS, MoD: interview with the Head of AHB and the writer on 29 July 1985.

14. Interview with the Head of AHB, 17 July 1985.

15 CHIEF OF THE DEFENCE STAFF

Neil Cameron's rise to the top of the British military establishment was extraordinarily swift, as has been seen. At the beginning of 1974 he was an acting Air Marshal, commanding a transport Group; by mid-1977 he had been promoted to Marshal of the RAF and appointed Chief of the Defence Staff.

He had finished his tour as Chief of the Air Staff on a high note, escorting the Queen at her Silver Jubilee Review of the Royal Air Force at Finningley on 29 July 1977. The CDS was then Admiral of the Fleet Sir Edward Ashmore, who had taken over the office when MRAF Sir Andrew Humphrey fell ill and continued to hold it after the latter died on 24 January. Ashmore was a strong man, well able to give a lead, and Neil Cameron benefited from serving with him on the Defence Council and under him on the Chiefs of Staff Committee.[1]

The problem which faced the Minister of Defence, Fred Mulley, when Andrew Humphrey died was that to give Ashmore (Acting CDS since 11 January) a full term of office would have upset the tri-Service sequence of appointments; the next Naval (Admiral Sir Terence Lewin) and Army (General Sir Edwin Bramall) nominees had already been earmarked as probable successors. On the other hand if Edward Ashmore were to continue in office for a few months – which seemed only fair to him – Neil Cameron would have more time to gain experience as CAS, on the Chiefs of Staff Committee and on the Defence Council, before becoming CDS. This, therefore, was the solution the Minister adopted: Cameron's appointment would be announced, and after relinquishing his CAS role at the end of July 1977 he would take up his new duties in September. At the Defence Council meeting on 9 February 1977 the Minister said that an announcement would be made later

that day that Sir Edward Ashmore had been appointed CDS
in the rank of Admiral of the Fleet and that Neil Cameron
would succeed him on 1 September 1977.[2] The latter thus,
in the first half of that year, fulfilled his last six months as
CAS and understudied for the role of CDS.

His successor as CAS, MRAF Sir Michael Beetham, has
commented in retrospect[3] that while this announcement
'came as a complete surprise' at the time, he felt that it was
'absolutely right' to choose Neil Cameron as CDS – not only
to preserve the RAF turn for the post, but because he had
the total confidence of the RAF hierarchy, who felt that he
was the best man for it. Cameron's own reaction, he felt, was
one of disappointment at not being able to complete a full
tour as CAS and so to make the impact he wished to achieve.
But he was a 'Whitehall man' and appreciated the wider
opportunities being presented to him as CDS. He said after
his retirement that he had 'never lobbied' for this post.[4]

The post of Chief of the Defence Staff was, however, for
an outspoken man like Neil Cameron, a lonely one:[5] he was
out in front, by himself, without the protection of colleagues of his own Service; and he was to find himself more
than once drawn into public controversy in the Press and
Parliament. The CDS had to speak for all three Services,
and had to be careful what he said, as representing the
British military establishment. As a spokesman for the
Services, Neil Cameron was very successful as CDS; as an
'establishment' figure, perhaps less so.

His relationship with the RAF was entirely impartial
while he was CDS and his behaviour towards his successor
as CAS – Sir Michael Beetham – was 'impeccable'; as the
latter has recalled:

> The relationship between CDS and the Chief of Staff of his own
> Service can be difficult. In our case it was a very cordial one – he
> never interfered. If, in formal briefing sessions of the Chiefs of
> Staff Committee, questions arose about the RAF – questions
> which he was entirely competent to answer, he always referred
> them to me. While he was a great believer in the importance of
> air power, he played the CDS role absolutely straight, and was
> respected both by his Service colleagues and also by the
> politicians – not only by his own Minister, Fred Mulley, but
> also by the Prime Minister, James Callaghan.

This scrupulousness as to his impartial role as CDS led him to resign his Presidency of the RAF Rugby Union: he felt that he should not be seen to be retaining any single-Service connections which might cause his impartiality to be doubted.

The diversity of things going on during Neil Cameron's time as CDS – September 1977 to August 1979 – can be gauged from the matters discussed at the Defence Council and Chiefs of Staff meetings. The Council, where the CDS and Chiefs of Staff formally encountered Ministers, was meeting more regularly in this period, at the behest of the Secretary of State; and it was to its meetings that the Chiefs carried their battle with the Government over Forces' pay. While this was a major theme in their discussions, however, the Council's overview of Defence matters – as a forum where 'a dialogue can take place between Ministers and top management on the various considerations and interests which need to be brought to bear on major issues'[6] – led them to talk about a variety of matters: reductions in the UK defence expenditure, the growth of Soviet military forces, the Offshore task, equipment collaboration (with reference to AST 403) and policy, air defence, and research and development.

At the Chiefs of Staff meetings the role of the CDS as chairman meant that he had to synthesise the discussions, taking a Defence view as distinct from a single-Service one. Neil Cameron's colleagues at the first meeting he attended, on 13 September 1977, were Sir Terence Lewin, CNS, Sir Roland Gibbs, CGS, and his successor as CAS, Sir Michael Beetham. None of them had had as much Whitehall experience as Cameron and his leadership was therefore significant, particularly in the matter of Service pay, which was to be one of the main issues during his term as CDS, due to the government's national pay policy. On the whole subject of the conditions of service in the Armed Forces – pay, accommodation and allowances – he gave a strong lead, urging the Services to speak with one voice.

When a national firemen's strike began on 14 November 1977 and the Services came to the aid of the civil authorities,[7] the Chiefs of Staff took the opportunity of emphasising (in January 1978) that the Services' role in the dispute had demonstrated that the case for a Forces' pay settlement was as strong as that of the firemen; and under Neil Cameron's leadership the Chiefs exercised their right of direct access to the Prime Minister on this matter – though not always successfully: in April 1978 Mr James Callaghan was unable to find time to meet them at short notice to discuss the Armed Forces' Pay Review, owing to his busy programme.

The firemen's strike and the fire-fighting aid given by the Services thus provided the new CDS and his CoS colleagues with the opportunity they wanted to press for pay comparability – an opportunity which they took in the spring of 1978.

In an interview which he gave at the end of his time as CAS[8] Neil Cameron remarked that the 'most important thing' to allay Service personnel's disillusionment over their recent (i.e. 1977) pay award was 'to regain comparability with the civilian sector just as quickly as we possibly can within the constraints of Government pay policy'. He said this before becoming CDS: he had thus nailed his colours to the mast, and after his Service career ended he recalled: 'Pay was one of the biggest issues. I was determined that it should come to the Chiefs of Staff: we fought it bitterly and eventually with success' – though not without using an unorthodox manoeuvre which brought the matter to the notice of the Press, Parliament and public.

On 17 March 1978 Neil Cameron had a private discussion on Services' pay with the Prime Minister, who had received a memorandum setting out the Chiefs of Staff views on the subject. A month later, on 18 April, the Press Association put out a report on the numbers of personnel leaving the Services. This was based on the Armed Forces' Pay Review Body report, which the Government was considering and which had been 'leaked' to the PA by the Chiefs of Staff without Ministerial authority. As a result the Prime Minister was questioned in Parliament about the 'alarming numbers' of men waiting to leave the Forces: he told MPs he had ordered an immediate inquiry and the Opposition demanded that the Government should take such reports into account in settling the Services' pay claim.[9]

The then CAS, Sir Michael Beetham, has commented on

this pay 'leak' that it exemplified how well Neil Cameron 'knew his Whitehall': there was 'a real pay problem; many skilled people were leaving the Services. The retirement figures were leaked at the instance of the Chiefs of Staff, but when the investigation into the leak began to home in on the man who had been put up to it (unfortunately the wording of the leak had been too precise) the Chiefs admitted to the Minister their responsibility.'[10]

Recalling this incident, the then Minister of Defence (Lord Mulley) has commented[11] that 'the leaking of the retirement rate figures just before the Cabinet was due to consider Services' pay was an annoyance and unhelpful. Eventually the Chiefs admitted to Frank Cooper (PUS) and then to me that they had been responsible and I told the Prime Minister.'

Subsequently the Minister of Defence told the Commons in a Written Answer on 16 May 1978 that 'the details published in the Press Association report, which gave some selective information about departures from the Services, were given to the Press Association by Service sources with the authority of the Chiefs of Staff. I have told the Chiefs of Staff that they should have sought the authority of Ministers in this matter. The Chiefs of Staff have accepted this and accordingly I regard the matter as closed.'[12]

On 25 April the Prime Minister announced an increase of 10% in the military salary with an increase in the 'X' factor[13] which would add a further 3%, with additional allowances bringing the total figure up to 14%. This was a pay award, not comparability; the fully comparable military salary had to wait for another year, coming into effect on 1 April 1979: it must have given Neil Cameron great satisfaction after his determined leadership of the Chiefs of Staff on this issue. The July 1979 issue of the Commanders' Brief (which he had instituted as CAS) referred to the new Government's[14] decision to pay Air Commodores (i.e. one-star rank officers) and below the fully comparable military salary as being 'significant'. Furthermore, it went on to comment on the opening and closing paragraphs of the official announcement – viz, 'one of the Government's first tasks must be to stop the very damaging outflow of officers and men from the Armed Services', and 'having fulfilled its undertaking by restoring the pay of Servicemen to the levels of their counterparts, it is the Government's intention to maintain it thereafter at those levels' – by saying: 'It is recognised that the restoration of pay comparability is not a panacea which will remedy all our recruiting and retention problems. But it is a healthy start and we can now concentrate on improving other areas of conditions of service.'

Services' pay, though a major issue, was only one matter discussed by the Chiefs of Staff, the agenda for whose meetings was wide-ranging. In the 1977–79 period the overseas policy matters discussed included the situation in the Arabian/Persian Gulf following the overthrow of the Shah of Iran, the withdrawal from Malta and the garrisoning of Belize; defence policy topics included the implications of disarmament and arms control talks, the defence of the United Kingdom, the deployment of cruise missiles (of which Neil Cameron was a protagonist) and *The Way Ahead* – the wide-ranging review of British defence policy which he delivered at Oxford University on 25 October 1978 and which will be referred to later in this chapter; matters of equipment discussed included the future of the aircraft carrier HMS *Bulwark*, the AST 403 – the Air Staff Requirement for a Harrier/Jaguar replacement (subsequently amended to a Jaguar replacement) – and international collaborative projects; while manpower problems on the Chiefs' agenda included the Army's overstretch on its commitment and the RAF shortage of junior pilots.

It was not only the pay issue that involved Neil Cameron in Press and Parliamentary controversy during 1978; it also occurred over something he said while on a visit to China and again when he was quoted in an article in a theological college magazine.

His was 'the first visit by a Defence Chief from the NATO integrated military command structure' to the People's Republic of China, as he described it in a draft autobiographical account.[15]

My visit to The People's Republic of China started in the Ladies' 'loo' at the Savoy Hotel. The occasion was the annual dinner-dance of the defence attachés, at which I was the Guest of Honour. My wife noticed that the Chinese Defence Attaché's wife was being isolated in the conversation because she could not speak English. She was sad at this sign of neglect on such a festive occasion and, hoping for contact, engaged the lady in her somewhat halting French. She did not know that Madame Fang Wen had been in Paris with her husband when he was Defence Attaché there. (Indeed Henry Kissinger in his book *The White House Years* mentions the part that Fang Wen played in the negotiations over Cambodia and Vietnam. The friendship developed, and the next time they met was at a Diplomatic reception at Buckingham Palace. Madame Fang Wen insisted that we meet the Chinese Ambassador. He asked us if we had ever been to China. The answer was No, we had not, and he suggested that we make a visit. Feeling that this was a typical pleasantry, we forgot the incident, but the invitation was of a more serious nature, because within ten days I was being asked for dates when I could go. I was delighted to accept and planning started forthwith.

I got permission to go from the Secretary of State for Defence, who was then Fred Mulley, but I felt that the Foreign Office were a little concerned that I would get off the leash and embarrass them in some way. They asked me if I was prepared to take a senior Foreign Office official with me. I agreed to do so and they nominated Hugh Cortazzi, who was head of the Far East desk and had a good deal of experience in the area. (He has since been our Ambassador in Japan). He proved to be a great help.

I was due in any case to inspect our troops in Hong Kong, so a useful itinerary was arranged. I was to have three days in Hong Kong and then travel by Royal Air Force VC10 to Peking. The visit to Hong Kong went off as planned and it was fascinating to see the efforts that were being made to keep Chinese refugees from crossing over into the British Protectorate. The Gurkhas as usual were in splendid spirits. A great deal of interest was generated by my visit and the Press were particularly persistent. The day before I left Hong Kong for Peking I had a large Press conference in the Commander's Headquarters. I let the Press know that I was going there on the invitation of the Head of the Armed Forces of the People's Republic, and that I did not intend to get involved in political issues.

The Chinese insisted that two Chinese navigators should join the VC10 to make sure it got to Peking safely. As neither of them spoke any English, and did not understand the navigational equipment of the VC10, it seemed to be rather a symbolic gesture.

Upon their arrival on 27 April they were met by a 'long line of dignitaries' and 'much handshaking took place'. The subsequent drive into the city by motorcade – 'down the centre of the road with horns blaring' – took forty-five minutes and they were accommodated in Diao Yu Tai No 6, one of seven Government Guest Houses in a large park some ten minutes' drive from the city centre. 'We were honoured to be accommodated in No 6 – normally reserved only for Presidents (President Nixon had stayed there on his recent visit)', Neil Cameron noted. He described in detail the 'standard welcoming ceremony' there – one 'with which we were to be greeted on many subsequent occasions during our trip':

Two long lines of sofas and armchairs were drawn up on either side of the room with small tables set out with sweets, cigarettes, fruit and Chinese tea – in traditional hatted tea-cups. The older Chinese are relatively heavy smokers and many of our hosts chain-smoked.

When all were seated our host made a short informal speech of welcome. We were issued with our programmes and then invited to find our rooms and have a 'rest' – a short one as twenty minutes later we were once again in our numbered cars (which the Chinese were particular that we stayed with) on our way to the Welcoming Banquet.

The rooms in the Guest House conveyed an impression of 1920s Grand Hotel style, with contemporary furniture to match – heavy carpets, heavy curtains and low lights. In each sitting-room were glass-fronted cabinets displaying magnificent items of pottery and glass. Then there were the cigarettes, the sweets, the fruit and the Chinese tea set out on a table. An enormous desk held all forms of stationery and sets of picture postcards. The bathrooms, built to palatial standards, were complete with every form of bathroom fitting and a vast range of toilet requisites.

That evening there was a welcoming banquet in the Great Hall of the People; the host was Yang Yung, senior Deputy Chief of the General Staff, and he and his military colleagues were assembled to meet their British guests at the door:

Handshakes all round and we took our places at the numbered tables. On the floor was a magnificent Chinese carpet measuring about 100ft by 30ft and in one corner a traditional Chinese vase, about eight feet tall.

During the banquet Yang Yung made a welcoming speech. He referred to the increasing contacts between China and the United Kingdom, each with its own different social system. Such differences should not affect the formation of a lasting friendship between the two countries, based on five principles of co-existence: admiration for the United Kingdom's independent spirit in its Second World War fight against fascism; the friendly contacts between the two Armed Forces which began with the Chinese visit to the Royal College of Defence Studies in 1977; the conflict between the two Super Powers with Europe as the key point; the inevitability of war; and the long march which the people of China were starting to modernise agriculture, science, technology, education and their military forces. Then the toasts – to the Queen, the Prime Minister, the Secretary of State for Defence, myself and my wife, Colonel and Mrs Jenkins[16] and other distinguished British visitors and guests.

I had to reply, and said how much we had been looking forward to our visit. I spoke of the interest created in the United Kingdom by it, the good progress in defence relations and our offer to the Chinese to come to Britain, the opportunity to discuss questions of defence philosophy and mutual defence interest, the chance to visit units of the People's Liberation Army and to see something of the great achievements of the Chinese people.

Then, after eating our way through nine or ten delicious courses, we returned to the Guest House immediately the banquet was finished. This was one of the advantages of Chinese hospitality: once a meal was ended, everyone went home.

Neil Cameron and his party had talks with the PLA (People's Liberation Army) leaders, led by Yang Yung and Wu Hsiu-Chuan, another of the Deputy Chiefs of the General Staff. Also present were the Director and his Deputy of the Foreign Affairs Bureau (FAB) of the Ministry of National Defence, one of the FAB Divisional Chiefs and Fang Wen, Chinese Defence Attaché in London[17]:

I was invited to speak first. I described the Soviet forces and their increasing modernisation. In answer to a question from Yang Yung I explained the NATO policy of deterrence, concluding with some indication of the new equipments we in the United Kingdom would be introducing into our Armed Forces.

Yang Yung in turn talked of the danger of confrontation between the Super Powers. He said that the Chinese considered that war was inevitable, not necessarily within three or five or ten years, but when the Soviet Union had accomplished its 'strategic position'. This war could be postponed but was still inevitable. The Chinese attitude towards this was 'firstly they were against it and secondly they were not afraid of it'. They would carry out Chairman Mao's policy – to prepare for war, 'dig deep tunnels, store grain everywhere and not seek hegemony'. They would dig networks of tunnels under every city to give everyone somewhere to shelter.

I extended a warm invitation to the Chinese to send delegations to the British Army Equipment Exhibition and the Farnborough Air Show that year, and to the Naval Exhibition in 1979.

CDS and his party were entertained that evening at a reception and banquet hosted by Vice-Premier Hsu Hsiang Chien, Minister of Defence, again in the Great Hall of the People. Greeted at the imposing North Door, they were escorted to the Banqueting Hall:

All the tables were circular and were numbered. Place-names displaying a fine standard of calligraphy were always used at these banquets. The first course, consisting of an assortment of cold dishes, was invariably laid out in advance. Individual hosts would take a selection from these plates and serve their guests, and as each course proceeded, top up their plates. It was expected that you would serve one of your hosts in this way from time to time.

To drink, there was usually a choice of beer or fizzy squash, with Chinese wine and Maotai (a white spirit made from millet or sorghum, of about the same strength as whisky). After one or two courses the principal Chinese host would make a speech of welcome. At its end he would invariably invite the party to 'gan bei' (literally, 'empty your glass' – which was not very large, but the custom was not strictly observed every time). Before drinking, the principal host at each table would clink glasses with all the guests and, following his speech, usually do a round of the other tables, toasting the visitors at each one.

After one or two more courses I made my speech in reply. I had to clink glasses with the Chinese at my table, and do the rounds to toast those at other tables. Throughout the meal, other members of both parties offered toasts at their tables and at other tables.

Of course, with the British party outnumbered at each table by up to six to one, it was not uncommon to be 'gan bei'd' on a dozen or more occasions. However, providing that Maotai and Chinese wine were not mixed, there was little after-effect the following day.

The speciality of this particular banquet was Peking Duck. We ate our way solemnly and steadily (and latterly unsteadily) through the claws, the feet, the tongue, the stomach, the lungs, the liver, the meat, finally reaching the greatest delicacy – the skin, crisp and dry and served with spring onion, rolled-up in a small pancake or inside a small bun covered with sesame seed. It was all quite delicious.

Again the welcoming speech by the Minister of Defence, and my reply. There was no doubt that the status accorded to CDS throughout this banquet was growing, as it would continue to grow throughout the visit.

On the following day (Saturday, 29 April) the visitors saw some of the practical results of Chairman Mao's advice to his people to 'dig tunnels deep and store grain every-where':

After the usual early rise we were driven in our motorcade to visit the Underground City. In Da Cha Sha Jie ('Jie' is Chinese for 'street') we parked outside what appeared to be an ordinary clothing store, though as yet there were few customers. The manager pressed a button behind one of the counters and a large trap door slid open, revealing lighted steps leading downwards – one of the entrances to the Underground City.

The present system was started in 1969, following a clash on the USSR/China border. This particular section was part of the much larger system covering practically the whole of Peking. We were told that about 10,000 people could be accommodated in this part, going down through some 90 entrances.

Generally, underground facilities duplicated those on the surface immediately above: for example, the dispensary was below the hospital and the kitchen below a similar one on the surface. The complex comprised kitchens, dining-rooms, and assembly areas with their own generators for power and with crude air filtration. Local wells had been dug within the system to provide fresh water, and in due course food storage areas were to be completed. The Government provided only the technical equipment – 'those things that you can make with your own hands, do not ask the Government for'. The actual digging was done by local voluntary groups in their spare time.

The total Peking system, said to be some 30km long, could accommodate four million people, and it was estimated that this number could be underground within five/six minutes following a loudspeaker warning. We were told that some practices were held, but it was not clear how these were organised.

Our hosts told us that there were similar underground tunnel systems beneath all the major Chinese cities.

After visiting Shenyang (formerly Mukden, principal city of what used to be called Manchuria), being shown round an aircraft factory there and being given a briefing on the USSR/China border situation by the Deputy Commander of the Shenyang Military Region, the British visitors attended a banquet hosted by the Region Commander and afterwards attended an evening performance given by the PLA acrobatic troupe – whose acts, CDS noted, 'were among the best I had ever seen'.

He and his colleagues had on the following day (Sunday, 30 April) an opportunity of seeing something of the Chinese Air Force when they flew by Trident to Yang-chun, HQ of 38 Air Division, where they were briefed on its role by Wang Chen-Hsiao, Divisional Commander, and watched a flying display by some of its F-6s (Chinese copy of the Russian MiG-19, produced at Shenyang). With an expert RAF eye he appraised their aerobatic capability:

The flying display opened with a solo performance by an F-6, lasting about eight minutes. The flying was smooth and the manoeuvres well executed, although the area covered was about five miles off either end of the main runway, with a considerable pause between each manoeuvre while the aircraft was re-positioned. The manoeuvres were mostly in the vertical plane and white smoke was used effectively to give trails from the wing-tips.

Once the solo aircraft had landed, two pairs of F-6s took off, joined up and gave a formation display. Although only two basic formations were flown – a Box Four and a Swan Four, position-keeping was good but with wider spacing than with British teams, and formation changes were executed relatively slowly. The performance lasted about ten minutes and was completed by a well-executed bomb-burst.

The aircraft then attacked ground targets on the far side of the airfield in low-angle strafing attacks at about 30-second intervals. This live firing looked impressive, but as the targets were flat on the ground it was not possible to see how successful the attacks were.

In describing his Yang-chun visit, CDS took the opportunity of mentioning the off-the-cuff remarks he would be called upon to make on such occasions, like those which got him into trouble on 1 May when he visited No 6 Tank Division near Peking. After the F-6 display:

We then went in to lunch, following the previous routine of having a short 'rest' first for refreshments. Each of these visits usually entailed a number of short 'public utterances' by myself, for which there was little hope of preparing anything in advance.

The start of any visit, on disembarking from the aircraft or cars, usually called for a short greeting. Then the party assembled in an ante-room, and after formal introductions, another few words would be called for. After the visit there was usually another rest and again some public pronouncement might be made, possibly a frankly expressed wish by the Chinese to tell them where they were behind the times and what they should do about it. Then there would be a lunch, or dinner, and again a speech was required before the toasts – which fortunately came early on in the meal. I was thus required to say something in public on a number of occasions each day, and it was only possible to prepare in any formal sense for the evening banquets.

When the British party got back to Peking that afternoon, CDS was told that time had been set aside for him to meet an important member of the Government, and 'the summons came shortly after 4.30':

We re-dressed in our uniforms, embarked in our cavalcade of cars and left for the Great Hall of the People. Only when we were on the move were we told that the meeting would be with the Chairman himself.

Hua Kuo Feng, who held the triple title of Chairman of the Central Committee, Premier of the State Council and Chairman of the Military Commission, was waiting for us at the door of the ante-room. Reporters and TV cameras were also present. The Chairman and his officials lined up at the entrance of the Hall and shook hands with each member of our party, including the two ladies. We then assembled in a vast semi-circle of arm-chairs for the preliminary exchange of courtesies and the now-customary group photograph. The ladies and the Press then left and the meeting – which was to last 1½ hours – started. We were told that this was the first occasion the Chairman had met a visiting military delegation and the longest talks he had held since becoming Chairman.

His welcome was extremely warm. 'This is only the beginning', he said. 'You have second, third and fourth occasions to visit China. You have honoured us with a military visit and at the proper time we will send appropriate delegations to visit your country'.

For the next 45 minutes the Chairman gave an impressive resumé of world affairs, emphasising in particular how a strong, united Europe was seen as important to China. 'A single chopstick breaks easily but a bundle is very much stronger', he observed. 'A single finger is weak but a clenched fist is strong'. We then had a wide-ranging discussion: he had a good grasp of world affairs, and we left the meeting feeling that there was no doubt that the hospitality and status afforded to our visit were far in excess of anything we had imagined.

On 1 May, after visiting the Great Wall – a fortification over 2,000 years old which stretches for 6,000km from the deserts of Western China eastwards to the sea, the British delegation went to the training area of No 6 Tank Division, 'whose task is to guard the approaches of Peking':

Again we walked between the ranks of clapping, flag-waving soldiers, partly hidden in the clouds of swirling dust, to a building overlooking the training area. Here, from the balcony, we watched the first part of a demonstration of heavy and light Chinese-built tanks covering high-speed driving, obstacle crossing and live firing. We then drove to a different part of the training area where seats had been arranged in a bowl surrounded on three sides by steep hills and where we watched the second part of the demonstration, of hill-climbing performance and manoeuvrability. We then had a chance to talk to the crews and look at their hardware.

From there we drove back to the HQ building and Mess for lunch, during which we discussed with our hosts the philosophy and concept of their tank operations, comparing their problems with those on the Central Front in Europe.

It was on this occasion that, in reply to a speech of welcome by the Divisional Commander, I made my well-reported remarks. I do not recall my actual words, which were an impromptu response to a toast made at the luncheon by the Political Commissar. However, a British Press Association reporter was present, and my remark that Britain and China 'both have a common enemy whose capital is Moscow' caught his fancy and was soon on the wire to London. Subsequently the reporter repeated the remark to me for confirmation, but did so in a manner which gave the impression that it was a paraphrase rather than a quote. Nevertheless, something very close to the alleged remark was made, so I considered that it would be inappropriate to deny it. It did cause a good few disturbances in the middle of the night for the remaining days of our visit – mostly answering questions from Downing Street and the Ministry of Defence.

Returning to Peking shortly after 3 o'clock, we changed and left for the British Embassy to hold a Press conference for the British reporters (*Daily Telegraph*, BBC and Reuters). I then briefed the EEC representatives. The German, Dutch and Danish Ambassadors were present, together with councillors from the French, Belgian and Italian Embassies – a good turnout for a public holiday.

After a visit to Shanghai on 2 May the British delegation was entertained to a banquet by the Far East Fleet, and saw the Fleet itself on 3 May before returning to Hong Kong.

CDS summed up his impressions of the visit by saying:

We were given quite exceptional treatment by the Chinese, genuinely warm and friendly and becoming more so as the visit progressed and we came to know our hosts better. I was accorded an outstandingly warm welcome. The senior Chinese officials said that 'protocol could do no more'. The visit was a memorable experience for us all, and certainly achieved its purpose of furthering defence relations between the United Kingdom and China.[18]

A warm welcome awaited Neil Cameron on his return to London – for different reasons. On 2 May *The Times* had reported that 'Labour left-wingers yesterday demanded the dismissal of Marshal of the RAF Sir Neil Cameron, Chief of the Defence Staff, for his suggestion in Peking that Britain and China had 'a common enemy at the door' in the Soviet Union. But', it went on to say, 'Dr David Owen, the Foreign Secretary, said he did not think the remarks would alienate Russia.' Clearly a storm had blown up in the Press and Parliament, and on 2 May the Prime Minister told MPs that British policy towards Russia and China would not be changed by CDS's remark about 'the common enemy' in Moscow. *Pravda* had demanded an early explanation from Britain for what it called his 'inflammatory' speech. In his replies to Questions, Mr Callaghan said that he gathered that Sir Neil Cameron 'was responding to a spontaneous toast by the local commander of the unit he was visiting, and he made an unscripted and impromptu reply'. His remarks 'should not be regarded as altering, extending, modifying or changing in any way our present relationships between Britain and China or between Britain and the Soviet Union'.

On 3 May there were further Soviet Press attacks on CDS, Tass calling his statement 'provocative, instigatory and openly anti-Soviet', *Izvestia* saying that for decades he had been rehearsing speeches with a definite tendency – to maintain the Cold War – and *Pravda* comparing him with a 'drunken hare', a reference to the fable about the hare which gets drunk and boasts that he is not afraid of anyone, even of a lion.

Neil Cameron and his party arrived back in London on 4 May, and the following day he was 'gently carpeted' (as *The Times* put it) by the Minister of Defence, Mr Mulley, 'seeking and receiving' confirmation that CDS 'understood the convention that policy matters should be left to Government Ministers'. For his part, CDS explained that his remarks were made 'off the cuff' in reply to an impromptu toast; there had been no question of his wanting to depart from Government policy.

By chance, shortly after the fuss over the China visit, an article appeared quoting some remarks by CDS about the Soviet Union – based on an interview he had given several months previously to *Areopagus*, the student magazine of the London Bible College. He was quoted as saying, 'Goodness knows the number of Jews being exterminated in the Soviet Union', and that, 'If one is looking at the situation from the point of view of this country's survival or of accepting the Anti-Christ of the Soviet Union, I just happen to believe my faith is worth fighting for.'

On 15 May the Secretary of State for Foreign and Commonwealth Affairs, in a Written Answer to a Parliamentary Question asking whether CDS's interview with *Areopagus* had been approved by his Department, said firmly that Sir Neil Cameron's remarks 'were his personal views, expressed in a private capacity'; and on 23 May the Secretary of State for Defence, asked what criteria he used 'to determine whether Chiefs of Defence Staff should be dismissed', said (again in a Written Answer): 'The essential requirement for the tenure of office of a Chief of the Defence Staff is that he should retain the confidence of Her Majesty's Government. Sir Neil Cameron retains that confidence.'[19]

In an article in the *Daily Express*[20] at the time of the 'China incident' Chapman Pincher had written:

Sir Neil is a man of fairly humble origins. His father, an assistant inspector of poor people's homes in Perth, died young and there was just enough money to buy the boy's uniform for Perth Academy.

He later worked as a bank clerk and joined the RAF just before the outbreak of war in 1939.

About 25 years ago he fought back from a dangerous heart ailment – believed to be the result of combat stress.

While many would have taken the opportunity to retire, he went on to the top of his profession.

In many respects, he was chosen to head the Chiefs of Staff because of that courage.

When he displays it now in the interests of his Forces, his

country and the freedom of the West he should be lauded, not censured.

Soon afterwards a flow of various delegations from the People's Republic started arriving in this country to visit UK military units and to see something of the defence industries. These visits were a great success and culminated in a visit of Mr Yang Yung himself. He was then seventy three. He was Neil Cameron's nearest equivalent as Deputy Chief of Staff of the People's Liberation Army (this included all three services). He had been on the Long March, from which his feet never recovered, and had been Commander-in-Chief in Korea. His wife, who accompanied him, was a Moslem. Neil Cameron regarded them highly, and arranged a fairly full week for them.

When Neil Cameron visited Iran, during his last months as CDS, he was sailing in slightly less stormy water politically. He was there only a few months before the collapse of the Shah's regime, and his own clear and concise account (hitherto unpublished) records the impression the country and its armed forces made on him:

In 1979 I received an official invitation to visit Iran from my opposite number there, the Chief of the Defence Staff.

It was a particularly interesting period because of the large scale arms sales by the United Kingdom to Iran, many firms in Britain having or negotiating large contracts with that country.

It was a time also of a great build-up in the Iranian armed forces, and there was much expectation in the West that Iran would become a strong force for peace and a deterrent to others in the Persian Gulf area.

Teheran was never my favourite place, but in Iran itself there are many delightful areas. The mountains overlooking the capital can be very beautiful.

I was particularly interested, when getting to know my opposite number and his Chiefs of Staff, in the tremendous veneration they held for the Shah. One felt that no decision was ever taken unless he had actually put his personal stamp on it. The subsequent collapse of the Iranian armed forces came as a great surprise when it actually happened, because I felt at the time of my visit that they had a fair grip on the situation.

I was privileged to have a session – a long one, indeed – with the Shah, and after giving him my greetings from the Royal Air

Force (of which he was an Honorary Air Chief Marshal) we got down to an hour-and-a-half's discussion on the effect of the Iranian arms programme on the balance of power in the area, and on some of the strategic issues affecting the West.

His detailed knowledge of military equipment was quite staggering: not just of airborne systems but also of naval and army ones – in the most minute detail, their performance was at his fingertips, and one had to remain on one's toes to stay with his line of argument. He seemed completely relaxed, and one felt later – recalling the interview – that he could have had no real idea of the situation which was facing Iran.

Within three months he had been swept away, and I cannot but believe that there were indications to him that all was not well. He gave me a long lecture about the 'indiscretions' of the BBC Overseas Service in broadcasting 'revolutionary material' to his people, ending with the command: 'Go back to England and tell them they must stop it'. I promised to do all I could. Sir Anthony Parsons' book (which I read subsequently) admits that the advice he had given at that difficult time had been wrong.[21] The same applied to the US Ambassador.

The Shah encouraged me to get out and see some of the great technological developments which were taking place in Iran: the fine new buildings and factories which had been put up in the desert, where all amenities had been provided. This we did, and were suitably impressed.

We also had a tour of air, naval and army units, and I was impressed by the number of aircraft that were available and seemed to be in flying condition. We also saw the large-scale training scheme for all three Services, particularly the Royal Iranian Air Force. We visited Shiraz, Isfahan and other important areas and inspected units there.

A few weeks later it was a shock to see in the British papers photographs of the first victims of the Ayatollah Khomeini's persecution – naked bodies laid out, among them that of the Commander of the Shiraz area, General Heim, whom I had dined with during our visit and who was one of the first to be massacred.

We also visited the great tented camp which had been constructed at Persepolis for the great celebrations of the longevity of the Peacock Throne.

In all, I was impressed by the tremendous steps which had been taken in Iran to modernise the country.

Some months later, reading the telegrams which were coming out of Teheran, I confess to having been surprised by the extent to which the situation had deteriorated, even when I was there. Looking back, it seems that the Shah had two options: one, to put the army into the streets and brutally suppress the Khomeini revolution; the other, to leave the country and allow it to develop as the mob wished. He did neither, until forced to leave. Perhaps many of the people are having second thoughts.

I have already mentioned the speed with which the military disintegrated when the Shah refused to allow them their head to put down the revolution. Clearly many of them were concerned about the probable outcome if Khomeini were once established, and the exodus from the armed forces was quite staggering. No doubt many of the senior officers had lined their pockets from large contracts negotiated with the United States, Britain and other countries, and soon found it necessary to disappear with their gains to the United States and elsewhere.

The Khomeini revolution produced a totally different strategic situation in that part of the world. With the large-scale Soviet forces on Iran's northern border, and with the post-war annexation of Azerbaijan in mind, one was conscious that the possibility of a Russian intervention in the event of an Iranian collapse would be of great strategic significance to the British and should be watched by the West.

Exactly what the West – largely in the shape of the United States – would do if the Soviet Union moved into the oilfields of Iran, is a matter of speculation. But it is not an easy strategic situation, even now that the United States have developed their Rapid Deployment Force.[22]

My last sight of Iran was from the airfield. The RAF VC10 was waiting to fly me out, and a large guard of honour, headed by the Chief of the Defence Staff and all his Chiefs of Staff, bade me a formal farewell. Within three or four months, all these officers had disappeared.

Meetings of the Defence Council and of the Chiefs of Staff Committee, and trips abroad, were two of the three main strands of Neil Cameron's two years as CDS: the third was his defence lecturing. In all he gave thirty-six lectures, of one kind or another, ranging from big formal occasions like a speech on British Defence Policy – *The Way Ahead* at Oxford University on 25 October 1978 – or one at the Chinese Embassy on 15 May of that year when he thanked his hosts for their hospitality during his visit to China, to speeches at the Oxford University Air Squadron dinner on 15 February 1978 or at the Sportsman of the Year Dinner in Edinburgh in January 1979, when he paid tribute to Scottish Regiments serving in Northern Ireland.

His paper on British defence policy in October 1978 typified his mature style as a speaker – characterised by wide-ranging views, the use of his first-hand experiences in China, Iran and the Far East to illustrate his themes, and his encouragement to his audience to express their own opinions.

The Way Ahead – which he himself described in an interview after his retirement[23] as a 'very important' paper – ranged over every contemporary aspect of political, international and economic affairs affecting defence policy: the growth of Soviet military capability (one of his constant themes) and its effect on the Russians themselves; the problem of energy supplies; the strategic importance of the Middle East; the impact of China on the world scene; the evolving situation in Africa; the problems of defence planning; NATO and the American commitment to Europe; British defence philosophy and technological changes.

Four times during this lecture he made references to subsequent discussion: he was always keen on the give-and-take of question-and-answer sessions, and he wanted to stimulate defence thinking and the expression of views in the Services.

On 9 May 1979 the Chiefs of Staff held a briefing for the new Ministers of the Conservative Administration returned to power as a result of the General Election on the 3 May: Secretary of State Francis Pym, Minister of State Lord Strathcona and Parliamentary Under-Secretaries Keith Speed, Barney Heyhoe and Geoffrey Pattie for the Royal Navy, Army and RAF respectively. This was the first time Neil Cameron had served in a senior post under a Conservative Government: in his PEG days, as ACDS (Pol), as AMP and as CAS and initially as CDS he had worked for Labour Ministers.

In his very last speech as Chief of the Defence Staff, an address to the RAF Club Dining Society on 27 June 1979, he made light-hearted reference to the 'leak' of figures of retirements from the Services and to the 'China incident', when he said that 1978–79 had been 'an interesting period':

> I didn't think Marshals of the RAF got put on carpets, but I managed to achieve two during that period: once as a solo effort for giving the Chinese a geography lesson; the other as leader of the Chiefs of Staff 'Gang of Four' on the last year's pay review.
>
> The China visit, it seemed, got some coverage in the Soviet and British Press and I now have a close association with the Soviet Press. *Pravda* has called me 'a drunken hare from darkest Albion'. When I got back from China I had a letter from a distinguished academic[24] who wrote that he 'didn't know which was the biggest insult, to be called "a drunken hare" by *Pravda* or "an intellectual" by the *Daily Express*'. Now, after a speech in Australia recently[25] Tass has called me 'this bellicose Cameron, the indefatigable firebrand'. Another Soviet newspaper has written: 'He knows nothing about the Services and is only seen on parades or reviews. From the professional point of view he is the most ignorant officer in Europe . . .'

Subsequently in this speech he again ranged over the whole gamut of the contemporary defence scene.

When he spoke at a seminar at King's College, London, on 13 November 1978 on 'The Priorities of British Defence Policy in the 1980s' – not realising then that he would return there as Principal in 1980 – he again made use of his recent personal experiences to highlight his views of the world scene.

'During a visit to Iran earlier this year', he said, 'the importance of the area was brought home to me and Iran was likened to "an island in a sea of strategic uncertainty". Since then there has been the coup in Afghanistan (with the Russians now a little closer to their long-term aim of direct access to the Indian Ocean), while the recent political troubles in Iran have further highlighted the political fragility of the area'. He went on:

> But no overview – however brief – of the world's scene today would be complete without reference to China, and the part this great country has to play in global strategic considerations. In my quite fascinating discussions with Chairman Hua . . . I

was treated to a masterly discourse on the Chinese appreciation of the developing world scene.

Hua strongly put across the point that he thought another
World War was inevitable and that a likely flashpoint was
Europe, and that only the extent of advanced preparations
would delay the outbreak. He also believed that China
and Western Europe could work together regardless of the
differences in political systems . . .

When speaking to the Joint Services Staff College and
RAAF Staff College on 13 October 1978 during his visit to
Australia and New Zealand, Neil Cameron reiterated one
of his most constant themes, the growth of Soviet military
power, which he said had been 'transformed from one
that was continental in character and scope' to one that
was now 'global in capability and increasingly offensive in
character'.

He made particular reference to the cruise missile, a
weapon for which he clearly had a high regard, saying that
the Soviets were worried about it

> as the number of cruise missiles that may be deployed against
> them could swamp and outflank their present air defence
> system, and with an estimated 500,000 personnel already
> employed in the air defence of the Soviet Union they have good
> cause to be concerned about the cruise. They hope to trap it, or
> limit its effectiveness, in some form of SALT agreement, and
> so far they have had some success. The West must be very
> careful not to lose the initiative they have in this most potent
> weapon.

He also reminded his Australian audience of the need for
military thinkers – another of his favourite themes:

> In some military circles it has become unfashionable to think
> deeply about the wider aspects of the defence and strategic
> scene. To those of you who will shortly be taking your first
> adult steps towards a military career, I would commend to you
> the need to cultivate and maintain the habit of thinking about
> the broader aspects of Service life. Initially of course you will be
> fully occupied just learning the basics of your profession; but
> do not let these pressures overwhelm the need for positive
> thought.

Here he was preaching what he himself had practised throughout the higher reaches of his Service career; it was his ability as a speaker and writer about RAF and Defence matters that had brought him to the attention of Andrew Humphrey and to his advancement to the Air Force Board and then to the post of CAS. His appointment as CDS had been, through tragic circumstances, in one sense fortuitous but nevertheless well deserved. How successful had he been?

When he made his last speech as CDS, an address to the RAF Club Dining Society on 27 June 1979 (already mentioned), he said to the members: 'It is always a pleasure to be in this Club of ours. There is a secure feeling of belonging and of being amongst the family . . .' In his familiar RAF world, as AMP and then as CAS, he had felt thoroughly at home; it was one he had lived in, and thought about, for nearly forty years. As CDS he was out on his own, speaking for the whole military establishment and much more vulnerable; but because of his courage and outspokenness – derived from his years of leadership dating back to wartime days – he made the office and its occupant better known to the public at large than it probably had been since the days of Lord Mountbatten, who was a charismatic figure in his own right.

Neil Cameron's leadership of the Chiefs of Staff over the Forces' pay issue, and his habit of never being afraid to say what he thought – as in the 'China incident' – brought him a certain notoriety in the Press and Parliament; he could be called a bold CDS because of his honesty. In his speeches, when what he said had been carefully considered and written down, he was more judicious but nevertheless hard-hitting in his views. As a military thinker, he took a global view, and he gave his mind and energy tirelessly to the exposition of military themes. Perhaps his thinking was not profound, but it was clear and strongly felt. He had the physique and bearing to impress his audiences and to give conviction to his words. The strength of his expression was verbal rather than literary: he was a speaker rather than a writer.

The Chiefs of Staff liked him, and he united them on crucial issues. The politicians, while they liked him personally and admired his character, were less sure of his political judgement: both the Prime Minister and the Minister of Defence had to defend him in the House of Commons.

In his two years as CDS, Neil Cameron worked hard and enthusiastically: he seems to have enjoyed his tenure of the post. Had he served for a full term, his activities might have made an even greater impact: certainly he made a positive and distinctive contribution to British military affairs.

Notes

1. Interview with Lord Mulley by the Head of AHB, 31 July 1985.

2. DCM(77) first meeting.

3. Interview with MRAF Sir Michael Beetham by the Head of AHB, 17 July 1985.

4. See chapter, 'On being a Christian' for Cameron's reaction on being asked to become CDS.

5. Interview with Sir Frank Cooper, former PUS, MOD, by the Head of AHB and the writer, 29 July 1985.

6. Future Role of the Defence Council – Commanders' Brief, January 1977.

7. At the peak of the operation some 20,000 Servicemen were involved. The Services' assistance continued until mid-January 1978 and they were involved in 39,612 incidents (*Statement on the Defence Estimates 1978*, Cmnd 7099).

8. In *RAF News*, 3–16 August 1977 issue.

9. Hansard, 22 May 1978, Cols 1131–1136.

10. Interview with the Head of AHB, 17 July 1985.

11. Interview with the Head of AHB, 31 July 1985.

12. Hansard, 16 May 1978, Col 104.

13. I.e. covering the special exigencies of Services life, like weekend duties and overseas deployments.

14. In the General Election on 3 May 1979 a Conservative Government was returned to power with Mrs Margaret Thatcher as Prime Minister.

15. A long (unpublished) description of the visit to China, from which these extracts are taken. The CDS was accompanied by Lady Cameron, Brigadier J. L. Chapple (PSO), Wing Commander J. D. Davis (Briefer), Flight Lieutenant J. C. French (ADC) and H. A. H. Cortazzi (DUS, Foreign and Commonwealth Office).

16. Col M. W. Jenkins, British Defence Attaché in Peking.

17. Who had been involved in the original arrangements for the visit, 'Subtle, but immensely courteous, inquiries were made by the Chinese authorities in London, mainly through their Defence Attaché, Mr Fang Wen.'

18. At the end of the draft autobiographical account of his visit to China Neil Cameron had noted in handwriting: 'Fuss in London Chinese terms for defence sales and "sack Cameron".'

19. Commons Hansard, Written Answers, 15 and 23 May 1978, respectively.

20. 3 May 1978, in which a leading article commented that what CDS 'said in Peking about the Russian threat was right, and if it helps to focus public attention on that threat he will have rendered a useful service'.

21. Sir Anthony Parsons *The Pride and Fall: Iran, 1974–1979* (Jonathan Cape, 1984), in which Sir Anthony says that 'our lack of perception derived not from a failure of information but from a failure to interpret correctly the information available to us. We were looking down the right telescope but were focused on the wrong target.'

22. Operation Eagle Claw, mounted by Delta Force on 24–26 April 1980 to rescue US hostages in the American Embassy in Teheran, failed disastrously through unserviceabilities and when two of the aircraft collided.

23. Interview with Air Commodore R. A. Mason at the RAF Staff College, Bracknell on 23 July 1980.

24. Professor Michael Howard.

25. To the Joint Services Staff College, RAAF Staff College and Senior Class of RMC Duntroon, 13 October 1978.

16 KING'S COLLEGE

The appointment of Principals to King's College tends to be accompanied by a mixture of equal parts of secrecy and speculation. The speculation is a sign of the healthy interest which academics properly take in their future leaders. The confidentiality which often surrounds senior academic appointments is much deepened by the involvement of the Prime Minister of the day and the Queen in what is, appropriately, a royal appointment.

This tells one much about the King's to which Sir Neil Cameron came as Principal on 1 August 1980. The College was founded in 1829 under the distinguished patronage of the Duke of Wellington, and by Royal Charter granted by George IV. University College, founded one year earlier, offered for the first time in England, outside Oxford and Cambridge, a university education. More importantly there were no religious tests or conditions of admission laid down. Although this brought university education within the range of Free Churchmen as well as free-thinkers, the influence of Bentham was perceived by many to be the guiding light at University College. Many established and worthy citizens of London valued the freedom to have their children educated to this level in London, but were reluctant to commit them to what might turn out to be a radical institution. Their response, under the leadership of the Duke of Wellington was to found a College which to this day enshrines in its Charter the following aim: '. . . to provide instruction of a university standard and to superintend postgraduate studies and to promote research in such branches of learning as may from time to time be determined by the Council and to provide instruction in the doctrines and duties of Christianity'.

The College was granted a Charter and lease of Crown

land to the east of Somerset House, and there it continues as one of the founding institutions of the University of London. For the four and a half years from 1980 until his death Neil Cameron gave unstintingly of his time, his experience, and his energy to the College and to the University of London. It is arguable that he steered the College through the most exacting and crucial period of its history since its foundation.

Sir Neil was the third successive Principal to be drawn to King's from outside the academic world, and one can only guess at some of the reasons which had led them from such different positions as BAOR (British Army of the Rhine), the Civil Service and the Ministry of Defence. General Sir John Hackett (1967–75) had of course a lifelong academic interest in classics, which could be more fully enjoyed as Principal of King's than as C-in-C BAOR. That King's has a distinguished Department of War Studies must have been an attraction to the former Chief of Defence Staff, but there were other much more compelling factors.

Without doubt Sir Neil was looking for a new challenge. Throughout his career he had found changes of direction a stimulus rather than a distraction and so it was to be for his time at King's. He was conscious of the fact that for reasons already given, he had not had a university education and he believed passionately in the value of training and education in depth. In his own words:

> The academic world always intrigued me. I have always encouraged my children to become expert in something however narrow the apparent specialization. (We had an expert in newts at King's and he was an international expert in the subject. People came to consult him from all over the world.) I also wanted to know if I could cope with an academic environment as head of a fair-sized College. To put it in another way I was trying to prove myself particularly because I had not had a University education, and the question was constantly at the back of my mind that I could have made University all right if it had not been for an extraordinary aberration in my learning when I was in my teens.

Academics being no different from civil servants or air transport units, they expect new leaders to prove themselves – however distinguished their careers in other fields. The new Principal found his opportunity within weeks of arriving. However, before turning to that, mention should be made of two further attractions which the post had for Sir Neil. The first has been well-foreshadowed in previous chapters. He cared deeply about young people, their welfare and their training – be it pilots entrusted to his command in some of the most gruelling theatres of war, or trainee officers at Cranwell, or the links with University Air Squadrons which he clearly relished.

A further attraction which was to be found in King's was its Christian foundation and the ethos which goes with that. Of course the college Charter permits no religious tests in student admission or staff appointments or bias in teaching, but Neil Cameron took a particular delight in such facts as that the major religious services at the beginning of term were packed out, or that the voluntary lecture series for the Associateship of King's College, on issues of a religious and theological nature, enrolled over five hundred students in his final year at College.

His decisiveness and his own sense of values and priorities were soon brought to bear on an issue being discussed within the College in the summer of 1980. Some were arguing that since 'times had changed' and although the College had a strong Faculty of Theology it no longer offered a full ordination training, the post of Dean of the College should either be scrapped or demoted to a part-time post. Sir Neil had no doubt in his mind that any such step would be retrograde and quickly banished any uncertainty on the matter. Soon after followed the excellent full-time appointment of the Rev Richard Harries as Dean of the College.

There are various ways of proving one's mettle amongst academics. Traditionally the most obvious way is through careful scholarship or innovative research, although these days raising large sums of money seems to be vying with these as 'performance indicators'. There is however a further rather different, albeit less externally ostentatious way of winning one's spurs – to protect the institution or one of its prize parts from external predators and to drive the invaders away.

Came the man, came the issue. Earlier in 1980 a University of London working party had recommended the closure of the King's pre-clinical Medical Faculty as part of a package reorganisation of medicine within London. Now one of the facts of academic life is that however much battles take place internally between Faculties over resource-allocation etc., in the face of external dangers ranks close, and King's was ready to do battle. Sir Neil led the attack from the front and the result was total victory. In an exceptional maiden speech to his first meeting of the Senate of the University of London he demonstrated to one and all within the College, and more widely in the University, that King's had a new and formidable Principal.

Nonetheless there was much to be learnt about the ways of academe and Sir Neil's own comments on his first reactions to both students and staff are worth noting:

In the Service of course there was the 'system' of rank and status (however false) to support you, but in dealing with students, being a Marshal of the Royal Air Force meant absolutely nothing and it was every man or woman for themselves. To discuss the issues of the day with twenty-five left wing students was an exciting experience and I learnt much. Having watched my son's politics and views move from extreme left wing to slightly right wing Conservatism it was reasonable to feel that the same would happen to those who regularly confronted me. Generally this happens and it is all part and parcel of a University education, but there is always the hard core who never change their views and go on to be lifelong protesters or anarchists. I have seen some excellent talent wasted in this way to the extent that no one when they heard of their political views was prepared to employ them.

On the whole I got a warm reception and a friendly welcome from the academics at King's and made many friends. The College was run by a Council (in my case delightfully chaired by Lord Jellicoe) which was made up of lay people usually of some distinction in the outside world, academics both professorial and non-professorial, representatives of the technical staff (and a surprising number of technicians work in the University field) and three student members. So it is a thoroughly democratic body of about thirty strong.

The Council are advised by an Academic Board of some one hundred plus and having been used in the Service to small committees I was glad this was not a decision-making body but an advisory body, although nonetheless a powerful one. The Board consisted of academics from all levels of the college plus student representation. It met twice a term. The academic spends much of his life exposing the weaknesses in students' work so it is not easy for them to cast off this technique when they are considering a paper on some element of College. Often they did not agree with each other, which did on occasions make it easier for me as Chairman to provide a summing up which got general agreement.

I was much surprised by the amount of time academics spend on committee work. Some clearly enjoy it. In a large University like London there is also the committee work at the federal level and though the main Colleges are independent the University Court controls the annual grant which comes from Government so there is an element of blackmail in the situation when it needs to be applied.

The College responded warmly to their new leader and the University was equally speedy in recognising that Sir Neil had much to contribute at a time of immense change and upheaval in higher education. Sir Neil was elected to the Court of the University and was soon one of the University's representatives on the national Committee of Vice-Chancellors and Principals. (The University is a federal institution, by far the largest in the country, consisting of a group of Schools or Colleges such as King's and University College, Medical Schools, and a variety of specialist institutes.)

In 1981 higher education nationally had at short notice to face up to large percentage cuts in recurrent budgets. London University took a substantial portion of these and it was clear that if the University was to have any prospect of remaining an effective teaching and research base, radical reorganisation was essential. The University had a new Vice-Chancellor – a Professor of English Language from University College – Randolph Quirk. He was a Vice-Chancellor of the highest quality who judged well the balance between the need for change and the demands of the autonomy and integrity of individual Colleges. The unlikely pairing of a former Chief of Defence Staff and a Professor of English Language went on to play a central role in the restructuring of the country's largest University and the dramatic changes in the shape and size of King's College which were part of that bold strategy for the future.

Within King's, Cameron came quickly to the view that to survive and to retain quality and excellence it was necessary to expand. This firm premise underlay his approach to the many problems facing the University. Expansion meant additional staff and students and the space and resources to go with them. In a period of diminishing budgets the only way to achieve this was by marriage or merger. Various options were considered, and at first the metaphor of marriage seemed appropriate as a courtship between King's and one of the former ladies' Colleges, Bedford, developed. At first things went well but after two or three months formal discussion there was what appeared to some a rather abrupt disengagement and King's and Bedford set off in rather different directions, Bedford eventually merging with Royal Holloway College at Egham.

Much however was learnt from these negotiations and in due course a new partner was found. There was need also for a new metaphor, for 'marriage' could hardly be used to describe the reunification of King's College and one of its former 'offspring', Queen Elizabeth College. By May 1982 the first draft statement of intent was ready for signing but Sir Neil was suddenly admitted to hospital for open-heart surgery and his Vice-Principal had to conduct the final negotiations on his behalf.

The operation was completely successful but three months were to elapse before Sir Neil was back at his desk. By any standards this was a remarkable recovery from very major surgery and those who expected their leader to return somewhat reduced in vigour and commitment still had much to learn about the Principal of King's College.

Merging, however, was not confined to one link. As a consequence of the medical faculty battle mentioned earlier an agreement was drawn up for King's to reunite with another of its offspring and on 1 August 1984 the King's College Medical and Dental Schools were formally re-incorporated into the College as the King's College School of Medicine and Dentistry. A path had been followed which had many potential dangers but the leadership of Neil Cameron, combined with the detailed negotiations brought to a conclusion through the fine informal touch of the then Head of Administration, Myles Tempany, allowed a happy and speedy reunification to be completed.

In the meantime the negotiations with Queen Elizabeth College were complicated and enriched by overtures to and from Chelsea College, and the metaphor of 'marriage' was finally, and on grounds of decency, buried in favour of a *'menage à trois'*. Of all London Colleges, Chelsea had been perhaps the most severely buffeted by economic and consequent academic storms and it was important that a future role for it be defined. Minds in both Queen Elizabeth and King's were divided about the wisdom of entering even further into the uncharted waters of merging. The scale of change within London and King's was quite unprecedented and there were many who wanted to give the highest priority to riding out the turbulence of two reunifications (Queen Elizabeth and the School of Medicine and Dentistry) before even considering the claims of Chelsea. Again decisive leadership was essential and was forthcoming.

The negotiations between King's, Queen Elizabeth and Chelsea were at times delicate and at times blunt. The three Principals began to meet in regular conclave and the whole panoply of working parties and negotiating groups began to function. There was opportunity enough for distraction from the main issue which was the creation of a College of the highest academic quality out of three merging partners, but Sir Neil kept the pace of discussions and movement at the required level.

There were however distractions and one of the most welcome was the conferment of a Peerage on Sir Neil, or Lord Cameron of Balhousie as he became, in the New Year's Day Honours List 1983. It was an honour which was shared, in reflection, by the whole College and messages of congratulation poured into the Principal's Office – the internal delight was clearly shared in the world outside as telegrams and letters arrived from throughout the UK and well beyond. A further and even more precious recognition came in 1984 when the Queen bestowed on him her personal honour by creating him a Knight of the Thistle. He wore his nationality lightly and had little time for the 'professional-Scot-abroad', but the delight which he felt at this particular honour was apparent to those many in the College who had come to perceive the warmth and humanity which lay within an essentially shy exterior.

The honour and the ceremony surrounding its conferment came at a time of declining health. In March 1984 he was admitted to hospital for abdominal surgery. The diagnosis was of course a confidential matter but when he was able to return to College some three months later it was clear that his strength of spirit was being tested to the full. He was supported by a close and loyal team and continued at his desk till the end of 1984.

It would be easy to tell a story of tragic and painful decline and there is no doubt that much pain was endured by the Principal. Equally members of the College closest to Lord Cameron were well aware of the heroic battle which he was fighting. Yet such a picture is too bleak to represent the reality of the situation. He had returned to College in June to carry on as Principal and that is what he did, whatever the personal cost. In those six months much was achieved.

Most particularly the College prepared for merging and the three Colleges gradually anticipated formal merging in all sorts of ways. For example, a single comprehensive academic, financial and space plan was drawn up and, through many details and even more committee hours, agreed. Anyone who has experience of the academic world would well know how highly such an achievement is to be prized. This plan, already in operation is the basis for the future unified College.

In addition the preparation of the necessary Private Bill through Parliament was completed and again many fine points of sensitivity and collegiate pride and self-identity were resolved. In all of this Lord Cameron's experience and respected leadership helped smooth the path and prepare the way. A foundation stone of academic merging was the possibility of spatially merging the three Colleges and in this a grand strategist was needed who knew well the doors which led to the corridors of power. Here Lord Cameron's contribution was outstanding. King's has long coveted the splendid rooms and architecture of Somerset House of which it is effectively an extension. Successive Principals have dreamt grand dreams and, some would say, will continue to do so. The vision implicit in this of a great College based in that fine historic building seized Neil Cameron and although success is still to be found in the future, the discussions have progressed in a way which is quite new. A further and perhaps more pragmatic part to the vision was the identification of a large publicly-owned building to the south of the Thames, within ten minutes walk of the Strand site, which is capable of allowing the College to consolidate on one location. Again, the practical politics of interdepartmental discussion within the Civil Service is a precondition of bidding successfully for the building and the resources necessary to convert it to academic use. The triumvirate of Lord Cameron, Earl Jellicoe, the Chairman of the College Council, and Sir Frank Cooper, a senior member of the Council, proved to be a formidable team in setting the initial moves in train. It would be a fitting tribute to Lord Cameron's vision of a single great College in the centre of the nation's capital if there were to be an early positive outcome to these negotiations.

However, the final six months of activity sapped what remained of his physical strength, although it seemed to make little impact on his spirit. Like Moses, he was the leader who knew of the promised land and who led King's – and with it, in due course, Queen Elizabeth and Chelsea Colleges – to the brink, but he did not himself enter it. The Colleges merged formally on 1 August 1985. The combined academic range is now much greater, for the potential of the new institution is much more than an aggregate of the not inconsiderable strengths of its component parts. He had the foresight to see that what has now come to be was essential if excellence is to be preserved as resources diminish. Those with smaller minds and narrower perspective had to be led by a man of vision and King's was well blessed in the Principalship of Neil Cameron.

At the beginning of the academic session 1984–85, Lord Cameron gave his customary opening of session address to the staff. His concluding remarks tell much of the man and his time at King's:

This will be the last opportunity I will have to address the King's College staff at the start of the session as I will have retired by this time next year.

My five years have passed all too quickly. It has been a great honour to be Principal of King's College and I have valued every moment of it.

It is often said that King's is a very friendly place, and that has certainly been my experience. Right from my early days here the support I have had from the staff of this College has moved me greatly.

We have tried to read the future in the University of London and the future of the academic world. We have attempted much and I believe King's with its great history is now safe from anything the UGC and others can do to it.

I hope to be around for a bit yet, but I take this opportunity of wishing you all well.

As much was communicated here by what was left unsaid, as by the words uttered. The poignancy of the occasion was not lost on the assembled staff and the warmth of the response to these closing sentences was the overt sign of the manner in which Neil Cameron had won the hearts as well as the respect of his colleagues.

17   MAN OF MANY PARTS

Above and beyond his normal duties, Neil Cameron was always actively and effectively involved in a bewildering number of organisations. Only a selection of these can be described in detail here, but to them should be added the fact that from 1983, he had been the Chairman of the Council of the Chest, Heart and Stroke Association.

President of the British Atlantic Committee

After retiring from his post as Chief of the Defence Staff, Lord Cameron began to take an active interest in the work of the British Atlantic Committee and was elected President of that body in succession to Sir Frank Roberts in December 1981.

The BAC is a non-governmental body and a registered charity whose purpose is to promote knowledge and understanding of the North Atlantic Treaty alliance and the central role it plays in ensuring the security and democratic freedom of the United Kingdom. It describes itself as an advocate of increasing interdependence within the alliance, of the twin goals of defence and *detente*, and of the maintenance of peace between East and West. The BAC was formed in 1952, when similar organisations were set up in each of the member countries of the alliance, together constituting the North Atlantic Treaty Organisation. It also has a youth wing, British Atlantic Youth, which maintains links with youth groups both in the United Kingdom and in other allied countries. Lord Cameron himself said of it, 'NATO is our business: we are fortunate to have among our ranks a good number of members who have served NATO in the highest appointments – UK permanent representatives, military commanders, officials who have worked the machine from the inside and know it, so to speak, inside out. There can be few groups in Britain with more concentrated experience of NATO's problems.' And on another occasion, – 'The work of the British Atlantic Committee is undertaken by its members, private citizens who in their individual capacities voluntarily give of their time and talents to help formulate its policies and forward its activities.'

Matters of defence strategy were of prime importance to Lord Cameron and he was chairman of a BAC study group which in 1981 produced a report entitled '*A Global Strategy to meet Global Threat: A British Initiative.*' This publication sounded a warning against the Soviet ability to intervene militarily worldwide: it was followed in 1984 by a second BAC study, '*Diminishing the Nuclear Threat: NATO's Defence and New Technology.*' This was a call for NATO to rely less on nuclear weapons by increasing the effectiveness of precision-guided and target-selecting weapons as vehicles for conventional warheads to offset the Russian superiority in armour.

Under Lord Cameron's leadership the British Atlantic Committee continued to expand and increase its activities. In the summer of 1982 the charity status of the Committee was challenged and it was through his clarity of view and firmness of purpose that the decision was taken to establish a separate non-charitable campaigning body, Peace Through NATO, while retaining the traditional educational role for the British Atlantic Committee, which kept its charity status. It is typical of the breadth of the man that, having launched the new body, he was willing also to be its first President.

Although defence strategy remained a dominant interest for him, he was also a strong supporter of the important task of the British Atlantic Committee, that of keeping the public fully informed of the role of NATO as the effective peace-keeping alliance in Europe. He was particularly interested in expanding this work in schools and universities and lent his support to several measures towards fulfilling the right of young people to have accurate knowledge of the alliances undertaken by their governments. Never happier than when he had too much work to do, he was always ready to give advice and subsequent support to the Committee and its officers.

Chairman of Trident Trust

The Trident Trust is an educational charity registered with the Department of Education and Science – so called because it gives practical support to young people in schools by bringing together the three resources of Industry and Commerce, Voluntary Organisations and Educational Authorities. In addition it offers three kinds of opportunities to young people before they enter the working world: work experience, voluntary service and personal development. Following the Ditchley Conference in 1970, where representatives from Education Authorities, Industry and Commerce and Voluntary Organisations met to discuss the problems facing young people at the time, a pilot project was established between the Hampshire Education Authority and IBM in 1971. In 1972 the Trust was formed and five more projects were started; by 1983 there were thirty-two.

In the Chairman's Foreword to the Trident Trust Annual Report for 1983, Lord Cameron wrote: '1983 has been a year of consolidation. After ten years of operation we have had a very thorough look at the work that we have been doing. The changing patterns of education have also been very much in our mind. The conclusions we have reached have confirmed the views expressed by those who originated the Trust. However, we clearly see that there are a number of areas where, if we can find the resources, we can do much more to help teachers to develop the bridge between school and adult life. It has been a year of expansion in that we have been able to help 15% more young people than last year and the demand from local authorities and schools is still growing.'

The Royal Air Force Museum, Hendon

Dr John Tanner, its Director, notes that Sir Neil Cameron's first official connection with the Royal Air Force Museum was in January 1975 when, as Air Member for Personnel on the Air Force Board, he sat with the Trustees as ex-officio member until April 1976. In effect, he was holding a watching brief for the Royal Air Force, and the heavy weight of his official duties gave him little opportunity to do more than this. Nonetheless, his clarity of mind and power of expression were frequently brought to bear, and his forward vision was clear. In the autumn of 1979, having by then vacated the posts of Chief of the Air Staff and Chief of the Defence Staff, it was suggested that Sir Neil be invited to serve on the Board of Trustees, a suggestion which was passed with acclaim. His first full meeting took place in January 1980, when Marshal of the Royal Air Force Sir Denis Spotswood announced his retirement and proposed Sir Neil as his successor in the post of Chairman. This, too, was a proposal passed with acclaim, and from the next meeting of the Board in April 1980, Neil Cameron was its effective and driving Chairman until his resignation in July 1983. It is doubtful whether anyone other than Neil Cameron could have led the Trustees and staff of the Museum through a period of such productivity: the conclusion of the Battle of Britain Museum Appeal; the negotiations with the Department of Education and Science on the subject of fiscal control, which under Lord Cameron's guidance went so well; the creation of the Manchester Air and Space Museum; above all, the setting-up and opening, by Her Majesty Queen Elizabeth, the Queen Mother, of the Bomber Command Museum, on the due date and during the lifetime of Sir Arthur Harris, the Command's wartime AOC-in-C. These were prodigious achievements indicative of Neil Cameron's status as a man of intellect, leadership and vision. All this was tempered by a constant and frequently expressed regard for the staff who worked for him with total devotion.

Leisure Time

Although he was always a Scot at heart, from the time of his tour as PSO to D/SACEUR, Neil Cameron developed a tremendous enthusiasm for France and for everything French. From then on, he took the family there every year for their holidays. The sight of an English car loaded down with camping equipment attracted much more attention then than it does now. Occasionally there might be a sortie into Germany or Italy, but France was always the favourite and, in particular, Provence. By no means a natural linguist and without enough spare time to study the language, he never spoke French fluently, but his obvious goodwill or perhaps his talent for sign-language almost invariably produced a good-humoured response. If it did not always get him what he wanted, his reaction, in such relatively rare cases was philosophical. A few weeks a year spent by the sea in Provence was the only real relaxation that he allowed himself. He was always a keen swimmer regardless of the weather and he loved the sea. Whenever his official trips abroad took him anywhere within reach of it, he would always try to find time for a swim.

Although his busy schedule seldom allowed him to attend live performances, classical music gave him a great deal of pleasure. Sunday evenings at home were a rare chance to listen to his favourite records – usually operas or choral works, although if he had a preference for the work of any one composer, it must have been Elgar. On one particular occasion, when the RAF Benevolent Fund was holding one of its Anniversary Concerts at the Royal Festival Hall on 7 April 1978 he took a personal interest in the programme. He was particularly pleased that his favourite violinist, Yehudi Menuhin, was able to take part, and afterwards made a point of meeting the conductor, Sir Charles Groves.

Rugby Football

One of Neil Cameron's lifelong interests was Rugby football – an interest he made no attempt to disguise. Air Chief

Marshal Sir Kenneth Cross, who was a distinguished player and in later years held virtually every office in the RAF Rugby Union, becoming its Vice-Patron, recalled that 'whatever heights Neil rose to in his professional life and however important the offices he held, once work was done it was to rugby football that he turned for relaxation'. Referring to his playing days Sir Kenneth commented that 'he reached first-class standard playing for Richmond and for the representative Royal Air Force XV against many of the great clubs in England and Wales. It was one of his rare failures, and a major disappointment, that he failed to make the Air Force team against the Army and Navy at Twickenham and so never won a Cap. He was unfortunate to coincide with a period when the Service was exceptionally well off for wing forwards.'

When his playing days ended, Neil Cameron took part in the administration of the RAF Rugby Union, showing the same enthusiasm, energy and efficiency that had characterised his play on the field and his professional activities. Air Commodore D. M. Strong, who was Chairman from 1954 to 1956, has recalled that Cameron was invited to become Honorary Secretary when he was serving at the Air Ministry in 1952. The Chairman at that time was Group Captain C. L. Troop who happened to be in the same Department as Cameron and realised that with his keenness for the game he would make an ideal secretary. He remained secretary for four seasons, and Strong considers that 'apart from his enthusiasm for the job which was abundantly clear, he seemed to be effortlessly in control of all its aspects. In those days of National Service each year brought a new intake, some of whom were potential members of the RAF Fifteen. Cameron soon forged links with club secretaries throughout the country – including Rugby League clubs – and his network of intelligence gave him early warning of all promising players who would be included in the annual intakes. The work of the Selection Committee was made so much easier because the Secretary produced a list of all members of the season's intake who might be worthy of a trial for the RAF XV. Cameron had good rapport with the players, who all appreciated the friendly and helpful manner with which he attended to

their affairs. In short, he was a quite outstanding Secretary.'
Four years later, on promotion to Group Captain and
appointment to command Abingdon, Cameron was
elected Chairman of the Committee of the RAF Rugby
Football Union and in this office became the man primarily
responsible for all aspects of the game in the Service. Sir
Kenneth Cross takes up the story again: 'Needless to say,
the health of the Union was never better, before or since. It
was not only the Royal Air Force that benefited in this
period. He took an intense interest in his RAF Abingdon
team and no doubt his encouragement had much to do with
the team's success in winning the RAF Cup. On a higher
level, 1961 happened to be the year for the Air Force's turn
to manage the Combined Services team to play against the
touring South Africans. Neil's management was not only
impeccable. It was inspired, and resulted in the team
playing splendidly against this very strong international
side. The Navy and Army Chairmen of the day, both ex-
players of international standing, were so impressed with
Neil's handling of the team that they offered to forego their
turns in running the Combined Services XV, leaving it with
the Royal Air Force as long as Neil remained Chairman.'

To complete the story, it was in 1976, as Chief of the Air
Staff, that Neil Cameron was invited to become President of
the Union, an honour he greatly appreciated. Sir Kenneth
Cross remembers that he maintained his interest in the
game to the end of his life and was a familiar sight at
Twickenham for all the major games, particularly the inter-
service matches. As a Scot, his enthusiasm for the national
team never wavered and his joy when the team beat the
'ould enemy' England was something even the English
appreciated. As a player, administrator or supporter his
activity was the same – wholehearted. The players, his
fellow Committee men and his many rugby football friends
were fortunate to have been associated with him.

Christian Life and Work

In the midst of all these activities, it was Neil Cameron's
Christian faith which formed his principal frame of

reference. After his serious illness in hospital, he became convinced that 'the first requirement was to establish a personal relationship with God, and by this I don't mean getting down on one's knees once or twice a day, but constantly consulting God as one goes through the day on all sorts of things.' He has described how he prayed a most solemn prayer from the heart for guidance when he knew there would be a chance that he might be asked to become Chief of the Defence Staff. This picture is confirmed by the then Resident Chaplain of St Clement Danes Church (the Ven Glyndwr Renowden – later Chaplain in Chief of the RAF) who has written:

> It was his practice to worship in the central church of the Royal Air Force, St Clement Danes, of which he was a keen supporter and a Managing Trustee of the Appeal Fund. I recall very well the morning when he took over as Chief of the Defence Staff – he arrived at the church very soon after it was opened on that day and very quietly and unobtrusively he spent some time in prayer and private devotion. As he left the Church I spoke to him and he said quite simply – 'I begin a new job today, I just came to ask for God's blessing and his guidance.'

Neil Cameron was prepared to give not only his name but his active support to a number of Christian organisations. He was a Vice-President of the Officers' Christian Union, on the governing body of the Society for the Propagation of the Gospel, and president of the Soldiers and Airmens Scripture Readers' Association. It was also a happy chance that he, who had once attended Boy's Brigade meetings on Friday evenings, should become a Vice-President of that organisation. He attended day conferences, chaired meetings and spoke at local gatherings of these organisations. In these ways he sought to witness to what was most central in his life. But those who knew him testify that it was above all the example of his whole personality, permeated by faith, that left the most lasting impression.

Neil Cameron's faith was all of a piece with the rest of his personality and it therefore took on all his directness, naturalness and charm. Because his faith was so integrated with his whole being he was able to relate easily to people from different backgrounds of belief and non-belief and to respect practising Christians of other traditions.

He moved easily in evangelical circles but was always honest and never overstated the case for what had happened to him. He said that as a boy of sixteen he had accepted Christ as his personal saviour but 'on reflection I now doubt if I really understood exactly what this meant'. About his time in hospital he wrote, 'There was no great conversion in my case'. Yet, clearly, that time was the decisive turning point in his life.

He was well aware of the damage caused by the wrong kind of evangelism, yet he himself was able to talk about his faith in a way that was entirely natural. Every year at King's College London there is a pre-sessional residential conference at Cumberland Lodge for a certain number of new students. One of the highlights of this conference is the President of the Students Union interview with the Principal. The interviews with Lord Cameron were invariably enthralling experiences and he was able to speak with as little embarrassment about the miracle that had happened to him in hospital as he did about his disastrous academic record at school and his time in the air during the war.

No doubt it was in part simply a matter of chance that Neil Cameron was confirmed into the Church of England: the C of E Chaplain was available. Yet it went deeper than that. Neil Cameron had a strong aesthetic sense. He liked things to look nice and be done decently. When there was a special service in the Chapel at King's College London, one of his first concerns was that there should be lovely flowers, well arranged (which they were – by his personal secretary, Sandra Gee). He particularly appreciated the fine music in the Chapel by the King's College Singers under their Director, Ernie Warrell.

The poet Edwin Muir, in his classic spiritual autobiography *The Story and the Fable*[1], described his upbringing in the Orkneys, his loss of faith and its gradual recovery. It was only when he went to live in Rome however, surrounded by Christian art, that he came to believe in the incarnation. His early religion had been moral and intellectual. This needed to be complemented by a grasp of the visible and tangible. Similarly, Neil Cameron had a strong visual sense which found its natural home in the ordered beauty of the services of the Church of England and its sacramental principles, whereby the outward and visible conveys to us the inward and spiritual. His first Holy Communion, in hospital, meant much to him: 'at my first Holy Communion I felt God had really forgiven me'. He was also to write, 'I have found regular attendance at Holy Communion a wonderful means of refreshing the soul and for renewing confidence and faith.' Together with this went his love for the Bible. In his briefcase he carried some lines from Psalm 63 'O God . . . remembering how thou hast been my help . . . then I humbly follow thee with all my heart, and thy right hand is my support.' (vs 7–8, NEB).

Neil Cameron much valued the fact that King's College was a Christian foundation. Not only were there the regular chapel services but almost opposite his office was the interesting Victorian Byzantine chapel. It was his custom, on his way to work, to kneel quietly for a minute or two, commending the day and its many decisions into the hand of God. During his last illness he drew on this faith more and more. To the outside world he may have appeared his usual quick, vigorous self. But to those who knew him best he sometimes seemed to keep going by the force of will, nervous energy and faith alone. It was at this time too that he found the Secretary of the College, Myles Tempany, such a support. It was another sign of Neil Cameron's width of Christian vision that he and Myles Tempany, a devout Roman Catholic, received so much from each other at a fundamental level of moral and spiritual conviction.

Neil Cameron's time at King's coincided with the height of the debate over the ethics of nuclear weapons. He knew that we lived in a world in which, sadly, evil is a reality. Soon after the appointment of a new Dean of the College, Neil Cameron had the idea of a joint book on the subject of the Christian and nuclear weapons. In the event, because King's was so well stocked with expertise in the field, the book was widened out into a series of King's essays called *What Hope in an Armed World?*[2] with Neil Cameron contributing the chapter on 'Deterrence and Superpower Balance'. He was as decisive on this issue as on any in his eventful and courageous life. The values inherent in

Western civilisation must be defended against potential tyranny.

But he had hope for the future, both for the progress of life on this earth and for himself beyond this present life. Shortly before he died Myles Tempany left him after a visit with the words, 'I'll be seeing you.' Neil Cameron replied, 'If we don't meet again here we'll definitely meet again in a better place.'

Notes

1. Hogarth Press, 1954.

2. Pickering and Inglis, 1982. All quotations, unless stated otherwise in the text, are taken from an article written by Neil Cameron 'My Christian Faith and Service Life' printed in a special edition of *Contact*, the magazine of the Officers Christian Union (July 1980 issue).

Index

NB: Ranks and titles are given as stated in the text.